Experimental Dining

Experimental Dining

Performance, Experience and Ideology in Contemporary Creative Restaurants

Paul Geary

Bristol, UK / Chicago, USA

First published in the UK in 2022 by
Intellect, The Mill, Parnall Road, Fishponds, Bristol, BS16 3JG, UK

First published in the USA in 2022 by
Intellect, The University of Chicago Press, 1427 E. 60th Street,
Chicago, IL 60637, USA

A catalogue record for this book is available from
the British Library.

Copy editor: MPS Limited
Cover designer: Aleksandra Szumlas
Cover image: Bombas & Parr/Nathan Pask
Production manager: Georgia Earl, Debora Nicosia
Typesetter: MPS Limited

Hardback ISBN 978-1-78938-343-0
ePDF ISBN 978-1-78938-344-7
ePUB ISBN 978-1-78938-345-4

Printed and bound by Lightning Source

To find out about all our publications, please visit our website.
There you can subscribe to our e-newsletter, browse or download our current
catalogue and buy any titles that are in print.

www.intellectbooks.com

This is a peer-reviewed publication.

Contents

Figures

Acknowledgements

There are a number of people without whom I would not have been able to complete this book. First, I offer thanks to those artists who have given me their time to discuss their work: Mike Knowlden of Blanch & Shock, Sam Bompas of Bompas & Parr, Olivia Winteringham of KILN, Siân Tonkin of Companis and Kaye Winwood. I also offer my gratitude to Jamie Desogus of Harborne Kitchen, with whom I have had a number of fruitful conversations and the chance to try out some of the ideas of the book in practice. I want to extend my gratitude to the restaurants I visited for this project: the staff at The Fat Duck, Noma and Alinea were very welcoming and generous with their time. I particularly want to thank Jonny Lake, James Winter and Otto Romer at The Fat Duck.

I am exceptionally grateful for the patience, diligence and friendly professionalism of the staff at Intellect and offer especial thanks to Aimée Bates, Georgia Earl, Tim Mitchell, Debora Nicosia and Jelena Stanovnik.

I am grateful for the opportunity to discuss my work as part of the 'How To Do Things With Food(s): Food as Research/Food in Performance' working group at ASTR in 2014 and the 'Documenting Performance' working group at TaPRA in 2016, as well as at the 'Digesting Ritual' conference at the University of Surrey in 2018 and at the Performance Philosophy Biennial in Amsterdam in 2019. To the convenors of those groups and conferences – Joshua Abrams, Kristin Hunt, Georgina Guy, Johanna Linsley, Adam Alston and the team running Performance Philosophy – I offer my thanks. I am also grateful to the University of Bristol and the University of Birmingham who provided funding for research trips. This book is an extension of my doctoral thesis, and I wish to offer my gratitude to Paul Clarke and Josephine Machon for their reflections during the examination process.

No work happens in a vacuum. In both direct and indirect ways, we are supported and encouraged by many people around us. Sometimes there are reflections on work, other times there are conversations about ideas and sometimes we are buoyed up by the love and solidarity of friendship and care. There are a number of colleagues and friends who have helped me and shaped my work over the last few years. In particular, I want to thank Cara Davies, Cristina Delgado-García,

Panayiota Demetriou, Eleftheria Ioannidou and Caroline Radcliffe. On a personal note, I want to thank my family for their continual support and encouragement throughout the process of researching and writing. Over the time of working on this project, I received a great deal of care and sustenance from Emily Gent, Annabell Allen and Maya Krishnan and to them all I offer my sincere gratitude.

Finally, there are two friends who have offered me considerable mentorship, support and guidance: Liz Tomlin, who has been incredibly supportive and the kind of mentor who inspires and nurtures, and Simon Jones, who has shaped my work and thinking in so many ways. To Liz and Simon, the greatest of thanks.

Introduction

Early in the afternoon of Sunday 19 August 2012, I was presented with the final course of a meal at Dinner by Heston Blumenthal, the Michelin-starred restaurant in London where each of the dishes is a contemporary reimagining of a historical recipe. The dish was a dessert called 'Tarte of Strawberries (*c*.1591)'. The dessert was served on a white circular plate and consisted of, on one side of the plate, a quenelle of vibrant red strawberry sorbet resting on a bed of crumbled, golden brown biscuit. On the other side of the plate was a rectangle of the same biscuit topped with macerated strawberries, pearly white cream, wild strawberries, crystallised violets and mint, honey cress and a light-pink and lacy strawberry tuile. Eating this dish was the first time I had been overtaken and overwhelmed by food, struck by *something* that I could not articulate. I felt unsettled and unnerved. I felt tangential to my own body, as though cleaved apart from my own sensory experience, forced to encounter it as estranged. I experienced a kind of nostalgia, but could not say exactly for what. I was affected, awakened and agitated by the food, to the point where I called on the waiter to tell me exactly of what the dish consisted, in the hope of regaining some control.

I begin this book with this moment because, for me, it was a personal experience of the potential of food to operate according to an artistic or aesthetic logic. It went beyond an everyday appreciation of dining as sustenance or maintaining the body and was seemingly operating outside of my everyday modes of appreciating food. I can articulate some of the various ideas and contexts that intersected in that experience: that it creatively reworked a historical recipe in a way that appealed to my palate and tastes; that it mixed together different tastes, flavours, textures and temperatures in such a way that the whole seemed to exceed the combination of its constituent parts; that from the restrained order of the visual presentation on the plate burst a series of intense sensations; that the crystallised violets triggered an emotionally infused nostalgia for a sweet I had eaten as a child; and that I dined with a partner with whom I was relaxed, comfortable and able to share my experience.

Experimental Dining offers an interrogation of the artistic work of experimental restaurants. Working predominantly from an experiential perspective, the book investigates the work of four Michelin-starred experimental, technoemotional restaurants (a term to which I will return). It is not uncommon to encounter terms like 'theatre', 'theatrical' and 'artistic' in relation to haute cuisine, especially in restaurant reviews and in television food programmes, where the terms are used loosely and often as a way of articulating the 'spectacular'. This book focuses on creative, experimental restaurants in relation to performance in order to move beyond spectacle and to consider both how performance unlocks a way of thinking about creative food practice and how this practice with food can, vice versa, open space for reflections on the embodied, experiential and reflective experience of performance. The opening example of 'Tarte of Strawberries (*c*.1591)', while personal, opens up some of the complexity of an artistic dining experience – some of the various factors, contexts and sensations that intersect in the experience to produce something artistic. *Experimental Dining* examines not only how the restaurants and their practice deploy sensations, embodiment, contexts and discourses as constitutive elements of the work but also how they use the experience to trouble itself; in other words, to make the experience an issue for itself.

Experimental Dining takes as its focus four of the world's most highly rated restaurants: Ferran Adrià's elBulli (Cala Montjoi, Spain), Heston Blumenthal's The Fat Duck (Bray, UK), René Redzepi's Noma (Copenhagen, Denmark) and Grant Achatz's Alinea (Chicago, USA). The restaurants are understood as engaging in modes of performance practice, considering the design and setting of the restaurants, the performances they house, the enacting of their performance events and performances of the food objects they serve. While 'performance' is the overarching framework for the analysis and arguments, the book draws on work from philosophy, cultural studies, food studies and sensory studies as a means of engaging with the detail of the experience. Performance is understood as an arena wherein different ideas, concepts and practices are brought together in confluence, in lived experience and as something that can take both itself and other things as an issue or focus. Performance can reflect upon and take issue with itself and its own practices as well as being the means by which other ideas and practices are explored, examined and critiqued. To understand these restaurants as performance allows for thinking both about how they make use of and deploy strategies, practices and ideas associated with performance studies and about how performance can operate as a framework, a container, a home or a space for ideas, concepts and practices seemingly outside of itself. The book interrogates the experience of the performances in and of these restaurants, with a particular focus on the entanglement of sensory, embodied and reflective experience with the broader cultural and ideological discourses that both frame and produce those seemingly individual, personal and intimate encounters with the work.

The Restaurants: elBulli, The Fat Duck, Noma and Alinea

The four restaurants that form the core focus and case studies for the book have each received two or three Michelin stars, the sought-after culinary accolade that is often taken around the world as the absolute system for rating the quality of a restaurant – two stars standing for 'excellent cooking, worth a detour' and three (the highest award) for 'exceptional cuisine, worth a special journey'. elBulli, The Fat Duck, Noma and Alinea have all appeared in the top ten of the prestigious 'World's 50 Best Restaurants' and in 2010 they were in the top seven places on the list, with three out of the four taking the top three places. Each of the restaurants mobilises its own approaches, techniques, concepts and practices in different ways; they have their own practical and conceptual identities. There are, nevertheless, continuities between them. They all engage in significant research and development processes, serving a crafted tasting menu (a series of smaller courses that are more experimental than classic or everyday cuisine) and they utilise new technologies, ingredients and working methods to produce an 'experience' that is carefully crafted, constructed and considered.

The four restaurants take an experimental approach to cuisine, dining and gastronomy, and their practice both utilises and diverges from histories of food preparation processes and dining contexts. While each restaurant does, to greater and lesser extents, make use of cuisines from around the world, they are largely grounded in a Western/French classic tradition, which was the hegemonic approach to fine dining throughout the twentieth century (in part reinforced by the Michelin rating system). In his article on Western haute cuisine periods and movements since the beginning of the twentieth century, the journalist Pau Arenós charts the development of experimental cuisine in three distinct styles or approaches: 'Codified Classicism', 'Nouvelle Cuisine' and 'Technoemotional Cuisine' (2009: 320–22). For Arenós, 'Codified Classicism' was the predominant approach to fine dining in the first half of the twentieth century and was the result of the French influence of Auguste Escoffier. 'Nouvelle Cuisine' began its influence around 1960 and Arenós splits it into four generations: the French 'Fathers of Nouvelle Cuisine' (including Paul Boucuse and Alain Chapel); the 'Followers of the 1st N.C. generation (1970–80)' (including the Roux brothers, Michel and Albert, and Pierre Koffman in the United Kingdom and Juan Mari Arzak in Spain); the 'Followers of the 2nd N.C. generation (1980–2000)' (including Christer Lingström in Sweden, Thomas Keller in the United States, Santi Sanataria in Spain and Marco Pierre White in the United Kingdom); and the 'Followers of the 3rd N.C. generation (2000–08)' (including Eric Ripert in the United States, Mathias Dahlgren in Sweden and Michel Roux Jr and Gordon Ramsay in the United Kingdom). The final development, which is the main focus of this book, is 'Technoemotional Cuisine (c.1990)', which Arenós marks as the Spanish influence on haute cuisine, beginning with the work of Ferran and Albert Adrià at elBulli and the 'Followers of the 1st Technoemotional cuisine generation (2000–08)', including Heston Blumenthal, René Redzepi and Grant Achatz.

elBulli

Located in the Cap de Creus natural park, by the ocean, in Cala Montjoi in the north-east of Spain, elBulli was established in the early 1960s by a German homeopathic doctor, Hans Schilling. The restaurant was surrounded by elements of nature (trees, rocks, the coast and the sea) with very few buildings in the vicinity. It was awarded its first Michelin star in 1976 for its classic French cuisine under the head chef Jean-Louis Neichel, gaining a second star in 1982 after Juli Soler joined as the restaurant manager the previous year, serving nouvelle cuisine under head chef Jean-Paul Vinay. Ferran Adrià joined elBulli in 1983, leaving for a period in 1984 before returning as chef de partie and then promoted to co-head chef alongside Christian Lutand after Vinay's departure. At this point, the second star was lost (though it was regained in 1990). In 1985, Ferran's brother, Albert Adrià, joined as a stager before becoming creative director of the workshop and head of the 'sweet world'. In 1987, elBulli began an experiment that significantly changed the mode of working at the restaurant as well as the type of food they were serving. They decided to open the restaurant for just six months of the year and to use the other six months (from the end of the summer season in September) to relocate to Barcelona for a period of research and development at elBullitaller, the research and development workshop. This work was supplemented by the establishment of another workshop in Cala Montjoi in 2003, to continue the development of dishes, concepts, approaches and presentations while the restaurant was open to diners in the summer.

From 1987 to the closure of elBulli in 2011, the restaurant was at the forefront of experimental cooking, taking a pivotal role in the development of what is often called 'molecular gastronomy' but also known as 'modernist cooking' or 'technoemotional cuisine'. In 1990, when they regained the second Michelin star, Ferran Adrià and Juli Soler bought the restaurant from the Schilling family and became notably more experimental with the cuisine, partly as a result of trips to encounter the work of French chefs Michel Bras and Pierre Gagnaire. The creative team at the restaurant, led by the Adrià brothers and Juli Soler, was expanded in 1996 when Oriol Castro joined the elBulli staff, beginning as a stager. Over the first half of the 1990s, elBulli made significant changes to their work and the restaurant, including the building of a new kitchen (designed by the architect Dolors Andreu to Ferran's specifications), expanding the space of the kitchen and engaging in discussions with the sculptor Xavier Medina Campeny, which led to the use of Campeny's workshop, in Barcelona, for creative research. In 1995, elBulli used the kitchens of Talaria restaurant in Barcelona for their creative workshop. In 1997, elBulli received its third Michelin star, which it retained until its closure in 2011.

The experiments conducted at elBulli and elBullitaller went beyond designing new food and techniques for its production. They engaged with a range of the contexts surrounding the production and consumption of food and arguably were the most prolific restaurant in terms of exploring the artistic potential of food and its settings. From 2000, elBulli engaged in a long-term project to document each of the dishes it produced, later publishing their catalogue with images of the final dishes and details of how to prepare and serve them. In 2002, they introduced what Adrià et al. described as 'a personalized tasting menu for every guest' and no longer offered an à la carte menu (2008: 184.5).[1] The following year they established a science department at elBullitaller, led by chemists Pere Castells and Íngrid Farré and throughout the first decade of the 2000s they experimented with new dishes, new cutlery and crockery and engaged in various interdisciplinary collaborations with scientists, designers and artists. In 2007, elBulli was invited to take part in Documenta 12 in Kassel, Germany, the contemporary art exhibition that takes place every five years. For this, guests were flown from Germany to the restaurant, as Adrià felt that the experience of the restaurant and its work was significantly grounded in its locality. Over the course of the 2008–09 season, a documentary was made, following the work of the restaurant over the year, entitled *El Bulli: Cooking in Progress*. In May 2008, Albert Adrià was replaced by Mateu Casañas as head pastry chef until the restaurant closed its doors for the last time on 30 July 2011.

By the end of its life, elBulli was serving around 50 diners per day, spread over 15 tables. They were open for approximately 160 days per year, serving on average 8000 guests, with 1500 different dishes per day and offering a wine list comprising 1666 wines. It would be easy to present Ferran Adrià as a pioneer in the field of gastronomy, and there is some truth to this. He led the restaurant through a long period of experimentation, the results of which were disseminated across restaurants around the world. As head chef of elBulli, he was an influential figure and chefs from all over the world would visit the restaurant or do 'stages' working in its kitchens. Indeed, both René Redzepi of Noma and Grant Achatz of Alinea did training placements at elBulli. Heston Blumenthal presented his work with liquid nitrogen in 2004 at Madrid Fusión, a conference held at the Palacio Municipal de Congresos, where Ferran sat in the front row of the audience. They later went on to collaborate on the 'Statement of the "New Cookery"', alongside food-scientist Harold McGee and chef Thomas Keller, published in the *Observer* on 10 December 2006, and

Blumenthal participated in one of the round-table discussions about elBulli documented in *Food for Thought, Thought for Food* (2009). While elBulli was engaging in prolonged investigations into food and its artistic potential, they were also collaborating with chefs, artists and academics. In other words, while their influence on global cuisine should not be diminished, the work sits within a broader context of explicit sharing and collaboration.

The Fat Duck

The small village of Bray in Berkshire is home to two of the United Kingdom's seven three-Michelin star restaurants: The Fat Duck and The Waterside Inn (the latter run by Alain Roux, with the other three-star restaurants all operating in London), as well as Heston Blumenthal's The Hind's Head pub (one Michelin star). The Fat Duck was opened in 1995 by Blumenthal, after two years of searching for premises. At the time of buying, it was a 450-year old pub, originally called The Ringers then called The Bell when it was purchased by Blumenthal. Before running The Fat Duck, Blumenthal had no intensive training as a chef. His only work in restaurants had been a week at Raymond Blanc's Le Manoir aux Quat-Saisons in Oxfordshire, where he met Marco Pierre White and formed a relationship that allowed Blumenthal three week's experience at Pierre White's Canteen in preparation for opening The Fat Duck. Other than this, Blumenthal is self-taught as a chef and, as a restaurant manager, he attended a course at Leiths Cookery School in London and read Hugh Pitt's *The Complete Restaurateur*.

The Fat Duck is a small restaurant, almost indistinguishable from the houses surrounding it, except for a sign hanging above the door and a small notice on the wall. One steps directly from the street into the restaurant. Over the road from the restaurant is the development kitchen, where new ideas are explored and a significant amount of the preparations for each service take place. Blumenthal no longer works in the kitchens of The Fat Duck, which is now under the leadership of the head chef Edward Cooke. Unlike Ferran Adrià, who continued to run elBulli throughout its existence and did not allow the restaurant to continue under the guidance of another chef when he finished, Blumenthal has passed on the day-to-day running of the restaurant, though continues to be a presence in its work and in the restaurant's identity. Previous head chefs at The Fat Duck include Garrey Dawson, Jonny Lake and Ashley Palmer-Watts. Palmer-Watts went on to be the head chef at Dinner by Heston Blumenthal in Kensington, which is now (at the time of writing) run by another former Fat Duck chef, Tom Allen.

The Fat Duck began cooking classical French cuisine, but moved into experimenting with food and 'molecular gastronomy' after gaining its first Michelin star. Around this time, Blumenthal contacted Peter Barham, Professor of Physics at the University of Bristol. At the time, the kitchen at The Fat Duck was very small and only had two direct gas stoves. As a self-taught chef, Blumenthal frequently turned to chefs' books and Harold McGee's *On Food and Cooking* for advice. To cook green beans, the standard advice from cookery books was to bring water to a rolling boil, add salt and then add the beans. The stoves at The Fat Duck were unable to maintain a rolling boil when more than a few beans were added and Blumenthal had found no significant difference in the beans whether the water was rapidly boiling or not, whether salt was added to the water or not. He consulted McGee's tome and when he failed to find the answer, contacted Peter Barham. That conversation began a relationship that led to Blumenthal visiting the labs at the University of Bristol and Barham visiting the restaurant around once a month. The Fat Duck has continued to foster collaborations with scientists, as well as designers and artists, much like elBulli, all in service of developing their practice.

Noma

In August 2003, René Redzepi undertook a 17-day trip around the Faroe Islands, Greenland and Iceland with cookery writer Claus Meyer and chef Mads Refslund. This was a research trip to explore the cuisine of the North Atlantic and to meet potential suppliers in preparation for the opening of Noma. It was during the trip to Greenland that Redzepi happened upon the fundamental conceptual and artistic drive for Noma, grounded in Nordic food cultures and locally-sourced ingredients. In 2003, Redzepi was working as a sous chef in a restaurant in Copenhagen when Claus Meyer offered him the post of chef and partner in a new restaurant, working with Meyer and Kristian Byrge (who went on to be founder and creative director of Muuto, a Scandinavian design company). The restaurant was to be located in a warehouse known as Nordatlantens Brugge (the North Atlantic Wharf) on the waterfront in Christianshavn, Copenhagen. The restaurant remained here until 2017, when it closed in order to move 1.5 km away to a new site on the waterfront.[2]

Noma was established to explore and serve Nordic cuisine, using, as far as possible, only ingredients from the Nordic countries. Indeed, the name Noma is a contraction of 'nordisk' and 'mad' (Nordic and food). Noma received two Michelin stars in 2008 and has maintained that ranking since (although with a hiatus as they moved locations, as happened with The Fat Duck in 2016 when it closed for renovations and relocated to Australia). Noma was named number one in the World's 50 Best Restaurants for a number of years (2010–12, 2014). Before it received awards, it was run in a very different way: the servers would answer the phone and take bookings and there was no reservation list. This changed when it began to receive accolades and the booking system is now operating months in advance. The overriding ethos of Noma is its grounding in, and construction of, the Nordic. It also seeks to foster a relationship with its immediate location, with the chefs often foraging for food in the city of Copenhagen.

The restaurant foregrounds the 'natural' and 'rustic' in its design and its food. The aesthetic includes roughly hewn wooden beams, furs, clay crockery and bare wooden tables. It seems to eschew the trappings of classical haute cuisine (of waiters in suits, highly polished cutlery and neatly pressed and pristinely white tablecloths) in favour of something earthier and representative of the 'natural world' from whence the ingredients come. This 'natural', 'rustic' and 'earthy' narrative is foregrounded throughout the experience they curate in terms of both the aesthetic and their conceptual approach to dining.

Alinea

Alinea opened in Chicago in 2005, a co-venture between chef Grant Achatz and his business partner Nick Kokonas. Achatz studied at the Culinary Institute of America in New York, as well as with Thomas Keller, working at Keller's The French Laundry in California as a sous chef. In 2000, he worked alongside René Redzepi as a stager at elBulli, on the recommendation of Thomas Keller. Kokonas was introduced to Achatz's food at Trio in Evanston, Chicago, where Achatz initially garnered his reputation and that led to their collaboration on Alinea and the later opening of restaurants Next (in 2011) and Roister (in 2016, with chef Andrew Brochu) and the cocktail lounge Aviary (in 2011).

Alinea's style and approach, like that of elBulli, The Fat Duck and Noma, is grounded in its geographical and cultural context, while drawing influence from and reflecting upon classical, French-inspired culinary traditions. A particularly distinctive feature of Alinea is its experimentation with the ways of serving food, often foregoing the traditional plate in favour of innovative designs for serving a dish (including a moulded ceramic in the shape and style of a napkin, a metal wire on which is pinned hanging bacon and even painting a dessert directly onto the surface of the table).

At the beginning of 2016, Alinea closed for renovations, to reopen in May of the same year. The restaurant adopted the name of the grammatical symbol of an alinea (the pilcrow or paragraph mark) as a way of continually phrasing the restaurant as a 'new start'. In light of this, the renovations were conducted to refresh the restaurant. It has been called Alinea 2.0 and Alinea Reboot, but for the restaurant, the renovation was a continuation of their attempt to be at the forefront of cuisine and fine dining. It has continued to hold three Michelin stars and Achatz has won a number of awards for his work, including the 'Outstanding Chef in America' in

2008 and Alinea remains on the 'World's 50 Best Restaurants' list, was named the Best Restaurant in North America in 2010 and in 2016 received the James Beard Foundation Award for Outstanding Restaurant.

Philosophical Approach

This book sits at the intersection of a number of disciplines: performance studies, cultural studies, sensory studies and philosophy. In utilising ideas from these disciplinary approaches, the book explores how they might speak to and with one another to offer a richer account of the aesthetic and experiential practice of each of the restaurants. There is an implicit argument that these different disciplinary perspectives are not mutually exclusive, but overlap, intersect and are confluent in live(d) experience. The book engages with the symbiotic relationship between the minutiae of sensory experience and broader cultural, political and ideological discourse, arguing that they are bound together and mutually produce, reproduce, reiterate and consolidate one another. 'Performance' becomes the house or frame for how this more theoretical argument is put into, explored through and troubled by the practice of the restaurant as an artistic-aesthetic undertaking. In a later section of the introduction, I turn explicitly to food, art, aesthetics and performance. Here I introduce the key theoretical-philosophical approach of the book, which is grounded in the work of Martin Heidegger.

Heidegger's work began as a development of the phenomenological project of his tutor, Edmund Husserl. Heidegger's issue with Husserl was that, in the examination of phenomena and experience in phenomenology, there nevertheless needed to be an interrogation of the underlying ontological assumptions on which those experiences rest. Heidegger's first major work, *Being and Time* (published in 1927 and first translated into English in 1962), was an ontological investigation of the nature of Being through the experience of beings. In other words, Heidegger interrogated various aspects, facets, traits and qualities of the experience of 'human' existence and experience. In *Being and Time*, he argued that 'Only as phenomenology, is ontology possible' (1962: 60). It is only by means of investigating phenomena, the experience of being, that any understanding of being can be achieved. *Being and Time* is ontologico-phenomenological: a hybridisation of ontology and phenomenology, of being and experience, where each is grounded in, and inseparable from, the other. Dasein, Heidegger's term for the kind of Being associated with the human, means 'being-there': a fundamental experience of existence that finds itself 'there' (which implies a spatiality and temporality, those two coordinates of 'there-ness'). Dasein is not synonymous with 'human' because, as a term, it is not focused on a species, a biological category, but rather a processual experience, a practice or process of being.

Heidegger's model of Dasein, as proposed and explicated in *Being and Time*, is sketched out below and is the model that grounds the approach and reflections of this book. As Heidegger identified with his critique of Husserl, there are always grounding assumptions and presuppositions in experience and scholarship; those things that are taken-for-granted, often unacknowledged, the set of fundamental premises that are required for sense to emerge (what we might think of like a Kuhnian 'paradigm' or a Foucauldian 'episteme'). In using Heidegger's thinking, I am attempting to become aware of and articulate some of those presuppositions that underlie my understanding of what it is to be an experiencing entity, because this book is an examination of aesthetic experience. Heidegger's thinking is therefore used as a model of, approach to and perspective on the experience and constitution of experience. *Experimental Dining* is not an ontological investigation, but rather a phenomenological and aesthetic one, so while Heidegger's writing is used as the basis and facilitator for phenomenological and aesthetic reflections and analysis, I do take some of his ontological premises for granted, though I also add to his model with material from other disciplines that nevertheless is congruent with Heidegger's model of Dasein.

At the heart of Heidegger's conception of Dasein is the idea of 'Being-in-the-world'. The hyphenation of the term fulfils both a grammatical and a conceptual function: it both cleaves apart and binds together the respective terms. Dasein, as 'being-there', requires a 'there' in which to be and that 'there' is a 'world'. For Heidegger, the world is a structure of significance, understood both materially (those things or objects that we might encounter) and more figuratively (like a world-view, which Heidegger explains via the example of the world of a mathematician, which signifies the possibilities and potentialities of understanding and activity available to the perspective of mathematics [1962: 93]). The idea of world combines these as the space where Dasein 'lives'; Dasein is always already 'in' the world and that 'in', for Heidegger, is not reducible to a purely spatial relationship, but rather connotes a residing and dwelling in, and familiarity with, the world (80). Being-in-the-world is a compound expression that acknowledges that Dasein and world are never free of one another. Dasein cannot be conceived without considering the world into which it is thrown and within which it becomes itself. The world only has significance and substance as a kind of ordering principle for Dasein, a means of (broadly speaking) 'understanding' what things are, how they work, how we work, how we behave and what constitutes being (as both noun and verb).

In *Being and Time*, Heidegger articulates two modes of Dasein, two modes of Being-in-the-world, which he designates as the 'authentic' and 'inauthentic'. These are not two absolute experiences and positions of Dasein, nor are they a spectrum from one to the other. Instead, they are ways of Being-in-the-world that are always in tension with one another and never absolutely inhabited by Dasein. Despite the connotations of these terms, Heidegger does not suggest a morality with them. In Heidegger's formulation, inauthenticity is not a 'lesser' mode of being (68). It is Dasein's 'average' or 'everyday' mode of Being-in-the-world (69). In the inauthentic mode of Dasein, we give ourselves over to the structure of significance of the world; that ordering principle that is not strictly our own, but according to the logic of which, we think, act, behave, understand and experience. It would be impossible to live a life while interrogating everything we do, think, feel or experience and, indeed, that interrogation itself almost invariably comes with the forms, histories and structures of a language that is inherited or learned. So, we are always already finding ourselves operating within a worldhood of signification, giving ourselves over to the structures, practices and ideas of the world, often in a way of which we are not consciously aware. This is the inauthentic mode of Being-in-the-world, where Dasein cannot be understood outside of its formation and constitution in relation to the world.

Heidegger goes on to term this inauthentic Dasein as the *'they*-self', distinguished from the 'authentic self' (167). The *they*-self is one that dissolves into the world of the *they*, which is a form of public understanding and practice – not particular others, but more like a shared cultural practice and way of understanding that only has existence to the extent that it is utilised and put into practice by individuals.[3] Heidegger offers particular examples of this deferral, this giving oneself over to the *they* (which he describes as a kind of dictatorship), where we take pleasure, make judgements about art and find shocking what *they* do (164). This is Dasein's everyday, inauthentic and unowned experience. The specific worldhood that we inhabit provides coordinates for understanding, experiences and making sense, for actions, thoughts and responses. It becomes a kind of shorthand that makes life continuously liveable.

Heidegger's *they* is part of the structural form of his ontology of Dasein and the world of the *they* permeates inauthentic experience. In the context of the experience of the restaurants, I explore how the sensations and the ways of making sense that can be manifested in those experiences are in part framed and produced by the *they* or what we might alternatively call 'ideology'. Ideology and Heidegger's *they* are not synonymous and cannot be used absolutely interchangeably. However, there are consistencies and crossovers between them. In *Experimental Dining*, I use some of Slavoj Žižek's writings on ideology as a way of pushing further the interrogation of *how* the *they* (as worldhood, as a horizon of significance and sense-making) is manifested not only in broader narratives of sense, understanding and politics but also at the level of individual, sensory and reflective experience. In Žižek's *The Sublime Object of Ideology*, he argues that 'An ideology is really "holding us" only when we do not feel any opposition between it and reality – that is, when the ideology succeeds in determining the mode of our everyday experience of reality itself' (2008: 49). By using Žižek's writing on ideology, I inflect Heidegger's *they* with a distinctly political orientation, for the purposes of examining the experience of the restaurant. In this particular world of haute cuisine and the experimental, Michelin-starred restaurant, I understand the particular ideological frame of the *they*, using Žižek, in terms of contemporary capitalism, neoliberalism, the commodification of experience, the production of desire and enjoyment and the use of scientific knowledges and technological practices as a form of understanding and control.

Heidegger's inauthentic *they*-self has the potential to be read in a deterministic way. We can never escape our Being-in-the-world, because there is no being of Dasein that can be conceived as independent of its thrownness into the world (we cannot conceive of a person who is not in-the-world, either in a material or socio-cultural sense). But Heidegger does offer a different mode of Dasein: the authentic. The authentic is Dasein's mode of 'owning' itself. While the inauthentic is falling into and losing oneself in the world of the *they*, the authentic is Dasein's grasping its potentiality to be itself (1962: 220). It is a form of freedom – a freedom to choose for itself, to take hold of itself (232). As a way of thinking about experience, the authentic is a retreat from and challenge to the world of the *they* and to grapple with one's own existence, where one's being becomes an issue for itself. So, again, Dasein cannot be conceived as separate from the world, but instead Heidegger argues that the authentic mode is not detached from the *they*, but rather a modification of or estrangement from it (168).

Žižek's writing on ideology supplements and expands the workings of Heidegger's *they* and the authentic/inauthentic modes of Dasein. It is not just knowledge of the *they* or ideology and its operations on, in and through us that shift us from an inauthentic to an authentic experience. Drawing on Peter Sloterdijk, Žižek develops Marx's classical formulation of ideology ('they do not know it, but they are doing it') to propose a form of 'ideological cynicism', where 'they know very well what they are doing, but still, they are doing it' (2008: 24–25). For Žižek, ideology is not necessarily a 'false consciousness' but rather being itself, supported, maintained and structured by this 'false consciousness' (15–16). To be aware of it is not necessarily to break out of that inauthentic mode, because ideology is not just in what we believe (about the world, about politics, being or experience), but also in the enacting, experiencing and staging of those beliefs. In other words, ideology has a performative quality. Žižek uses the phrase 'as if', where we act 'as if' entities have power, significance or particular meanings and that enacting produces the very substrate on which it is supposed to rest (34). I argue that this is not just in the grand narratives of a culture (Žižek gives the examples of the President, the Will of the People, bureaucracy, the working class [34]) but is equally at work in the most intimate, personal, embodied and sensory experiences. What we experience, how we experience and how we understand and reflect on those experiences can also operate according to this 'as if' performative logic-staging, even in seemingly intuitive and spontaneous perception and experience, an embodied life practice that is not our own. It gives the sense of substance, significance and meaning as if these were simply true, apparent and real, where they actually emerge as a relation between self and world.

To experience according to an authentic mode of Dasein is, then, not merely to become aware of the ways in which we are intimately held by ideology, because even in becoming aware, our bodies can still perform themselves according to an ideological logic. Rather, the authentic is something estranged, unsettled, not free of the world but a different way of engaging with it. It is an experiential and reflective awareness of the aspects, traits and qualities of experience that do not absolutely conform to an ideological worldhood. The authentic institutes ways of both sensing and making sense that run against the grain and counter to the everyday, inauthentic modes of being. It challenges submission to a logic, narrative or paradigm of sense that is in service to an ideological agenda (which is never just a structure of understanding and meaning, but one that is perpetuating structures of power, dominance and agency). The tension between the authentic and inauthentic modes of Dasein is not just ontological or experiential but is also infused with a politics concerning structures of power, questions of agency, and the political and ideological interpellation of the individual, even at the level of seemingly spontaneous sensory experience.

The grounding theoretical position, which underlies the reflections and analysis of *Experimental Dining*, is a model of experience that, in its everyday or average mode, is framed and produced by ideology, by the realm of the *they*. But there is nevertheless the possibility of a different mode of experience; one that takes itself as an issue, that does not take for granted (in experience or reflection) absolutely the ideological worldhood of sense, that can become estranged from the fabric of this social reality that guides our attention frames our perceptions and provides a horizon of significance and meaning. This can never be free of the world but is instead an experience that can become aware of the determinations of the *they* and interrupt or disrupt the continuous performance of self and experience. It moves towards, though can never absolutely inhabit, the Heideggerian authentic. Heidegger's later work, *Mindfulness*, seems to develop this notion of the authentic in a more directly historical and political context, thinking of it as the 'struggle' of 'en-owning' against the machination (coercive force, power and mastery) of Modernity and modern technicity (2016: 11–12).[4] This model of experience – of everydayness and of estrangement, disruption and the struggle against the machination, power and politics of ideology and the *they* – is the theoretical position that underscores both my analysis of and reflections on the work of the restaurants and figures in the following discussion of what constitutes the 'artistry' of gastronomy and dining.

Food, Art and Performance

In Michel de Certeau, Luce Giard and Pierre Mayol's *Practice of Everyday Life, Vol.2: Living and Cooking*, they argue that eating is not just the maintenance of the 'biological machinery' of the body but also that it makes 'concrete one of the specific modes of relation between a person and the world, thus forming one of the fundamental landmarks in space-time' (1998: 183). Food and dining operate as a site for the intersection of multiple discourses and practices of personal, socio-cultural, economic and political ways of Being-in-the-world. While the act of eating can be understood from these different perspectives separately (as a personal, intimate and sensory encounter, as manifesting a particular socio-cultural heritage or position, and as operating within a particular economic framework), in practice they are entangled with one another. They are inseparable, reliant upon one another, and bound together in the constitution of the dining experience.

In Martin Jones' book *Feast*, he offers an account of Marin Harris' pyramidical structure for understanding culture, which moves from the base of the physical, environmental and biological maintenance of life, up through structures of social organisation (families, tribes, nations) to the apex of 'superstructural' elements like art and religion (2007: 4–5). While each of the 'higher' levels of culture rests on that base layer, which includes the acquisition of food and sustenance, the model nevertheless maintains a strict cultural hierarchy. This cultural hierarchy has, traditionally, excluded food from the apex of the pyramid, from being considered as an artistic material. It conceives of food practices as too entangled with the necessities of sustaining the body and the baseness of personal taste to be eligible to produce the heights of aesthetic experience. This division of 'high culture' from the basic 'necessities' of the body is mirrored in the history of the senses in the Western tradition, which has divided the senses into the 'higher' senses of sight and sound and the 'lower' senses of taste, smell and touch (see Howes and Classen 2014: 67). The higher senses are believed to offer distance and so are connected to aesthetics (the distanced or disinterested aesthetic ideal) while the lower senses are associated with low culture, manual labour and the basic subsistence of the body. In this cultural tradition, the actual consumption of food, which crosses over from distanced contemplation (mainly through sight, but also through sound) into embodied, haptic consumption and the encounter of the chemical senses (smell and taste), can be thought as seemingly too primitive, too close to necessity, too close to the body itself, to be worthy of aesthetic attention.

While this may be the position under the disinterested aesthetic gaze encapsulated in Immanuel Kant's significant writings on art, by the twentieth century, it was certainly troubled.[5] To say that food is *not* a material for art (beyond perhaps the distanced rendering of it in fixed form in, say, still life painting) is to invoke a particular cultural history of art from the Western tradition. It recollects: the division of the artistic from objects and tools of utility; the position of food as a scarcity, reserved for the majority for the sustenance of the body rather than to be frivolously wasted in artistic endeavours; the history of the cultural hierarchy of the senses, valuing the distanced intellectual contemplation of sight and sound (which itself was invariably associated with the able-bodied, privileged, White man); the converse association of the lower senses with the working classes, with women and with those who were considered 'Other' to the heteronormative White man; and the Cartesian subject, whose body was a mediator for the true locus of self in the contemplative, elevated mind. To think of dining and eating food as an artistic endeavour or aesthetic experience is a challenge to this tradition.

Experimental Dining addresses both the artistic and the aesthetic in relation to food and the restaurants. The 'artistic' is understood as an arts *practice*: the techniques, methods, tools and materials of making. This broad category can be further split into sub-disciplines of specific arts, such as painting, music, sculpture, etc., each with its own historically grounded constellation of materials and practices with which it is associated. The 'aesthetic' refers to the *experience* of art, following the root of aesthetics in *aesthesis*, meaning sensation or perception.[6] This aesthetics includes the historically dominant senses of sight and sound but folds them into a broader embodied experience of multisensory perception, the relation and entanglement of the senses to and with one another in the production of experience.

In Mary Douglas' sociological study, *In the Active Voice*, she argues that food belongs to the applied arts (alongside clothing and architecture) rather than the fine or pure arts (like the visual arts and music), because it includes a defining quality of the applied arts as manifesting a 'tension between the requirements of function and the requirements of design' (1982: 106). This distinction between the fine and applied arts speaks to a cultural and economic separation where the fine arts, with their lack of direct or obvious utility, enable the pure, disinterested, aesthetic gaze because they are seemingly not reducible to fulfilling basic and useful needs. Indeed, the sociologist Pierre Bourdieu, in his seminal work *Distinction: A Social Critique of the Judgement of Taste*, argues that

> The aesthetic disposition, a generalized capacity to neutralize ordinary urgencies and to bracket off practical ends, a durable inclination and aptitude for practice without a practical function, can only be constituted within an experience of the world freed from urgency and through the practice of activities which are an end in themselves [...].
>
> (2010: 47)

This reveals a number of things: the class structure that is inherent in the determination of the fine and applied arts; the association of the fine arts with distance from economic necessity; and the 'naturalisation' of a socio-cultural, historical and political distinction, which reserves the fine or pure arts for those privileged enough not to be tied to urgent issues of necessity. The use of food in or as art seems to be, then, a proclivity of the privileged – those for whom food can be an object and experience of the aesthetic attitude and not mere sustenance and subsistence.

Food has classically been contested as an artistic medium and dining as an art form, because of its necessary relationship to the body, its role in the sustenance of the body and its place within an everyday life practice (though that classical position has been significantly challenged over the last century in both artistic practice and scholarship). This form of argumentation reveals the cultural and class hierarchy of both Harris' pyramid and the senses; neither of which are absolute but are a result of a cultural history that maintains the positions of power and privilege for those not directly involved in the labour of production and a life practice of mere subsistence. However, all art forms can be said to have an articulation that has an everyday or instrumental quality, not just in the applied arts where that instrumentality is made explicit (for instance, applied theatre, clothing, pottery) but also in the pure arts (for example, the role of music and dance in religious rituals, which can maintain a socio-political order, or painting and drawing as a means of decoration or cartography). What is important is not the artistic material and practice itself, but the ways in which it is deployed and framed. To think of food and dining as an artistic material and practice is not to argue that *all* food does this, but rather that there are particular contexts, methods and frames that allow them to be deployed as such.

The split between the artistic and aesthetic as a split between production and experience mirrors the tension in aesthetic theory between craft and art (which, for Boisvert and Heldke, is a distinction that has 'come to hold exalted, honorific status' in conceiving art [2016: 70]). This also speaks to the split of fine and applied arts. The practice of art, the skill and craft of production is given a lesser cultural status than the work itself and its experience (the aesthetic). But they are, of course, inseparable. The craft, skill, production and making of art, while alone not enough to confer absolute status as art, is nevertheless integral. There is a class hierarchy in modes of skill and making, where the painter, the sculptor and the musician work 'for art's sake', while the carpenter, the weaver and perhaps even the chef are positioned as dwelling in craft alone. To consider food as artistic is in part to acknowledge and legitimise the modes of craft to which it is subjected by the chef, not just the everyday activities of preparing food in the domestic kitchen or even in the high street restaurant, but the finely honed skills and the special technologies of the high-end kitchen. To consider the experience of dining as aesthetic is to acknowledge and legitimise the ways in which the experience goes beyond everyday eating (sustenance, direct appeal to personal taste and pleasure) to reach the sensory and conceptual realm historically associated with the fine arts. In experimental, Michelin-starred restaurants, there can be very little claim that the food served is for the sustenance of the body; it is not just an everyday or quotidian craft and experience but something different (though whether this is artistic-aesthetic or part of an economy of experiences is an issue to which I will return).

In Heidegger's 'The Origin of the Work of Art', he argues that the essence of art is in its *alētheia*: truth as unconcealment or disclosure (2011a: 102). The *work* of the work of art is to reveal, disclose or unconceal through setting up its own world (108), a material and conceptual space that engages with and reveals the more general world within which it operates. This is in contrast to the 'applied or industrial arts that manufacture equipment' (102) and in contrast to art that enters 'world-withdrawal' or 'world-decay' (106), which ceases to engage with the world and transforms from an art work (which houses in it the doubling of 'work' as noun and verb) to an object. The artwork is still a 'thing' ('a bearer of traits', 'the unity of a manifold of sensations' and 'formed matter' [98]), so still includes a craft and skill of making but is not the making of equipment with usefulness and utility (109). It is the establishment of the world of the work of art, which does not disappear into easy usefulness as part of an unthinking, on-going life practice, but rather sets forth and discloses what Heidegger terms the 'earth' ('In setting up a world, the work sets forth the earth. [...] The work moves the earth itself into the open region of a world [...]' [109]). The earth is the background that lets all worlds come into being. We might think of it as a materiality that contains possibilities to come into being and be expressed in particular material and cultural modes. That materiality could be said to include (though Heidegger does not state this) bodily materiality (bodies, organs, nerves, brains, electrical signals, sensory streams), those things that are the fundamental facilitators of the emergence of Being-in-the-world, without which no world would be possible and only in the realm of which can any world be possible. For Heidegger, the work of art is an enacted, philosophical process of uncovering, unconcealing, disclosing and revealing the earth in its world; bringing it forth and preserving it in the artwork; consecrating a material and conceptual space outside of or beyond our everyday interactions with equipment of usefulness (where equipment serves, unthinkingly, the structures of meaning and involvements of the world).

In *Experimental Dining*, I take the Heideggerian model of art as the basis for arguing for an artistic and aesthetic understanding of the work of the experimental restaurants. Heidegger's conception of art is of an object that is created (123) and is the 'creative preserving of truth in the work', the 'becoming and happening of truth' (127); the disclosure of the earth through the world of the work. As a model for thinking about the art and aesthetics of the experimental restaurant, I am using the Heideggerian 'earth' relatively loosely, to think of how the work of the restaurants, in the world of the work they establish (both the broad frame of the restaurant and individual acts and dishes housed in that world) unearths, reveals or discloses something about itself, about the nature of experience or about the broader worldhood within which the work operates. In other words, the model of art being deployed is an argument that an artwork (as opposed to an object in world-withdrawal) is an engagement with and unsettling of the world (of ideology, of the *they*), which may take the form of unsettling and estrangement. Heidegger's model of art encompasses the acts, crafts and skills of making (its createdness), which can either lead to a work of art or to an object in world-withdrawal. In the first case, the artwork is disclosing, revealing, troubling, unsettling, estranging and moving towards the authentic mode of Dasein, which is not free of the world, but troubling an easy or continuous experience by encountering the world in such a way that its worldly workings begin to be revealed. It can draw attention to, expose or unearth the production and practice of bodies, the senses, cultural frames, political positions, histories and ideologies, taking experience as an issue for itself in experience. The object in world-withdrawal, on the other hand, conforms to the logic of the inauthentic mode of Dasein, which is not an engagement with or questioning of the world but continuing its ideological framing, positioning and ways of understanding.

In *Mindfulness*, Heidegger expands his writing on art in relation to modernity, implicitly referencing ideas of authentic and inauthentic Dasein from *Being and Time*. Heidegger anticipates the emergence of the economy of experiences (codified, as a plan for businesses, by the economists Pine and Gilmore in *The Experience Economy: Work is Theater and Every Business a Stage* [1999]). Where the artwork is the 'clearing of being' (2016: 27) in the manner of unearthing within the world of the work (as in 'The Origin of the Work of Art'), in modernity art can be, instead, a mere 'installation' (23), an organisation of elements and a way of organising beings, so that art contributes to the machinational production of being.[7] In this mode, art becomes 'lived-experience' and 'training-in-lived-experience' (25). As such, Heidegger establishes a tension between the artwork that engages in that creative disclosure and preserving of truth in the work, on the one hand, and, on the other, the kinds of experiential art that merely continue the makability of being; constructing, producing and reproducing the commodifying logic of modernity (capitalism) and, under the guise of art, elevating 'lived-experience' to a position of the seemingly aesthetic and using this apparent 'art' to continue cultural and political training of the individual; in other words, interpellation.

Heidegger's prefiguring of the economy of experiences unearths a way of thinking about the commodification of experience itself, not just the economic valuation of experience and the co-opting of experience within a neoliberalised economic framework but also that an economy of experiences, the selling of experiences themselves, institutes a mode of 'training-in-lived-experience'. It is both a training that 'lived experience' is something produced and purchased (not something that can merely be encountered as part of a life lived) and that we are trained through the purchasing of experiences how a life ought to be lived (that experiences have worth only to the extent that they are purchased and to the extent that they are understood and appreciated according to the commodified pleasure principle of hedonistic late capitalism). While Heidegger obviously does not frame his theorisation in terms of the experience economy of late, neoliberal capitalism (that would perhaps be too prescient), the theorisation nevertheless lends itself to a reading of art, culture and experience within that ideological framework. Most important here is the tension he established between artworks and 'lived-experience': artworks are the revealing, disclosive unconcealing through the world and work of the work and 'lived-experience' is an inauthentic giving-over to the worldhood of the *they*. In 'lived-experience' Dasein is given over to the culturally and politically deterministic logic of the ideological – Dasein becomes an experiencing machine that can be produced and deployed in a way that is not fully owned by itself. Indeed, the experience economy could be said to conform to the inauthentic mode of Dasein, which in *Being and Time* Heidegger articulates as constituted by curiosity, an unceasing seeking of novelty and subject to the all-knowing mode of language he calls idle talk, which always understands, is never confused and can speak about anything (1962: 216–17). The motivating tension in *Experimental Dining*, for thinking about the artistic and aesthetic workings of the work of the restaurants, is a tension between the disclosive, unsettling and revealing work of art and the conformity of the restaurants to the logic of the experience economy, selling an experience that appeals to curiosity, satisfies (at least momentarily) a desire for novelty and can be easily understood through idle talk. It is clear that they do enter into an experience economy, but I argue that at least some of their practice enters into the realm of artwork, unsettling the commodification of experience from within.

So far, performance has been noticeably absent from this discussion of food and art. While Heidegger's 'The Origin of the Work of Art' focuses on painting (notably Van Gogh's *A Pair of Shoes*), his theorisation can be read in relation to performance, because the work of art is enacted, unfolding in time, requiring a level of 'immersion' into the world of the work, not something fixed or static and doing its revelatory work in the interaction between viewer and work. The presentation of a dish in a restaurant, if it is to be compared to any artform, might intuitively seem closest to sculpture. But performance is a more appropriate and convincing framework for understanding the restaurant's work as artistic and aesthetic. Increasingly, the convergence of food and performance has become an interest in performance studies, from the issue of the *Performance Research* journal 'On Cooking' in 1999, through the establishment of working groups on food and performance as part of the American Society of Theatre Research to the Live Art

Development Agency's 2016 study room guide, 'Food & Performance', as well as a number of articles and book chapters in recent years that address the convergence.

At the beginning of Barbara Kirshenblatt-Gimblett's article, 'Playing to the Senses: Food as a Performance Medium' (in the issue of *Performance Research* 'On Cooking'), she argues that 'food and performance converge conceptually at three junctures': first, 'to perform is to do', the execution of a task, 'to make food, to service food'; second, 'to perform is to behave', the social activities and practices, 'to behave appropriately in relation to food at any point in its production, consumption, or disposal'; and third, 'to perform is to show', the theatrical displaying of action and behaviour, inviting the exercise of 'discernment, evaluation and appreciation' (1999: 1–2). This is mirrored in David Szanto's chapter, 'Performing With(in) Food', where he discusses the ways things perform, including the performance of a plant coming to fruition, and how bodies perform, including the gestures and utterances, in relation to scripts, of cooks and eaters (2018: 226). Szanto goes on to move towards a fourth area missing from Kirshenblatt-Gimblett's taxonomy of food and performance, by discussing how 'food performance becomes a means by which to bring attention to the senses, to destabilize divisions among what and who is performing, and [...] it also shows that the experience of reality is produced when sensing and cognition perform together [...]' (231). In other words, the fourth convergence of food and performance is that to perform is to experience: to perform the embodied, experiencing being that engages with the food in a multisensory way. The body itself (in its embodied consciousness) is the site of enactment of the multisensory unfolding of the aesthetic experience of eating. To consider the experience as performance is to acknowledge that the encounter with the food object is performed: it is enacted, it unfolds on, in and through the body, and the body itself is implicated as the site of the aesthetic experience of the artwork, performing its sensing and the processes of making sense.

In her chapter 'Food and Art: Changing Perspectives on Food as a Creative Medium', Yael Raviv notes that 'The discipline of performance studies has been developing ways to study and discuss time-based artwork' and that the intersection of food and art addresses the blurring of art and everyday life, intimacy and participation (2018: 208, 197). To frame the restaurants' work as performance is to acknowledge both the perspective of performance studies in reading the particular practices, objects and experiences within the work (the meal as a performance event; the performances of bodies within the space of the restaurant; the performances of objects; the dramaturgical structure of the experience) and to think about how an overarching frame of a performance event houses different artforms and practices within itself (the plastic, visual and sculptural arts in the design of the space and individual dishes; the musical arts in the noises and soundscapes of the space). Any object or material within the restaurant carries the traces of performance, its createdness, its having been made, and the food objects have the quality of the ephemeral unfolding of performance, without the attempt to even appear as a static or fixed object. The ephemerality and transience of the food are always at the fore of the experience: a plate served and later removed; the crucial timing of the presentation of a dish so that it holds its shape and temperature; the consumption and transformation from object to sensory experience in the act of eating. The convergence of the restaurant and performance is apparent in this ephemerality, as well as in the foregrounding of embodiment in the experience, in the bringing together of different artistic practices within an event and in the unfolding of a meal, where individual elements are experienced and reflected upon in relation to the unfolding, overarching narratives or ideas of the whole event.

Experimental Dining examines the restaurants as sites of performance practice, thinking about dining in the restaurant as a performance event, which utilises food, eating and sensory experience both *in* performance and *as* performance. The book explores the tension between, on the one hand, the artistic practice and aesthetic experience of the restaurants as estranged from the everyday, unsettling, disrupting, reflecting on and revealing the everyday, and, on the other hand, the everyday logic of the commodification of experience, which is not artistic-aesthetic in the Heideggerian sense, but rather an experience offered (and purchased) for the sake of novelty and curiosity, for 'lived-experience' that appeals to spectacle, emotional satisfaction and for the sake of the accumulation of cultural capital. Laurie Beth Clark and Michael Peterson define their use of the term 'food performances' as a Brechtian alienation, which can use new techniques and technologies to create new dishes, to render the familiar as unfamiliar or draw attention to 'the problematics of food itself' – it becomes an avant-garde food practice 'when it denaturalizes the act of eating' (2017). The artistic-aesthetic performances in and of the restaurant occur when it engages in this process of 'denaturalising', 'de-second-naturing'[8] or in Brechtian estrangement. In Fredrik Jameson's account of Brecht's estrangement, he writes that it is 'To make something look strange' and that it 'implies the antecedence of a general familiarity, of a habit which prevents us from really looking at things, a kind of perceptual numbness' that, in estrangement, gives way to 'the freshness of experience and the recovery of perception' (1999: 50).[9] The restaurants' artistic-aesthetic practice is one of estrangement, both sensually and conceptually, unsettling and defamiliarising the everyday and re-sensitising the diner to the possibilities of sensation and thinking outside of the world order of quotidian tastes, everyday food practice and the continuous, unthinking experience of one's own embodiment.

Arguments and Structure of the Book

There are a number of arguments running through *Experimental Dining*. It addresses the staging of the meals in each of the restaurants, considering the various performances at work and the dramaturgical construction of the meal. The book argues that the work of the restaurants operates both as part of an economy of experiences, conforming to the ideological order of commodification, pleasure and enjoyment through the deployment of 'science and technology' as a form of control and understanding, and that it engages in an artistic-aesthetic practice, utilising creative practices and performances to unsettle, de-second-nature, make strange and explore the very ideological and experiential framings within which it operates. Rather than thinking of the experience economy and artistic practice as diametrically opposed, they are treated here as simultaneous possibilities of understanding and experiencing, in part grounded in the approach and practice of making the work and in part a result of the approach and perspective of the experiencing diner. This argument constitutes an interrogation of claims to theatre and the theatrical in experimental and spectacular restaurants, though framing this instead as performance, given that performance and performance studies are broader terms that allow for different kinds of practices beyond those just associated with the stage.

In order to make the case for the restaurant, the dining experience and the food as performance, running alongside the analysis of the restaurants is a selection of performance and artistic works that have involved food or drawn attention to the aesthetics of sensory experience beyond sight and sound. These works are largely in the area of experimental, avant garde practice or from performance art and live art, from the turn of the twentieth century to the present. The choice of this period is for a number of reasons. First, as explored by Georges Bataille in *The Accursed Share*, the Industrial Revolution significantly changed food production processes and politics (1989: 24, 27–38). Mechanisation led to greater surpluses and excesses in food production, through changes to agricultural processes and food storage and preservation. The politics surrounding the expenditure of that excess led to a greater consideration of food production and consumption, as well as greater experimentation with food as a material in the arts. Second, as Allen S. Weiss has argued, from the latter-half of the nineteenth century, European art was marked by: a shift in focus to the internal experience of art, moving away from just questions of representation and addressing intoxication and synaesthesia; the hybridisation of artforms, following ideas of the total work of art; and the questioning of aesthetic hierarchies (2007: 200). These shifts in the understanding of art and the conceptual focus of artists provided the coordinates and conditions for experimentation outside of classical aesthetic ideals. Finally, as Daphne Ben Chaim has argued, a key aspect of twentieth century theatre was an exploration of 'distance' (the physical, emotional and intellectual positioning and relation of the audience to the artwork), which she traces to the early twentieth century theatrical experiments (1984: 78). While notions of 'distance' in the arts were not new at this time (indeed, Kantian disinterestedness can be understood as a modality of distance), the artistic and theatrical experiments within the historical avant garde brought to the fore greater experiments with distance and the positioning of the audience, which set the stage for performance work across the twentieth century up to the contemporary proliferation of participatory, relational and immersive practices.

The artistic and performance practice referenced and explored through the book operates in a number of ways. First, it offers a historical precedent and context for some of the explorations and experiments with food, dining and the senses in the restaurants. Second, following Heidegger's understanding of art, the works themselves raise ideas through their work of revealing, uncovering and disclosing and, as such, form a means of articulating ideas that can be applied to the restaurants' practice. Finally, in bringing together explicitly artistic or performance practice with the restaurants, not only can the arts provide a perspective on the restaurants' work, but the restaurants themselves can offer a way of thinking about performance. In particular, given the rise of immersive practices, which bring the sensate and reflective body of the audience-participant into the world of the work, the restaurants' explicitly multisensory practice can open new ways of thinking about and making art and performance, dealing with the complexity of embodied, sensory experience in immersive practice.

The book is structured according to a conceptual conceit. Each of the chapters deals with a different temporality in relation to the experience of dining, moving from the preparations for the dining event, through the minutiae of perceptual experience to the broader ways in which individual elements are arranged and ordered as an overarching event and the political and ideological discourse within which the work takes place. This structure is not to argue that the experience occupies different, discrete temporal strata, but rather is a means of interrogating, step by step (as it were), the different temporal modalities of the experience. The separation of the chapters is a structural device, a way of teasing out the complexities of the experience while nevertheless acknowledging that they are entangled with one another. It proposes that individual 'moments' of perception are not free of broader narratives and discourses and that the broader ideological and dramaturgical thrusts of the event of the meal cannot be understood without their constituent (and constituting) parts. In part, the structure of the book mirrors the structure of a tasting menu, with individual courses or chapters arranged to build upon one another, with various connections between the main chapters and 'palate-cleansing' interludes between the chapters. These interludes are shorter pieces addressing a particular practice, issue or idea, forming a bridge between the preceding chapter and beginning to lay the ground for the chapter to follow.

The first chapter, Preparation, examines some of the foundational assumptions of the restaurants and the ways in which the ground is prepared for the dining experience. In this chapter is consideration of the conceptual drive of each of the restaurants, thinking about what they are attempting to achieve and the broad principles of their practice. This is followed by an examination of the construction of the world of the restaurant as a site of performance, reflections on the creative approaches and methodologies they employ and ending with an examination of the term 'technoemotional cuisine' (rather than the more generally used term, 'molecular gastronomy'), as a way not just of naming but of thinking about the work of the restaurants. Chapter two, Presentation, addresses some of the performances of the restaurant, including reading the front of house staff as performers, the menu as a script and performance text and the performances of the presentation of the food itself. These various performances are considered in particular in terms of how they facilitate, frame and produce the experience of dining. The third chapter, Perception, turns to the multisensory and embodied experience of eating, considering the aesthetic dimension of the multisensory encounter with the food and how notions of reception (processing, understanding, interpreting) are always already at work in and framing perception. The chapter begins with an exploration of immediacy and how notions of immediacy and presence (often used as an ontological basis of performance) are troubled by the dining experience. This is followed by an examination of how language, particularly in consciousness, enters into, frames and unsettles experience. The chapter ends with a discussion of the intersection of dining and sex, both thought of as sensory and sensual encounters, and the creative approach of deconstruction in gastronomy and where it intersects with philosophical deconstruction as a process of de-structuring, revealing and undermining self-evident presence. The fourth chapter, Processing, turns to how the whole dining event is built, examining the processes of making sense of the dining experience, the deployment of narratives in and through the meal (especially in the curation of the tasting menu) and how the experience can be understood as an artistic-aesthetic event (in the Heideggerian sense). The final chapter, Payoff, examines the political discourses and economic frameworks within which the restaurants operate, considering how they frame, shape, guide and produce the experience. This chapter considers notions of pleasure, enjoyment and excess (the luxury of the Michelin-starred restaurant), the food politics of seasonality, localism and the organic and ends with a direct engagement with the restaurants as part of an economy of experiences, including the commodification of lived-experience and the accumulation of cultural capital.

The first interlude, between chapters one and two, addresses Italian Futurism and how the Italian Futurists' work with food offers a historical precedent for technoemotional cuisine. This interlude takes up the ideas of technology, emotion and the politics of the work from the preceding chapter and moves into the following chapter in exploring particular examples of the presentation of the food in Italian Futurism as an artistic material. The second interlude examines Blumenthal's work as a celebrity chef on television, focusing on an episode of his programme, *Heston's Feasts*, to explore the audio-visual presentation of the food and the implied sensuality arising from it, bridging from the presentation of food in the previous chapter to the sensory and sensual encounter with the food object. The third interlude makes use of some of the ideas from the Perception chapter to offer an analysis of *Pop-Up Love Party*, a performance event by Zuppa Theatre Company that operated at the intersection of food, performance and philosophy (it was a performance of Plato's *Symposium* with an accompanying tasting menu of dishes). This interlude is a particular case study, which explores the application of practices and principles from the restaurant in performance and leads in to the following chapter in thinking about the narratives of the dining performance and the relation of individual elements to the whole event. The final interlude explores the documentation and exhibiting of elBulli's work, to think about how the restaurant's practice was transformed into an artistic exhibition and how the exhibition reflected upon and attempted to capture the sensations and narratives of their work and, in so doing, transformed it explicitly into material of cultural capital, which in the final chapter is addressed as a core part of the economy of experiences.

Experimental Dining is an attempt to interrogate the positioning of experimental, Michelin-starred restaurants as offering an artistic and aesthetic experience. It works through issues of art and performance and issues of experience. I draw on my own experience of dining as the basis for the reflections, as well as cookbooks, catalogues, films and television programmes. While the restaurants cannot be extracted from the economics and politics of a level of privilege, given their cost and their elite position within gastronomy, nevertheless the experiences of dining were unsettling, exciting, sensually rich and a site of engaged creative practice.

NOTES

1. The references to *A Day at elBulli* are decimalised as this refers to inserts in the book that are not included in the book's pagination. The decimalised number refers to the page location within the insert.
2. The reflections on Noma throughout the book are based on the restaurant's site before the move in 2017.
3. In Macquarrie and Robinson's translation of *Being and Time*, from which I am working, Heidegger's *they* is sometimes italicised, other times in speech marks, sometimes both. When referring to Heidegger's *they*, rather than its more common usage, I will italicise the term.
4. Heidegger's *Mindfulness* was written as part of what he called 'The Turn' in his work and thinking in the 1930s and 1940s. In 'Letter on Humanism', Heidegger states that this turn

is 'not a change of standpoint from *Being and Time*' (2011b: 157). Rather it encapsulates a development of his thinking and a shift in the kind of language he deploys but with significant continuities that can be traced from the earlier work.

5. The use of Kant's writing on art and disinterestedness occurs in a number of writings on food and art; for instance, see Baggini (2014: 227–28), Boisvert and Heldke (2016: 76, 79–81, 90–91, 94), Jouary (2013: 19–27) and Spence (2018b: 239).

6. The distinction between artistic and aesthetic is articulated by John Dewey in 'Art as Experience', with the former referring to 'the act of production' and the latter 'perception and enjoyment' (2008: 310).

7. Heidegger writes that 'art has the character of *Da-sein*' in that, in art as the 'clearing of being', it 'holds the decision for man's [sic] other way of being' (27). There is an apparent continuation of the two modes of Dasein here; where the installational art, that continuation of the makability of being, is the inauthentic, and the true artwork, that disclosure, is the decision for an authentic mode of being.

8. To use Simon Jones' term, 'de-second-naturing', which he defines as 'True discontinuity, the actually felt interruption of *out-standing standing-within* is felt as both a *mood* of de-naturing and an *instant* when-where one's self is forced out of its self, interested in (in the sense of *esse*/being *inter*/between) the world' (2012: 36–37, original emphasis).

9. Ironically, in this case, Jameson's discussion of estrangement comes after discussion of Brecht's adversity to intellectual theatre, which involves mere pleasure and entertainment and which he terms 'culinary' (1999: 47).

1

Preparation: The Creative World of the Restaurants

Before the aesthetic experience of the work of the restaurants can take place, the artwork itself needs to be created. This chapter examines the creation of the artwork of the restaurants through consideration of the grounding assumptions they employ as the foundation for both the work itself and how it is understood by those who make it. It also explores the construction of the restaurant space itself as a site and world of performance practice alongside the methods, approaches and practices used to create the work. The chapter begins by exploring the overarching conceptual positions of each of the restaurants, how they position their own practice and what each of the chefs and restaurants is attempting to do or explore. This is followed by analysis of the creation and curation of the world of the practice – the material, conceptual and artistic construction of the restaurant as a site of performance and a site, like in immersive practices, that performs, that houses other performances and operates as a frame for the performances and experiences it contains. The penultimate section of the chapter addresses the creative practice of developing and making the food: the methodologies, skills and craft of artistic production. The chapter ends by turning to Pau Arenós' term, technoemotional cuisine (an alternative to molecular gastronomy), which I argue is a more useful term in that it encapsulates the approach and ideological positioning of the restaurants, as well as housing within it the possibility for an artistic and aesthetic understanding of the practice.

Restaurant Philosophy

On 10 December 2006, chefs Ferran Adrià, Heston Blumenthal and Thomas Keller, with food scientist Harold McGee, published in the *Observer* their 'Statement on "New Cookery"'. In this statement, which reads like a manifesto, they set out the four principles that they believe underpin 'New Cookery', by which they mean the work of their own and others' avant garde restaurants. Unlike some of the manifestos of artistic practice from the historical avant garde, which tended to overtly state the political position of the work, this statement engages a politics that is presented as self-evident – not a radical statement of the 'new', but a seemingly reasonable account that attempted to de-radicalise the work of 'molecular gastronomy', to demonstrate it as a 'natural' evolution of cooking techniques. Helstosky argues that modernist cuisine (one of the many names used for experimental, molecular gastronomist cooking) is fundamentally an attempt to reinvent cooking (2017). However, in the statement, this new trend in gastronomic practice is presented as an evolution rather than revolution, a return to histories and cultures of food preparation and a continuation of its ongoing development. In some ways, the work of the chefs is revolutionary, adopting new approaches, techniques and technologies, but it is also an evolution, building on, and not a radical break from, traditional, historical and quotidian food practices and cultures.

In the statement, they write that the four key tenets of their work are as follows:

1. Excellence, openness and integrity.
2. Valuing of tradition and building on it in 'the ongoing evolution of [their] craft'.
3. Embracing innovation.
4. The belief that 'cooking can affect people in profound ways, and that a spirit of collaboration and sharing is essential to true progress in developing this potential'.
(Blumenthal 2009: 126–27)

The statement is an attempt, on the part of the chefs, to shift the frame of their practice from the scientific to gastronomy as an artform, countering the predominantly 'scientific' frame that lingers through cultural understandings of molecular gastronomy. They argue that dining, because it 'engages all the senses as well as the mind', can be understood as 'the most complex and comprehensive of the performing arts' (in Blumenthal 2009: 127). Their suggestion is that the dining experience is a performing art and that, in addressing all of the senses (rather than just the classically higher aesthetic senses of sight and sound), the tactile and chemical senses can be considered as part of the complexity of the aesthetic experience. Throughout the statement is an underlying preoccupation with 'pleasure', that everything is ultimately in service of the deliciousness of the food and emotional affects for the diner. Their politics is one of easy pleasure, of pure hedonism, irrelevant of the processes and conditions of production. For the chefs, the *artistic* aims of their work are always subservient to a pleasure principle.

In the summer of 2005, elBulli set down in a 23-point document their own definition of the philosophy of the restaurant. In the document, they articulate their approach to food, covering: its artistic potential, the desire for quality, the preference for vegetables and seafood over red meat and large cuts of poultry, the desire to 'preserve the purity' of ingredient's original flavour, the desire for knowledge and collaboration, to appeal to all of the senses and the desire for creativity and breaking of conventions (Adrià et al. 2014g: 87). For elBulli, 'The tasting menu is the finest expression of avant-garde cooking' (Adrià et al. 2014g: 87) in that it engenders small and delicate yet powerfully flavoured courses and therefore allows for a greater range experimentation in the meal. It allows a broader range of gustatory practices to be explored in a single meal.

Two of the 'defining' qualities of elBulli, as articulated by the Adrià brothers and Soler, are the 'technique-concept search' and 'the sixth sense' (2014g: 396). The first of these is what they see as the pinnacle of creativity, in producing new practices or ideas for preparing and presenting food, through utilising new techniques or practices in the kitchen and developing new concepts. What constitutes a concept in each of the restaurants is never quite clear though often seems to involve some kind of idea that is rendered in practical form. At elBulli, the 'technique-concept search' was a movement away from relying on the recipes of others (other chefs and culturally inherited recipes) and involved an interrogative research and development process, exploring new methods of cooking, unusual or unconventional ingredients and creative ways of presenting food to the diner. The 'sixth sense' was elBulli's term for the conceptual appreciation of their food and consisted of, amongst other things, 'trickery, surprise, irony, provocation [and] decontextualisation' (400). For Adrià, the 'sixth sense' was an attempt to reposition diners in relation to the food, to transform dining from sustenance and a social act to an activity that foregrounded the sensorial and aesthetic dimensions of experience (400). It was the twin drive towards the 'technique-concept search' and the 'sixth sense' that marked the innovative nature of elBulli's practice. The first was manifested in the practice of the chefs, in the kitchen, whereas the second was about the positioning of the diner in relation to the experience. However, they coalesce in the drive for innovative cuisine that goes beyond traditional production processes and enters the domain of conceptual art and aesthetic experience. In both cases, there was an attempt to disrupt the everyday practice and experience of preparing and eating food.

In a similar way, the work at The Fat Duck can be categorised into those two perspectives of the drive in the kitchen and the drive in the dining room, coalescing in the work. Blumenthal writes that '[…] one of the key questions that still drives the Fat Duck [is]: *What is flavour, and how do we perceive it?*' (2009: 87, original emphasis). Unlike Adrià's broadly artistic focus in the search for technique-concepts, The Fat Duck is driven by a psychological and physiological inquiry into the workings of flavour and how that can be transformed into an experience for the diner. For Blumenthal, the overarching aim of the work, once it reaches the diner, is to provoke a pleasurable emotional response. Alongside the 'deliciousness' of the food, he wanted to 'engage the emotions, provoking curios-ity, amusement or even a child-like sense of wonder' (Blumenthal 2009: 140). The underlying ethos of The Fat Duck is to bring together the pleasures of eating with the pleasurable feelings of curiosity, amusement and wonder. Blumenthal reflects that the pleasures of dining are grounded not only in the multisensory encounter with the food but also that they are framed by the specific contexts of the experi-ence and the memories brought, or associations made, by the diner (Blumenthal 2010: 6). Indeed, an overarching concern for Blumenthal is to trigger memories (in part as a means of intensifying the sensory experience). This invocative attempt includes both personal and cultural memory, though inevitably more the latter than the former. Cultural memory, which we might rather think of as a heritage and context, is utilised to intensify pleasure and satisfaction. The position adopted by The Fat Duck is that an element of familiarity contributes to enjoyment. Of course, the predominantly British heritage and history that underscores The Fat Duck's work means this particular appeal is made to those who somehow iden-tify with that cultural frame. The conceptual impetus of The Fat Duck is to draw on cultural and culinary histories, scientific and psychological knowledges and to make use of new technologies to create an experience for the diner that is pleasur-able, carrying traces of the familiar in service of the pleasurable while nevertheless producing something out of the ordinary.

The overarching concept of the work of Noma is that of Nordic cuisine. This is instituted at various levels, through the choice and sourcing of ingredients, through the preparatory methods to transform those ingredients into the dish and the construction of the scenography of the restaurant. For Redzepi, this was an overtly political act to counter the dominance of French and Spanish cuisine in European fine dining (in Skyum-Nielsen 2010: 11). Redzepi writes that the 'time and place' of the contemporary Nordic region was the foundation on which Noma would layer 'conceptual thoughts about the dishes, such as innovation [and] technique [...]' (in Skyum-Nielsen 2010: 13). In a similar way to elBulli and The Fat Duck, Noma is positioned in relation to a particular geographic and cultural heritage, coupled with new techniques for the preparation of dishes. However, where elBulli and The Fat Duck use 'history' as a creative impetus, Noma's work attempts to preserve their regional history in the dishes. In practical terms, this can amount to the same thing (the use of regional or national histories, heritages and tastes as part of the creative development of dishes), but there is an important difference in how the chefs conceive of the work. In Adrià's and Blumenthal's writings, they often foreground the pleas-ures of eating, to which Spanish or Catalan and British food traditions (respectively) are in service; in Redzepi's writings, the Nordic is almost invariably at the forefront.

In contrast to these, Alinea is framed as being a break from being overly deter-mined by historical lineages and contexts. While their work is inevitably entangled with its various contexts, Alinea professes to continually attempt to break away and discover new modes of food preparation and presentation without recourse to a historical or contextual narrative for justification. It is the search for innovation in and of itself rather than contextual reflection and reconfiguration that drives the cuisine. In Achatz's edited book, *Alinea*, which is both a recipe book and a series of reflections on the restaurant, Mark McClusky writes that 'Alinea's food doesn't evoke, it provokes. It's not comfort food that looks to the past; it's challenging food that looks to the future [...]' (2008: 19). There is a useful tension established, here, between evocation and provocation although McClusky is too direct in suggesting that Alinea engages only in the latter and not the former. While elBulli, The Fat Duck and Noma frame their work as evocative (to bring to consciousness or recall the past or an idea of a location) and Alinea presents theirs as provocative (to stimulate a reaction), both seem to be at work in all of the restaurants. There is a balance between the comforting familiarity of the evocative, utilising common ingredients and preparations to evoke personal memories connected to and encouraged by dining (in the manner of the Proustian madeleine), and the provocative, where unusual ingredients, combinations, concepts and presentations are designed and deployed to provoke a more intense reaction to and reading of the food. In the case of the evocative, the diner is positioned as a genteel receiver of pleasure whose engagement with the dining experience operates at the level of a certain emotional satisfaction aroused by the food. In the case of the provocative, the diner is called to engage more directly in making sense of the experience and to be awoken to the possibilities of sensory stimulation beyond the usual confines of the everyday.

In utilising cultural food heritages and appealing to conventional tastes, the restaurants are continuing a particular ideological position in their practice. In Claude Lévi-Strauss' *The Raw and the Cooked*, he explores how the 'empirical categories' of raw and cooked, fresh and decayed, moistened and burned, are themselves the result of cultural performances, 'adopting the standpoint of a particular culture' (1969: 1). The very means by which we conceive of something as *food*, as edible, as distinct from inedible, raw, over-cooked or decayed/rotten, is culturally determined. Indeed, even the choice of 'raw ingredients' carries the traces of a cultural frame of what constitutes the edible, rendering the 'raw' in some ways always already 'cooked' (in Lévi-Strauss' sense as ready to be eaten). While there is some flexibility around the liminal points between the categories of 'raw' and 'cooked', they nevertheless rely on cultural narratives to mark the distinctions between them. However experimental the restaurants' work is, there is still an appeal to cultural narratives of edibility and the pleasurable and the use of conventional ingredients and cooking processes. The work of the restaurants is never absolutely new or original because it relies upon and makes use of cultural histories of food preparation and consumption, which themselves figure in the production of the tastes of the diners and their enjoyment. We can read this as ideological, rather than merely a process of enculturation, to inflect it with a politics: one that naturalises tastes derived from 'national cuisines', suggesting that tastes, which themselves have been produced through familiarity with a national-cultural cuisine, are simply true, thereby intimately connecting a practice of the body with(in) a national framework. In using this to appeal to pleasure, the restaurants are utilising those tastes and culinary heritages in service of selling a pleasurable experience.

Explicitly for both elBulli and The Fat Duck, there is a rhetoric employed around the role of childhood in determining the diners' tastes in, preferences for and enjoyment of food. Understanding the formation of the subject through childhood experiences, often (though by no means exclusively) practiced within a particular cultural framework, the restaurants deploy a rather static notion of the subject and tastes, as though the tasting adult emerges fully formed from childhood and that the pleasure of the experience needs to conform to those immaturely formed tastes. This then appears to be the basis of the restaurants' playful approach to food histories and conventions. While they might play with, rework and in some ways depart from those traditions, they cannot stray too far from the cultural performances of raw and cooked, precisely because they are so ingrained. They enjoy making use of the spectacle of surprise, but for this surprise to appeal and work for more than any given individual diner, it requires a foundational knowledge of a cultural heritage of cuisine (how can we be surprised by a deconstruction of a classic dish if we do not know the reference point that is the focus of its activity?). For surprise to work as something pleasurable and delightful (which in the restaurants is the guiding principle; it cannot slip into shock and disgust), it must remain on the pleasurable side of the line of tension between the creative or new and the traditional. For each of the restaurants, in the pursuit of pleasure, there is a constraint on the creativity of the practice: it cannot radically transgress the performative narratives of raw and cooked, narratives that are taken to be almost absolute, given that they appeal to a seemingly spontaneous experience of pleasure.

There is a tension that underscores the work of the restaurants. The generic understanding of the practice of molecular gastronomy, as a radical practice and revolution in cuisine, is countered by the restaurants themselves in order to reassure (potential) diners that the experience will nevertheless be pleasurable and will appeal to pre-existing food tastes and cultures. The restaurants explore new ideas, practices, ingredients and presentations, but always with a view to the diners' experience of pleasure and a degree of familiarity. There is an attempt to balance the evolutionary against the revolutionary and the evocative against the provocative.

In part, this is driven by the need to sell the experience to diners and the experience itself cannot be *too* unsettling; it needs to remain on the pleasurable side of novelty. There is, however, still a degree of the unsettling and of estrangement in the work, as it does not merely perpetuate food heritages, traditions and cultures in a recognisably traditional form, which is precisely what makes it *unsettling* rather than an absolute rejection and bold originality. The artistic production and aesthetic experience, respectively in the creative work of the chefs and the sensory and reflective encounter of that work by the diner, navigate this tension between the traditional and the new although in some cases moves more clearly into one realm than the other.

Constructing the World

The construction of the space of the restaurant is important in two regards: first, it is a curated and created work in its own right, and second, it is the site that contains, frames and provides the conditions for the performances and experiences that operate and are enacted and performed within it. In Heidegger's formulation of Being-in-the-world, he conceptualises Dasein as always already 'thrown' into the world; it always finds itself already 'there' (1962: 174). Heidegger writes of this in a generic sense, as a theorisation of how Dasein is never free of the world, never able to be conceived as a fully autonomous individual that can be separated from the world. It is not some particular space in Heidegger's theorisation although in practice it is always some particular world. As such, the world has a significant bearing on experience. Not only must experience take place within the world (across the continuum of Being-in-the-world, never entirely conceivable at merely one or the other end of the spectrum) but also the world itself furnishes experience with its spatial, temporal and conceptual horizon (its significance). In his writing on art, Heidegger inflects the notion of world slightly differently from its deployment in *Being and Time*. He writes that the artwork opens up and sets up a world, where the Thingly qualities of art are granted their significance in the open space of the world of the work, which itself is the working quality of the work of art (2011a: 108–09). This world of the work of art is distinct from the more general worldhood, in that it enables disclosure and uncovering; it is a consecrated world that engages with the more general world. While for Heidegger this is largely a conceptual world opened by the work of art (though of course that can never be thought as separate from its material conditions and articulation), it can be extended to think of it as an inhabitable space, a space in which the audience, spectator or, in this case, diner can dwell physically as well as conceptually.

In this section, I turn to the construction of the worlds of the restaurants, their scenographic construction, in order to think of them as akin to site-specific performance, where the site is not set at a distance from the audience (or in this case the diner), but rather is a space to be navigated and experienced from within, operating as an encompassing spatial and conceptual horizon for the individual acts and experiences within it. This in turn becomes a background or frame for those performances, providing a grounding. I do not claim the grander ontological thrust of Heidegger's theorisation (which deals with being as such constituted and conditioned by, and related to, the world) but rather utilise his model to think about the experiences that take place within these particular worlds. I do argue that the spaces go beyond being merely a material site, by thinking about how the creation and curation of the spaces contribute to the processes of making sense of the experience, both through locating the experience and through operating as an artistic world of performance. The tension of the two worlds from Heidegger (the general world of Being-in-the-world and the artistic world of the opening established in/as the work of art) is manifested in the restaurants: they continue some of the (often unnoticed and everyday) workings of restaurants (the general world) and operate as an artistic world, where they set up a space outside of, yet always related to or in tension with, the quotidian world.

The continuum of Being and world allows for a consideration of how our experience is grounded in and produced by the material and ideological context within which it takes place. Alongside this are the particular workings of the world opened up by the work of art, which establishes its own world, though can never be thought as entirely separate from the more general world beyond itself. Each of the restaurants pays attention to the construction of this world, from the architecture of the buildings within which they operate, to the furnishing of the spaces and the individual items of cutlery and crockery they use for specific dishes. However, it is important to emphasise that no matter how much the spaces are constructed according to a totalising world view on the part of the restaurants' staff and creatives, this is never translated into a totalised world. In Nick Kokonas' reflections on designing Alinea, he argues that they attempted to recognise and challenge *every* aspect of the conventional production of a dining space (2008: 44). But there is always space for that which breaks through, which was not considered or which has been forgotten – the unexpected, the unplanned, the erroneous and the incoherent and that which is 'misread' by the diner, understood in a different way from how it was planned. This is where we might depart from Heidegger, because lingering through his 'Origin of the Work of Art' is a sense of the totalised world of the work of art – that it is a coherent and consistent world. But the work of art can never operate in this totalised way because there are inevitably things beyond the control of the totalising perspective of the creator: materials in the work that are overlooked or forgotten, elements of the broader world that inform and enter into the material and experiential dimensions of the work and the resistance of the bodies and reflections of the audience or diners, whether by conscious effort or otherwise, to submit to the perspective of the artist.

In Anne Ring Peterson's chapter, 'Between Image and Stage: The Theatricality and Performativity of Installation Art', she implicitly builds on Michael Fried's 'Art and Objecthood' as she draws out the performativity of installation spaces by noting that they transform the physical space into a setting to be negotiated and that the work has to function as an object in a situation (2005: 215). She goes on that 'The viewer will continually be aware that the installation is an artificial construction, not part of a life world' (230). However, while the initial entry into the world of the work might seemingly operate in this way, it does not necessarily continue throughout the experience: the world of the work of art is never entirely separated from the 'life world' (it exists within and references that broader world and those who encounter the work of art are not reconfigured in their sensate embodiment, reflective interpretations or political positions, which are all implicated in the experience of the work of art) and awareness of the constructedness of the world can fade relatively quickly as we acclimatise to it. Indeed, the 'life world', or perhaps everyday or even inauthentic experience of the world, operates in the same way: it has the potential for attention to be turned to its constructedness, but we find ourselves fallen into it, dwelling in familiarity to the extent that constructedness does not occupy attention indefinitely. Artistic, spectacular or performance worlds can be more apparent in their constructedness, given that they work against the grain of the everyday, hence drawing attention to those worlds themselves, but the surprise or unsettlement of the unfamiliar can all-too-easily become merely the new background world to and of experience.

In Barbara Kirshenblatt-Gimblett's 'Making Sense of Food in Performance', she draws an analogy between the restaurant and a performance space, exploring 'Self-consciously theatrical restaurants' as stages (2007: 75). This analogy can be extended, given the use of front of house staff in both the theatre and the restaurant (although with slightly different functions), the distinction between onstage and backstage (the dining room and the kitchen, though also the kitchen and the prep kitchen) and, at elBulli, the designation of the restaurant manager, Juli Soler, as 'The Stage Manager' (Adrià et al. 2008: 42). The stage, the arena of performance, is the dining room, but it is much closer to immersive or site-specific practice than the traditional theatrical stage and auditorium; it is a world that is open to the bodies of the diners, not marked out as a world to be viewed from a physical and psychical distance. Unlike the classic proscenium stage, the curtain does not rise on the world of the restaurant, plunging the visitor into the midst of the world, but rather requires that the diner be invited into the world, facilitating and managing the transition from the everyday world ('out there') to the physical, conceptual and artistic space that both frames and constitutes a core element of the dining experience.

The diner always takes a journey to the restaurant space and that journey is part of the curation of the experience, framing it in advance. Each of the restaurants requires pre-booking, often months in advance. At elBulli, even if there were tables free for a particular service, they would not allow them to be taken by someone without a reservation, to avoid setting the precedent of being able to walk in and be served. In the early years of elBulli, Adrià would go into the dining room to greet the guests, but increasingly the guests wanted to visit him in the kitchen, which then became part of the structured experience. In visiting the kitchen, where the work of the chef takes place, the backstage arena is opened to the diner for their inspection and curiosity, not to break the magic of the food to follow, but to add to the intrigue: they visited the space where the food was prepared, but still have no sense of *how* it was done. In a way, it is an extra layer of the magic trick: showing the diner that the chef doesn't have anything up his sleeve before making their card appear. The diner sees the 'backstage' activities and apparatus of the show yet is still denied an explanation of the magical spectacle of the food served.

At The Fat Duck, the process of transition into the restaurant is less controlled but no less significant to the experience. The door to the restaurant opens out directly onto the pavement and road running through the small village of Bray. It would be easy to think the transition into the restaurant is more abrupt. However, the restaurant is triangulated with Blumenthal's development kitchen, which is on the opposite side of the road, and his pub, The Hind's Head (not to mention the reservation process, which begins the experience for the diner months in advance). The street itself, then, becomes appropriated as part of the 'Heston experience', with noticeable (though not imposing) signs indicating that this is 'Heston territory'. The front door of The Fat Duck opens onto the dining room, where the front of house staff immediately guide the diner. After crossing the threshold, the diner is in the hands of the staff and the experience.

Like The Fat Duck, Alinea opens out onto the street in Chicago's Lincoln Park, described by Michael Ruhlman as an 'affluent, residential neighborhood' (in Achatz 2008: 1). The restaurant has a sleek, modern exterior, with a big window and just a small sandwich-board sign to indicate its presence. The restaurant is near a theatre and, just as one does for the theatre, asks diners to buy a ticket rather than book a table. Achatz and Kokonas introduced the selling of tickets from an economic rather than theatrical perspective, arguing that it would mitigate the impact of 'no-shows or late cancellations' (2011: 395). However, framing the event in this way, by purchasing a ticket, does bring the restaurant even closer to the performance event. Purchasing a ticket pays for the event in advance, which in some ways could alleviate the consideration of cost during the meal itself. It also sits within the economics of the theatre, which is different from the more usual mode of payment and consumption, whereby money is exchanged for the product once the product is received. With performance events and at Alinea, one purchases the experience itself, irrespective of its quality, which can never be guaranteed in advance. While there is sometimes the opportunity to demand a refund after the event if it did not match up to one's expectations, purchasing a ticket is a statement of support and expectation. It also attempts to explicitly move the work of the restaurant from providing goods and services to an aesthetic event.

On entering the restaurant, the diner is greeted by a hallway of curved walls bathed in a red light. The entrance hall to Alinea is a little disorienting and clearly marks the transition from the street to the dining room. The corridor stretches ahead, with an archway at the end, to the left, which leads into the downstairs dining room and the base of the staircase leading up to the dining room on the first floor. Unlike at The Fat Duck, where the front of house staff greet the diner as soon as they cross the threshold, Alinea allows a moment for the diner to reorient themselves within this new world. The hallway is a slightly disorientating experience, though it does throw the dim dining room into sharper relief, more so than if one were to step immediately from the street into the darkened dining room.

At Noma, the entrance to the restaurant is wholly different from The Fat Duck and Alinea, which sit within a wider context of a neighbourhood. Noma was located in an old warehouse on the sea front in Copenhagen, hidden away from passing traffic and requiring a special journey. On entering the restaurant, the diner is greeted by the front of house staff *en masse*. Having stepped into the restaurant, the diner is confronted by a group of around 15 people, all smiling and saying hello to each guest. The diner is then approached by one of the waiting staff and taken into and through the kitchen. Unlike at elBulli, where Adrià greets the guests and talks to them, the chefs at Noma continue to work. However, as the diner passes, each chef looks up from their task, including Redzepi, to look at the diner and greet them, before moving back to work. The diner is made to feel like a returning guest, with the uncanny feeling that you were known in advance and are important to the staff. Much like Adrià's greeting of the guests, this establishes a sense that the diner is valued and that the experience is being crafted specifically for them.

At elBulli, the diner would first be greeted by a freshly raked gravel front. Before each service, the gravel would be raked to form a smooth surface, one that did not bear the traces of other movement. This small act of preparation established two different but complementary aspects of the experience. First, in demonstrating attention to detail in the space, it begins the experience of the restaurant with a sense of precision and control. Even though the world of elBulli is within the more chaotic and unknowable world of the everyday, the raked gravel, as a transitory space, suggested that the world into which the diner was entering was one in which there was a logical coherence, where each aspect of the setting was controlled and deliberate. Second, the raked gravel wipes away the traces of both previous performances (other services) and the daily grind of the work of the restaurant. It moves the space from its preparatory processes to the performance event. The gravel would bear the traces of the movements of only this set of people, who have gathered for this particular event at this particular place and time.

The large kitchen, small kitchen and terrace, which form the opening spaces of the meal at elBulli, are spread out before the diner as they enter from the car park. The diner is invited to the terrace for cocktails and snacks, before moving past this extended entrance space into the *comedor* and *salón* for the main part of the meal. These spaces have tiled floors (which, according to Lisa Abend in her book on elBulli 'show their age' [2011: 91], continuing the rootedness of elBulli in the histories of the building) and pebble-dashed white walls, with tables spread out and the room framed by dark wooden beams. There is a feeling of the outside being brought in, as the walls are styled in the same way as the typical exteriors of Mediterranean buildings and the beams are on show. The restaurant's grounding in its location is folded in once more in mimicking the location through the decor. For Adrià, 'A good dinner is inseparable from good scenography' (2008: 29). Indeed, the similarity to scenographic terminology is evident in two key terms in the establishment of the space at elBulli: *cambio de tercio*, a Spanish bullfighting expression meaning the 'change of stage', referring to a moment of transition, which at elBulli is the change from preparation to performance, to service (2008: 232), and *mise en place*, a more general phrase in restaurant terminology, referring to the preparation done before a service, the laying out of items for the performance, much like the *mise en scène* is the arrangement of the setting for performance.

At The Fat Duck, the inside of the restaurant has plain white walls and ceilings, interrupted by dark wooden beams and a central fireplace. The fireplace breaks up the space so that it is not one, single cube of a room, but is instead a U-shape, orientating the space around this central feature, which is balanced, on the opposite side, by the entrance to the kitchens. In the far corner from the front door is the sommelier's station, where glasses and bottles are laid out for the service, and the blank whiteness of the walls is broken by large, abstract colour paintings, with swirls of blue, green and yellow.[1] The pictures begin to slide from attention into the background of the experience but are purposefully there to break up the monotone of the walls. Blumenthal has written that the 'carpet and soft furnishings [...] made the place less harsh and jarring, more relaxed and comfortable' (2009: 80). There is an attention paid to a multisensory scenography, where the tactile is considered alongside the visual. For Blumenthal, this engenders a relaxation and comfort in the diner, attempting make them more receptive to an enjoyable experience. In order to do this, there is an implication of luxury.

Both Joseph Beuys and Jana Sterbak have produced sculptural works that can be read as articulating this mode of luxury of the restaurant and its potential to slide into the grotesque and to go beyond opulence. Jana Sterbak's *Cake Stool* (1996) is a metal stool with a plain cake sponge as the seat and Joseph Beuys' *Fat Chair* (1964) is a wooden chair, painted white, with a thick layer of fat on the seat. For Cecelia Novero, *Fat Chair* '[...] expressed the ideas of transformation from chaos to form, and vice versa, ideas that for Beuys exemplify processes of life, especially human social activity' (2010: 213). This evocative work marks out the connection between the body and its apparatus by drawing attention to the place where the fat of the human posterior meets with the seat of the chair. The layer of fat in Beuys' sculptural work is neither wholly of the chair nor wholly of the human. Disconnected from both and made strange, it lingers on the surface and, in its extraction from the everyday experience of a chair, focuses on the interaction of body and its object of support. Sterbak's *Cake Stool* follows the same logic, though through a cake rather than raw fat. It transforms the luxury of food prepared for you into a support for the body, implicating the labour of food preparation and how it is often taken for granted. In both of these works, the luxuriousness is troubled by following the implications of sitting in fat or cake; luxury becomes contaminated by the limits of an excess that slips into the grotesque or uncomfortable. Both of these works take the logic of luxurious comfort to an uncomfortable conclusion and, in comparison to the restaurants, reveal how the restaurants demonstrate a level of restraint to prevent this slippage into grotesque luxury.

There is a different kind of luxury at work in the design of Noma. Sign Bindslev, the architect commissioned to furnish the space, found furniture for Noma that continued the overarching concept of the Nordic: everything was made of 'natural' materials – iron, stone, wood and clay. The restaurant has dark wooden tables and a colour palette dominated by blacks, dark browns, greys and whites. The walls are painted a grey-white, interrupted by the beams that are the structure of the building, also painted grey-white. A number of the chairs have grey furs thrown over them. The restaurant spreads out through separate rooms, much like elBulli. Redzepi reflects that the design of Noma is 'casual', not a 'posh atmosphere', 'down to earth' and 'a pure and unpretentious experience' (in Skyum-Nielson 2010: 15–16). While not operating as the explicit luxury of The Fat Duck, there is nevertheless a mode of luxury at work. In presenting an expensive, world-class meal in these surroundings, Noma attempts to undermine itself, to self-consciously prevent the slippage into grotesque opulence. But the luxury engendered by the food and cost is, to an extent, in tension with the environment, with the stark wooden chairs and tables and bare wood of the floor and beams. By virtue of this, in a way it becomes more luxurious. It is part of the contemporary ideological process, as noted by Žižek, where the counter to capital is incorporated into the product itself. Žižek cites the example of Starbucks (2009: 53–54.), where the advertising draws out the 'ethical consumption' of buying their coffee: x-amount of profits will go to the growers, the coffee is fair trade, etc. It brings the counter to capital within the working of the product itself, thereby alleviating the guilt of purchasing. In the same way, the pared-down aesthetic of Noma brings the counter to the luxurious expenditure within the experience of the space itself.

The world of Alinea is starkly different to that of the other restaurants. The space is quite dark with spotlights offering targeted lighting, with plain and smooth white walls. The restaurant feels like a contemporary gallery space. There are intriguing clues to the experience that is about to unfold, with food hanging from the ceiling over the tables and a momentary glimpse through the glass at the far end of the dining room into the preparatory work of the kitchen. There are two dining rooms: one upstairs and one down, both dimly lit with spotlights spread out across the ceiling, leading to patches of space that are brighter. The homogenous space of the room is given densities and light relief. In planning the restaurant, Achatz and Kokonas gave thought to the lighting system, installing a system where the colour and intensity of the light could be carefully controlled. They considered how the light could be set differently at different times of the year or change colour and intensity over the course of a five-hour meal (2011: 241). Inevitably, the colour and intensity of light change the experience, not only in terms of the colour and visibility of the food placed on the table but also in establishing 'hot' areas of personal space around the table and in establishing the mood of the room. An early work by food artists Blanch & Shock explored the way that light could be a driving force in the development of a meal. In *Xicato/Light Collective Dinners* (2010–13), Blanch & Shock worked with Sharon Stammers and Martin Lupton of Light Collective and designer Flynn Talbot to produce three 'polychromatic dinners' for LED lighting. Each dish had a distinctive colour palette that would be highlighted by the LED lighting. Like at Alinea, the light focused the attention of the diners, orientating them towards the food, guiding the process of their perception.

For each of the restaurants, there is both a continuation of usual practices of dining spaces and something particular to their practice, something out of the ordinary, spectacular, luxurious or grounded in the specific geographic and cultural context of the restaurant. However, it can be argued that the worlds they establish, even in the use of the unusual, nevertheless continue an everyday or average logic. Heidegger writes that the everyday, the quotidian, is 'averageness' (Heidegger's term is *Durchschnittlichkeit*, which can be translated as indifference or ordinariness; it does not have the same pejorative connotations as 'average' in English, which speaks of class as well as the quotidian). This is the inauthentic, 'everyday undifferentiated character of Dasein', which is manifest when Dasein is busy, excited, interested or ready for enjoyment, when it is subsumed within activity (1962: 68–69). As the restaurants are selling an experience, the spectacular, unusual or distinctive elements of the world can be read, not as an interruption to the everyday, but a continuation of the everyday logic of the experience economy. In presenting for the diner a world of novelty, interest and enjoyment, to some extent these worlds are not consecrated spaces for the work of art but a continuation of the subjection of the diner to the neoliberal economic logic of the *they*. However, the tension between the everyday and the artistic, between the inauthentic and authentic, is nevertheless at work and there is the possibility for the restaurants not to fall into 'world-withdrawal' and to open space for disclosure (as with elBulli's gravel, the luxury of The Fat Duck, the tension between the luxurious and the rustic at Noma and in the attentional fluctuations of light at Alinea).

By way of comparison, there are a number of performance works that have pursued the domestic logic of food production in order to trouble, provoke and explore it. In Herman Nitsch's *Action 7: Action-Drama Dedicated to Dr. Wolfgang Tunner* (1965), the artist created a three-hour action work spread over six rooms in a domestic house, as well as outdoors, in collaboration with Rudolf Schwarzkogler (1999: 142–44). Various food items were used throughout the work in rooms not often associated with food consumption, including a bathroom and study. In the study, a lamb was prepared by being nailed to the wall and cut in the side, a motif used in a number of Nitsch's actions. This was accompanied by eggs and sugar, as well as the smell of menthol. In Bobby Baker's *Kitchen Show* (1991), Baker invites the audience into her own kitchen, where she works with various foods, showing and discussing the artistic and expressive qualities of food preparation. In Nikesh Shukla's performance, *Salt in the Sugar Jar* (2015), the audience were invited into the artist's home in Bristol, United Kingdom, to sit in the lounge and watch the kitchen as he prepared a meal while talking through his memories of his mother's cooking. In each case, to greater and lesser degrees, the everyday preparation of food is made strange, through an unsettling of the kitchen as a site of hidden physical and emotional labour, through exposing the emotional labour that can linger through food preparation and through unsettling the comforting familiarity of food in a domestic space. So, where the restaurants, in using the unusual and theatrical, can continue the everyday or average logic of the experience economy, these performance works take the domestic space and unsettle the unacknowledged and unnoticed experiences of the everyday.

These examples begin to reveal the interconnected nature of the physical/material and the conceptual in the world of the restaurant. The construction of the world relies on its material production and articulation but nevertheless invokes a conceptual realm, encouraging particular attitudes, on the part of the diner, towards the world into which they find themselves thrown (whether that is the continuation or estrangement of the everyday logic of sites of food preparation and consumption). Heidegger's conception of Being-in-the-world includes being always already 'thrown' into the world; finding oneself 'caught' in and 'taken along' by the world that forms the 'there' in which Dasein finds itself (1962: 400). This experience of Being-there includes: a state-of-mind, mood or attunement to the world; a pre-ontological understanding of the world, which furnishes any experience of the world with substance and significance according to a worldly organisational principle; and an ability to articulate this experience through talk or discourse, to articulate an interpretation of the experience (172, 182, 188, 203–04). Across the above discussions of the worlds of the restaurants are these three kinds of Being-there: a recognition of the mood or sense of the world (which for Heidegger is the foundation of Being-there, arising neither from 'outside' nor from 'inside' but as a relation across Being-in-the-world [176]); the elaboration of this sense in terms of the primordial understanding of the thrust, drive or concept of the restaurants; and, through language and discourse, an attempt at articulating assertions about and interpretations of the 'meaning' (what Heidegger terms the 'totality-of-significations' [204]) of the produced world.

The experiences of and within the world of the restaurant are subject to, rest on the conditions of and are framed by these modes of Being-there – modes that are experienced as interconnected, entangled and inseparable; and they are experiential. They operate neither completely in the material world of the restaurant, nor entirely in the perspective and position of the diner, but as a negotiated and relational in-between. This experience of the world of the restaurant sets the coordinates of all elements of the experience. It is the overarching frame for the experience of the meal and lingers in the background of each constituent part – sometimes as a background, sometimes emerging more clearly into the foreground, but nevertheless always colouring the experience. In David Leatherbarrow's 'Table Talk', he writes of setting a table that it has a prescriptive quality before a meal and inscriptive afterwards (2004: 212). In other words, the setting of the meal (which could be extended beyond setting the table to the setting more generally) has a certain quality of marking and prescribing possibilities of experience in advance and operating, after the event, as a memento or reminder of the activities it contained and allowed. In Heideggerian terms, it becomes part of Dasein's 'facticity', which is to say it is that 'factual' dimension of Being-in-the-world that, at this present moment, cannot be changed, an inescapable structure (1962: 82). This is not to assert that the situation could not have been otherwise, but rather an acknowledgement of things as they are; the circumstances in which one finds oneself.

In Heidegger's 'The Question Concerning Technology', he elaborates notions of 'setting' as framing. Heidegger uses *Ge-stell*, meaning 'enframing', which contains within it two modes of 'setting' – the term harboring its root in *stellen* meaning 'to set'. For Heidegger, this setting or enframing offers a 'challenging forth' as 'revealing' through a 'gathering together', preserving in its operation a 'producing and presenting', as *poiēsis*, to allow a coming forth into 'unconcealment' (2011c: 227). The process of enframing, the frame of the world that gathers together various parts and activities, provides a setting that is not necessarily merely installational, but a process of making (*poiēsis* as bringing into being and making) and, in that making, enacting a revealing, disclosure or uncovering. To think of the setting of the world of the restaurants in this way allows for a consideration of both the artistic qualities of the worlds themselves (including, for instance, the ways in which they continue and unsettle those traits and qualities that are taken for granted in the construction of the dining space) and consideration of how the setting frames the performances and objects within itself (how the conceptual space and world of the restaurants inflect, to greater and lesser extents, each element that takes place within it).

Creative Methods and Approaches

The inhabitable world of the restaurant operates as an important aspect of setting and framing the experience. Perhaps equally important, as a preparatory activity for producing the dining-performance event, are the creative methods, approaches and techniques used to develop the food, the dishes and courses to be served. As with the site or world of the restaurant, they have a dual role. They implicitly operate as part of the framing of the experience, making manifest in the practical activities attitudes and approaches of the world of the restaurant (concepts, ideas, underlying understanding of what is to be produced and why) and they constitute a core part of the experience itself (the food is a central component of the experience, the 'thing' that is to be experienced). In this section, I turn to some of the creative approaches and methodologies used by the restaurants for working with and producing food as an artistic material or medium, a core material in the dining performance experience. As with the development of any artistic practice, there are creative methodologies (though not always used in a way of which the chefs are self-aware) of devising, creating, developing and producing. I explore these as artistic methodologies, considering how they work and some of the underlying positions, ideas and assumptions that provide a conceptual and intellectual support for the chefs' own understanding of the practice.

In reflecting on their work at elBulli, Adrià et al. observe that, for them, creativity had two modes: the spontaneous emergence of an idea, which would not necessarily arise when engaged in creative activities, and a deliberate and purposeful process of developing ideas, often as a result of actually working with food, which could stimulate inspiration (2014g: 42). As such, the model of creativity was not the absolute originary and spontaneous enlightening of the artistic genius chef, but instead the result of a mixture of method, work, reflection, (sometimes serendipitous) connection-making and conceptualisation. It is perhaps for this reason that Adrià continually draws out a connection between organisation and creativity, arguing that they are intimately bound together. This is echoed by Grant Achatz when he writes that 'creativity is primarily the result of hard work and study' (2008: 27), by Heston Blumenthal when he discusses the scientific and chemical basis for his seemingly spontaneous cooking (2009: 146) and by René Redzepi when he writes that 'creativity is the ability to store the special moments, big or small, that occur throughout your life, then being able to see how they connect to the moment you're in' (2013: 119). In each case, creative practice is understood as a working practice. It is a process of development and never free of its circumstances.

There is an element of seeming spontaneity in their creative approach to food, in the development of dishes that exceed conventions of combinations of ingredients and presentations, but it is a spontaneity that can be rationalised and understood after the fact of its emergence. In *Event*, Žižek reflects on Borges' question over Kafka, as to whether the precursors to Kafka are really precursors or whether we retrospectively assign them as precursors. He writes that 'The properly dialectical solution of the dilemma of "Is it really there, in the source, or did we only read it into the source?" is thus: it is there, but we can only perceive and state this retroactively, from today's perspective' (2014a: 142). In other words, the apparently novel work, which seems to come as if from nowhere, can retrospectively be furnished with a narrative of its emergence, discovering and allocating its precursors only by way of the work they are said to prefigure. This is a useful perspective to take on artistic practice, including that of the restaurants, in reflecting on creative methods and approaches: that the creative development is not the laying and following of a pathway that knows its destination in advance, but instead a way of looking back at the path that was trodden that brought the artist to this particular point. The apparent emergence of the 'new' can be retrospectively conceived in terms of its conditions of possibility, but this is not to diminish its status as a new practice.

A core part of the creative production of food for these restaurants, and one that counters any claim to absolute originality, is that there is inevitably a reliance on the cultured world in which it operates. In the second volume of de Certeau et al.'s *The Practice of Everyday Life*, they implicitly draw on and extend Lévi-Strauss's argument of the cultural narratives of transformation from raw to cooked, arguing that even when eaten raw or in the harvesting of food, it is 'already a *cultured foodstuff*, prior to any preparation and by the simple fact that it is regarded as being edible' (1998: 167, original emphasis). While their focus is on fruit, this line of argument can be extended to all foods, that by virtue of being considered *as* an ingredient or as food, it is encultured as edible. There are various cultural transformations that take place in the process from chosen food object to the final, consumable dish, but the seemingly initial transformation (from 'natural' or 'earthly' object to potentially edible food) has always already taken place, even if it is the identification of a kind of proto-edibility, in the decision to test the edibility of an object. This inflects Heidegger's distinction between earth and world in art in a particular way: while the earth is that sustaining background to all activity, it cannot be accessed directly because all engagements and activities with its objects cannot help but bear the traces and carry the connotations of a worldly culture. The creative methodologies of the production of food are not, as many restaurants have it, the transformation of the natural earth into the cultured and artistic product, ready for consumption. To use Lévi-Strauss' terminology, the raw is always already cooked.

There is a kind of thinking at work in the preparations and creative explorations of food. In *The Five Senses*, Michel Serres reflects on this, writing that 'Cooking compacts, concentrates, […] goes from random chance, from flighty, improbable, inconstant circumstance to habit and compactnesss. Goes from diffuse, chaotic mixture to dense, ordered blend' (2016: 167). There is an ordering principle in the thinking manifested in preparing food, working through questions of taste (what is palatable), of cultural framing and ethics (what could or should be used as an ingredient) and of concepts (what ingredients can be brought together, how and why). Despite the experimentations with preparations and ingredients at each of the restaurants, there is nevertheless a limitation imposed (by virtue of their appeal to the satisfying, fulfilling and enjoyable) to bring a cultural frame and heritage of tastes to the preparations.

Although elBulli closed for six months of the year to develop new ideas and methods at elBullitaller, their creative work continued throughout the other six months while the restaurant was open. The other restaurants do the same, setting aside time and resources for experimentation while the everyday work of serving diners continues. At The Fat Duck, the development kitchen in Bray is used for testing new ideas, folding them gradually into the menu, as well as occasionally overhauling their tasting menu. At Noma, they have what they termed the 'Saturday Night Projects', where the chefs would work on a Saturday night after service for a few hours coming up with new ideas, testing them out and sharing them with one another. Each Saturday night, one chef from each section presents a dish or a new practice, with each chef presenting work around once per month (Skyum-Nielsen 2010: 14–15). Achatz has reflected that at Alinea the creative process also often begins after a service, where he would sit with books, a laptop, notepads and a glass of wine and make notes, sometimes documenting ideas that had occurred during the day's service (2008: 27).

In their reflections on their practice, each of the chefs at these restaurants has explored how they understand creativity – what it is for them to be creative in relation to food practice. What often emerges in these reflections are notions of interdisciplinarity, although it is never framed in those terms. In particular, elBulli have the term 'elBullivirus', which was used to describe the 'bridges' with other methods, disciplines and forms (Adrià et al. 2014g: 60). The term, coined by Toni Zegarra from the SCPF advertising agency, 'refers to the flow of influences from elBulli into other disciplines and vice versa' (Adrià et al. 2014g: 60). These included the 'Plastic arts virus', the 'Music virus', the 'Architecture virus', the 'Graphic design virus', the 'Publishing virus', the 'Education and health virus' and the 'Science virus' (Adrià et al. 2014g: 60–62), amongst others. There are two things of note here: first, in using the term 'virus', there are implications that different disciplines infect one another, not manifesting as a superficial symptom, but rather as the underlying cause; second, it acknowledges the inherently interdisciplinary nature of creative practice, articulating the openness of creative works to multiple and parallactic perspectives.

The search for new ideas and practices at elBulli, through the research conducted at elBullitaller, was categorised by the creative team as falling into four principal modes:

- Products: analysing and using new products.
- Technology: new equipment and new uses of existing equipment.
- Preparations: new ways of preparing or existing preparations taken out of context.
- Styles and Characteristics: new styles, characteristics or perspectives.

(Adrià et al. 2008: 515)

This categorisation is analogous to the areas of development and exploration in any artistic practice: 'raw' materials; technologies and equipment; modes and methods of enquiry and development; and aesthetic, stylistic, formal and conceptual articulations. Each of the restaurants has pursued various new methods and techniques for devising a dish, operating within these different spheres, with those processes of development lingering in the food itself. For example, Noma's dish, 'Blueberries Surrounded by their Natural Environment', which consisted of blueberries served with variations of spruce (Redzepi 2010: 289), was inspired by the provenance of ingredients and what they are found alongside when growing; the exploration of the product's 'production' inspired the dish. The technological developments at elBulli led to preparations that could only be achieved through the new technologies, knowledges and their deployment, including pioneering frozen savoury foods, spherification (whereby intensely flavoured liquids are contained within a thin outer bubble layer) and the creation of stable, flavoured foams and hot jellies (Adrià et al. 2008: 136.6). In terms of preparations, the production of bacon become the concept for Alinea's dish, 'Bacon', which referenced hanging pork to dry and cure it by serving bacon, with butterscotch and apple, hanging from a wire (Achatz 2008: 116–17). Each of the restaurants takes inspiration from within and outside of gastronomy for concepts, styles, forms and characteristics of the food (for instance, Blumenthal's dish 'Eel "Nichi"' was inspired by the film *Barefoot in the Park* [Blumenthal 2009: 198]). Like with other forms of artistic experimentation, the arenas of exploration are not independent of one another; but in drawing out the different spheres in which experimentation takes place (and the pathways they can open to new dishes as artistic practice), there is some acknowledgement of the considered and detailed development work of and in the kitchen, which is not reducible to merely the continuation of preexisting food cultures and practices.

One of the key tropes and practices of experimentation in the restaurants is an exploration of a particular ingredient, to dismantle it and see what creative ideas it might provoke or yield. At elBulli, this would consist of a detailed study of a particular ingredient, considering its qualities: its 'shape, texture, proportion, flavour, density, response to different cooking techniques and so on' (Adrià et al. 2008: 72.2). For instance, in *El Bulli: Cooking in Progress*, one can watch the initial process of exploration of a mushroom, where the chefs cut it and follow their intuition in reeling off a number of possible ways of cooking the ingredient: turning it into ravioli, serving it as leaves, coupling it with filo or noodle dough, as well as marking out its associations; that it looks like a fish or like leaves. At The Fat Duck, the development of the 'Saddle of Venison' dish, served with celeriac and sauce poivrade, pearl barley and frankincense tea also began with an ingredient: the venison from the hills of the Finnebrogue Estate near Downpatrick in Northern Ireland (Blumenthal 2009: 365). Beginning with the 'superb-tasting venison' (Blumenthal 2009: 365), it was coupled with frankincense as a counter to the richness of the meat. The qualities of the meat began the exploration and development. In both cases, there is an implication that the ingredient is both a thing unto itself, with various qualities and traits that can be put to good use, and a thing that would or could come into itself by the various processes of transformation of the chefs and their tools.

The embodied understanding of the chef is implicit in their practice in developing recipes and in delivering dishes. It includes an embodied understanding of the culture within which they operate and references their own production as a sensible subject, charting a course that overlays their own personal preferences with cultural palatability. For elBulli, this is encapsulated in their notion of the 'mental palate': 'cooking mentally, dialoguing with ideas and looking for synergies between them, or between ideas or dishes from other years' (Adrià et al. 2014g: 49). Blumenthal articulates a similar notion, described as 'banking flavour-memories', which encompasses 'developing a set of reference points for the level of depth and complexity that could be achieved in a dish' (2009: 34). This allows for the cognitive mapping of a dish, drawing on sensory, embodied memories to judge, in advance of an experiment, what might work. For de Certeau et al., cooking draws on multiple memories: 'of apprenticeship, of witnessed gestures, and of consistencies', as well as the 'programming mind', which allows for calculations of cooking times and anticipated results and the intervention of sensory perception, whereby the senses themselves intervene into the programming processes to make adjustments based on sight, smell and taste (1998: 157–58). The body of the creative chef becomes a trained and honed facilitator, drawing on that embodied knowledge of skill and memories that allow for the prediction of desired results. It is an embodied, disciplinary knowledge that is manifested in the acts of cooking, where personal experience and perception co-exist with processes of learning and training. It implicates both the skill or craft of the chef (in perception as well as activity) alongside the shared world of palatability, assuming that what is pleasurable to the chef will also be pleasurable to the diner.

The creative acts of the chef lead to the production of the work of food, but for that process to be considered artistic, it needs to go further than embodied practice and artisanal skill. Adrià et al. reflect that there are levels of creativity in gastronomy, moving from following a recipe to making alterations to a recipe, inventing new recipes and finally, as the pinnacle of their creative approach, inventing new modes of cooking and concepts (2008: 52). However, to conceptualise any of these as artistic, in Heideggerian terms, one cannot rely merely on the extent to which they are creative or offer something new; the quality of 'having been created', irrespective of the degree to which that process of creation is novel, is not enough to constitute an art*work*. Heidegger writes that, while the work's createdness is dependent on the performance of acts of creation, the creation of the artwork 'is to let something emerge as a thing that has been brought forth' as that which produces and preserves unconcealment, revelation or disclosure (2011a: 119). In a similar temporal logic to that in Žižek's reflections on Borges and Kafka, the work stands before its audience as having been created, but the significance of the performance of acts of creation is only instituted in light of the created work. As such, the use of creative methods and approaches is insufficient as a means of conceiving the restaurants' work as artistic, because the methods themselves are no guarantee of an artistic output. But they nevertheless can contribute to the Heideggerian artistry of an artwork, if they are a result of a process of uncovering or disclosure *in the process*, which is then preserved in the resultant work. If, for example, there is an uncovering of particular food cultures in the process (ingredients, palatability, tastes), the results of this exploration as an uncovering and a cultural challenge can be preserved in the work of the final dish, not merely a discovery of the process, but a subsequent aspect of the dish that arose from the discovery.

Technoemotional Cuisine

The work by these restaurants is often categorised as 'molecular gastronomy', a term in common usage to describe restaurants that employ new technologies and scientific knowledges in the production of the food. The term is a truncation of the 'Workshop on Molecular and Physical Gastronomy', which was first held in August 1992 in Erice, Sicily, established by Nicholas Kurti, Harold McGee and Hervé This, with Peter Barham joining after Kurti's death. The workshops (six of them, held between 1992 and 2004) brought together scientists to explore aspects of cookery. For Hervé This, the area of molecular gastronomy goes beyond the examination of the 'composition and structure of food' of food science to deal with 'culinary transformations and the sensory phenomena associated with eating' (2006: 3). There are a number of less popular, but still used, terms aside from molecular gastronomy: modernist cuisine, postmodern cuisine, new cuisine, future cuisine, avant-garde cuisine, twenty-first century cuisine and technoemotional cuisine. There is an attempt to capture, in the names, a sense of something contemporary, something modern, to suggest both novelty and revolution (rather than continuation and evolution). Each term inflects the practice in a different way. In this section, I explore specifically the term technoemotional cuisine, to think about what it encapsulates, how it inflects and positions the work of the restaurants and how it opens space for a critique of the ideological frame of the work and experience.

The term technoemotional cuisine was proposed by Pau Arenós and arose from his encounters with and reflections on elBulli and its followers. His extended definition and explication of the term is as follows:

> International culinary movements dating from the turn of the 21st century led by Ferran and Albert Adrià. Formed by chefs of different ages and traditions. The aim of the dishes is to create emotions in the diner for which use is made of new techniques and technology. They are discoverers or simply interpreters who have recourse to systems and concepts developed by others. The chefs take on risks with their attitude and preparations. They pay attention to the five senses and not only to those of taste and smell. Besides creating dishes, their goal is to find new paths. They do not seek confrontation with tradition – given that most of their dishes are evolutionary; on the contrary, they express their indebtedness to and respect for it. They have initiated a dialogue with scientists, but also with artists, novelists, poets, journalists, historians, anthropologists etc. They collaborate with agricultural and livestock farmers and fishermen [sic] as they seek the survival of the product.
>
> (2009: 323)

At first, this can seem like merely the collecting of traits, rather than a considered and consolidated conceptual position for framing and understanding the work of the restaurants. However, I argue that the term technoemotional offers a conceptual position and ideological frame for understanding the practice, which brings together the apparently unconnected elements of technology, emotion, sensory experience, interdisciplinary collaboration, food histories and producers. In each area, there lingers (sometimes implicitly, sometimes more overtly) the sense of the form of attitude and thinking that Heidegger terms the 'standing-reserve' that is associated with modern technological thinking. This is an attitude of 'setting-upon' nature, where 'the energy concealed in nature is unlocked, what is unlocked is transformed, what is transformed is stored up, what is stored up is in turn distributed, and what is distributed is switched about ever anew' (in 'The Question Concerning Technology' 2011c: 224). By this, Heidegger theorises an attitude or position whereby everything is understood in an instrumental way, a standing-reserve of 'energy' that can be used and deployed in and through technology, merely waiting for an instrumental use. It is a paradigm of 'regulating and securing' (225) rather than an openness to and entanglement with the world. Even the human (body) is positioned as a resource, to be set-upon and ordered as standing-reserve (227). Everything waits to be set-upon to yield itself for an instrumental purpose, to be used in a prefigured manner. This is the manner of technological thinking and I argue that this is what makes sense of the term technoemotional, not only in its use and deployment of technologies, but also in the selection of knowledge and practices from other arenas of activity (*using* the work of food producers, artists, academics) and the bodies of the diners *used* as the site of an experience (utilising their sensory apparatus and emotions), all in service of an experience to be sold, from which they might profit, conforming to the hedonistic logic of neoliberal economics (a supposedly free choice to pay for the pleasurable).

The term technoemotional speaks to the technological paradigm of thinking and activity argued and elucidated by Heidegger: the perspective that reduces everything to a standing-reserve, to something to be used in an instrumental manner in service of productivity, including the bodies of the diners themselves. Lingering through this is an illusion of control – that the scientific knowledges and technologies can be deployed as a way of controlling and guiding the experience, an attempt to force an experience that submits to a prefigured aim or goal. In the following reflections, I explore the two constituent elements of the term, the technological and the emotional, arguing that this dual framing of the work of the restaurant reduces the artistic production to the logic of the technological and the aesthetic experience to the level of the emotional, in both cases operating within the paradigm of the standing-reserve. However, this is not to say this is absolute in the practice itself. To frame the work as artistic-aesthetic instead allows for other qualities and traits to emerge: the unplanned, the eccentric, the accidental, revelation, disclosure and unconcealment. There is resistance to the perspective of standing-reserve in the work and experience, despite it operating as the predominant discourse of understanding (perhaps especially in the reflections of the chefs themselves).

There is a distinction, in Heidegger's writing, between the modern technological mode of understanding and the Ancient Greek root of technology in *technē*. In 'The Question Concerning Technology', he writes that *technē* is not only craft or skill but also a term for 'the arts of the mind and the fine arts' (2011c: 222). For Heidegger, *technē* should be understood in relation to *poiēsis*, which is making, 'bringing-forth', 'something poetic' and *epistēmē*, which is 'knowing in the widest sense' (2011c: 222). *Technē*, then, is both an act or activity of making and giving form, and it reveals and stages a mode of knowledge or knowing. This does continue in the contemporary technological paradigm, though in a particular form. Modern technological thinking takes technology as merely equipment, a means to an end, but for Heidegger it institutes an attitude towards the world (the attitude of standing-reserve, where everything is subject to the manipulations and exploitations of technological equipment). Technologies also make manifest that attitude (that mode of knowing, that *epistēmē*) and have the potential to reveal the mode of knowing and understanding that gives rise to them. For Heidegger, the 'revealing that holds sway throughout modern technology does not unfold into a bringing-forth in the sense of *poiēsis*. The revealing that rules in modern technology is a challenging, which puts to nature the unreasonable demand that it supply energy […]' (223). This is where the artistic-*technē* diverges from the modern-technological; the latter operates within a frame of knowing in advance, technological control, manipulation and instrumentalism, where the former is the opening of a space of 'investigative' revealing and bringing-forth.

The technologies employed by the restaurants, which in the cultural imagination are a core and distinguishing part of their practice, have the potential to conform to both of these technological modes – the equipment that attempts to 'extract' for productive purposes and the artistic revealing. For example, each of the restaurants employs *sous vide* as a cooking method, where ingredients are vacuum-packed and then slow-cooked in a low-temperature water bath. The technology began to be used in the 1970s but has now become a popular and prolific practice in high-end restaurants. As noted by Blumenthal, cooking meat *sous vide* allows for consistent, low-temperature cooking, which results in tenderness and juiciness in the cooked meat (2009: 429). The technology treats the meat as a standing-reserve, not just to yield energy through eating but to yield a particular experience that is desirable and pleasurable. The aim is determined in advance, resting on assumptions of what is good in terms of taste (tender and juicy meat). The technology becomes a tool for production, conforming to preexisting tastes. However, it can also begin to engage in revelation and disclosure through unsettling itself. The (relatively) new technologies of *sous vide* cooking allow for a heightened version of an established predilection (for succulent, tender and juicy meat) to be realised; the ideal of the 'perfect' cooking of meat, which with older cooking technologies could be approximated but perhaps never fully realised, is now able to be brought to fruition. The cooking is outside the capabilities of the domestic kitchen and everyday food preparation (at least for the most part – there are now domestic *sous vide* machines available, though it is fair to suppose that this is not a staple for most domestic kitchens). The technologies of production cease to be transparent. They are no longer hidden in their usefulness, because they produce something beyond the everyday interactions with culinary equipment. It has the potential to bring to the fore of experience questions of the technology itself: how was this achieved? what technologies and processes allowed for the realisation of this ideal? now I taste it, is it really the ideal I wanted, given its strangeness to my palate? The operations of technology are no longer obscuring, but their setting-upon the ingredient becomes a palpable aspect of the dining experience.

The technologies employed in the kitchen, operating beyond the everyday world of domestic food production (or even that of high street restaurants), can begin to undo themselves, not in becoming un-ready-to-hand (Heidegger's formulation of technologies that fail, cease to work and become unusable, a negation of the ready-to-hand, which is equipment with which we can interact and of which we can make use without theorisation, in a structure of involvements with which we are familiar [Heidegger 1962: 98–103]), but in becoming conspicuous by doing their job too well. This has a revelatory or disclosive function, through unsettling and exposing the assumptions of productivity upon which the operations of the technologies rest (what we want to achieve and why). Underlying each of the kitchen technologies is the paradigm of technological thinking and a mode of 'performance' that is understood not as artistic but, as Jon McKenzie proposes in *Perform or Else* (2001), an ideological world characterised by a drive towards performances that are efficacious, efficient and effective. In the kitchen, the technologies are often an efficacious, efficient and effective enhancement of and replacement for the embodied activities of the chef; the technologies build on and 'improve' the physical labour of the chef, replacing embodied training and learning with an automatic and efficient device. For instance, The Fat Duck makes use of Overhead Stirrers, used for stirring for a long time at either very high or low speeds. The technology replaces the inefficient labour of the chef, seeking a more efficient means of achieving a pre-articulated aim. In this, it begins to reveal the connection between *technē* and *epistēmē* noted by Heidegger: the technology is grounded in and externalises a way of thinking and behaving derived from the human, extending it, making it more effective and efficient, but nevertheless operating within the imaginative horizon of the activities of the human body.

Technology can be caught in a structure of involvements that allows it to be used for a purpose, unthinkingly, without need of theorisation and reflection. But it is grounded in *technē*, with its connections to *poiēsis* and *epistēmē*, so has the potentiality to reveal or expose itself, to unconceal its own operational foundations. However, there is also a constructive quality to technology, which is embedded in that connection to *poiēsis* and *epistēmē*, an ability to bring forth, produce and make knowledge as much as technology can reveal the modes of thinking and behaviour that give rise to it. As such, technology can have a performative quality as a kind of symbolic machine, which for Žižek is the 'place where the fate of our internal, most "sincere" and "intimate" beliefs is *in advance* staged [...]' (2008: 42, emphasis added). While always already grounded in the worlds from which they have been developed, technologies take on a 'life of their own' and begin to stage ideas, beliefs and knowledges, seemingly self-legitimising that knowledge if the technology works (for how could it not be true if it works?). For example, elBulli used a machine called 'Jungle Essence', which allowed for the extraction of the essential oils of an ingredient (see Adrià et al. 2014g: 226). The idea of an essence (commonly encountered in gastronomy, for instance in vanilla essence) rests on an assumption of an essential aspect or quality of an ingredient that stands in for the whole, as a synecdoche. However, to extract one part of an ingredient (an 'essential oil') and treat it as an essence is to stage an operation of uncovering or unconcealment that in fact *produces* the very essence it purports to reveal.

Alongside *technē*, the emotional is the other component part of technoemotional cuisine. In the reflections and writings of each of the chefs, the emotions sought are within a strictly delimited range of emotional experience, which are broadly pleasurable and enjoyable. Blumenthal sees his work with food as creating an emotional state in the diner, particularly in terms of curiosity and surprise (Blumenthal 2009: 140, 258). In Steingarten's article, 'Experiencing Alinea', he discusses this desire for an emotional reaction, clarifying that it does not seem to be *any* emotion, but rather those that are pleasurable (2008: 11). Adrià discusses four different pleasures of food, ranking them in a hierarchy, from the lowest of satisfying hunger, through the pleasures of the senses to emotional pleasure and finally, at the pinnacle, the pleasure of intellectual stimulation (Adrià et al. 2008: 318). The emotional is seemingly just one layer of pleasure for Adrià, though in framing the modes of engagement as a hierarchy of pleasures, there is nevertheless an implication of an enjoyable emotional response from the diner. This drive to enjoyable emotional experiences is part of the hedonistic logic of the experience economy – a pacification of the diner by means of purchased pleasure. To divert from pleasure would perhaps be too radical a direction for the restaurants, given that their experiences are predicated on gustatory and sensory fulfilment. However, in Olafur Eliasson's writing on Noma, he argues that, 'We are constantly confronted with a trivialized sensory world, largely the product of banal commer-cialization. [...] By contrast, what is continually being developed at Noma helps to keep our senses keen. Its ability to surprise and sow the seeds of uncertainty is of the essence' (2010: 8). So while the pleasurable drive of the work can be under-stood as conforming to the logic of commodifying experiences, it also contains a potential subversion of the ideological status quo by countering the dominant pacifying order of easy pleasure. The experiences enliven the sensate body, open new vistas of experience and can engender an experience of surprise or shock and so operate on the boundary of the pleasurable novelty of the experience economy, on the one side, and on the other offering experiences that, in being surprising and unusual, *can* (though not necessarily do) trouble everyday modes of understand-ing and experiencing.

The drive towards an emotional reaction in the context of these restaurants speaks to the wider contemporary political discourses of inclusivity. One has the ability to have an emotional reaction, irrelevant of one's comprehension of the various contexts at work around the food, of one's experience or cultural heritage. This is not to say that these things do not have an affect on what that emotional response is, but rather that the ability to have an emotional response is not predi-cated on a particular set of experiences and contexts. Both Blumenthal and Adrià have resisted, on multiple occasions, the title of 'artist'. This title frames their work in a particular way, which they avoid so as not to seem as though their work is only for diners with the appropriate cultural capital. Instead, by appealing to emotion, their work appears to be opened out for anyone to read in any way they want. This politics of individualism and inclusivity assumes that emotional expe-rience itself is depoliticised and free of political and ideological discourse, which is not the case given that an appeal to pleasurable emotions is a core component of commodified experience. In continually pursuing those things deeming pleas-urable, rather than, say, abject or disgusting, the work is intimately political, instituting the politics of pleasure, hedonism and 'personal fulfilment' above all else. This pursuit is grounded in and perpetuates the positioning of the diner as an average *they*-self, reducing the possibilities of experience to things that 'anyone' can pursue, through encouraging the diner to dwell in a limited arena of pleasur-able feelings, which themselves are taken to be merely given, simply true and not subject to artistic, aesthetic or theoretical critique. The only prerequisite for the experience is the ability to pay for it.

As a term, technoemotional encapsulates an approach to the restaurants' prac-tice and a strategy on the part of the chefs. It positions the work as using tech-nological modes of making and thinking in order to produce an experience that evokes or provokes a pleasurable emotional experience. The experiencing body of the diner is reduced to a component resource, to be used and deployed within the experience as its site and constitution, through the manipulations of technologies and scientific knowledges. The body itself is addressed as an experiencing machine. In hybridising the technological and the emotional into a single term, it unites processes of production and reception. It offers a counter to the perspective of the artistic-aesthetic. Whereas the technoemotional reduces the production and experience of the meal to a standing-reserve, elements to be used in order to release a pleasurable and profitable experience, the artistic-aesthetic is a mode of creating and experiencing that engenders an opening out, discovery, unconcealment and disclosure. It is a distinction between the Heideggerian inauthentic and authentic respectively. Both of these modes are at work in the experience of the restaurants.

NOTE

1.   Since my visit to The Fat Duck (which forms the basis of these reflections) some changes have been made to the décor of the restaurant: the paintings have changed and the sommelier station has moved to a position in front of the kitchen.

Interlude 1

Progression: Italian Futurism and Technoemotional Cuisine

The Italian Futurist movement was founded and led by Filippo Tommaso Marinetti, an artist who studied and worked in Paris alongside the Symbolists, before establishing Italian Futurism in 1909 with the first 'Futurist Manifesto'. The movement continued until the Second World War, with Marinetti continually at its forefront, and worked, like other movements of the historical avant garde, through various art forms to enact and put into practice its political and aesthetic aims, as articulated in manifestoes. Using music, painting, performance, sculpture and food, the Italian Futurists sought to not only represent but also forge the new Italy, with the artistic practice both articulating their vision of the modern Italian (almost always presented as the modern Italian *man*) and playing a role in the production of that identity and life practice.

The Futurist Cookbook, compiled by Marinetti with contributions from a number of Italian Futurist artists, offers outlines, scenarios and plans for multisensory performance events. There are a number of conceptual and artistic correspondences between the Italian Futurists' work with food (especially in their Holy Palate Restaurant) and the contemporary technoemotional restaurants. In this interlude, I explore some of these correspondences and use Italian Futurism as a historical artistic precedent for technoemotional cuisine, considering where the latter took up ideas and practices instituted by the former and where they diverge in terms of the political application and framing of the practices. The technoemotional restaurants (which are the focus of this book) have not explicitly positioned their work as a continuation of, or reaction to, Italian Futurism. However, to use Italian Futurism as a historical precedent for the contemporary practice allows for traits and qualities of technoemotional cuisine to emerge more clearly, particularly in terms of the technological capabilities and thinking, and to make the politics of technoemotional cuisine emerge more forcefully. Both the Italian Futurists and the work of the technoemotional restaurants make use of new technologies in cooking, attempt to manipulate the diner by means of these technologies and the dining experience, engage in an artistic process of questioning and (re)constructing everyday practices of eating and made use of multiple artistic forms within the dining experience. This interlude takes up ideas from the previous chapter, especially principles that underlie the production of experience, the construction of the world and the deployment of technologies, as well as setting the stage for consideration of the presentation of food (as a plastic or sculptural multisensory art object), which is taken up in the next chapter.

In terms of historical periods, the relationship between Italian Futurism and technoemotional cuisine could be framed as one between modernism and postmodernism. As a movement of the historical avant garde, Italian Futurism certainly engaged with practices associated with a modernist perspective: experimentation with artistic forms; engaging with and glorifying modern, industrial life; rejecting classic aesthetic theories of disinterested sublime beauty; and instituting a belief in what they understood as progress towards a utopian vision of the modern future (though, as I will go on to explore, this vision was both misogynistic and racist). Allen S. Weiss has argued that contemporary cuisine can be understood as postmodern, through its

> self-conscious reflexivity (experimentation to reveal the primary qualities of the component materials of a work), questioning of origins (the realization that all inventions are but variations, transmutations, or inspirations based on previous works), regionalism (the decentralization and relativization of techniques, materials, and styles), and exoticism (the juxtaposition and incorporation of foreign elements on an equal footing with native material).
>
> (2004: 25)

Technoemotional cuisine also engages with aesthetic traits of postmodern artistic practice, including irony, de- and re-contextualisation and deconstruction.

However, it is perhaps too easy to categorise according to the constellation of traits associated with these historical periods. Technoemotional cuisine engages with practices and approaches that could more accurately be described as modernist (the belief in the transformative power of new technologies, formal experimentation seemingly abstracted from its contextual frames, the reduction of the diner to a receiving and experiencing processing machine) – hence the uncertainty of the naming of this contemporary gastronomy, which has been called both modern cuisine and postmodern cuisine. Equally, while Italian Futurism was undoubtedly a modernist movement, it nevertheless manifested in its practice slippages from a totalising modernist determination (such as the mixing of literal and figurative modes of thinking, an awareness of the performative rather than essentialist understandings of identities and the reliance of their practice on the everyday life world that it sought to question, reject and reconfigure). The inconsistency of this modernist/postmodernist categorisation opens conceptual space for thinking about both the continuities and divergences between Italian Futurism and technoemotional cuisine. They do not share exactly the same models of politics, art and bodies, but nor are they absolutely incompatible.

Across the Italian Futurist practice was a materialist understanding of the world (both in their use of technological machines and understanding the body itself as a machine to be produced and deployed) and, at times, assuming that those materials have essential identities and qualities. They appeared to take the notion of an Italian identity as an essential trait though they also acknowledged that that identity could be performatively reworked by means of a politically inflected practice. Marinetti famously wrote a manifesto attacking pasta, the eating of which he felt produced a sluggish and lethargic Italian body (both an individual body and the body politic), engendering an 'ironic and sentimental scepticism', leading to a depletion of enthusiasm in Italians (Marinetti 2014: 34). In the same manifesto, he also wrote of other national cuisines: that beneficial to the English was a diet of cod, roast beef and steamed pudding, for the Dutch, cold cuts and cheese, and for the Germans, sauerkraut, smoked and salted pork and sausage (Marinetti 2014: 34). The implication of Marinetti's writing is that there are essential qualities to particular food preparations that appeal to largely essentialist notions of a body being of a particular nation, heritage and culture. However, the attack on pasta also assumes that this political body can be reconfigured by means of new foods, which themselves have essential qualities to performatively produce a different kind of identity. There is, then, a theoretical inconsistency in his approach, assuming that bodies and foods have essential properties and that the bodies and identities can be fundamentally changed (they are performative, responsive, not deterministically essentialised) by ingesting other foods.

This essentialist thinking can also be found in a number of their recipes, where they believed that the inclusion of particular ingredients would impart particular qualities to the diner, based on their reading of the ingredient. For instance, for the Futurist's dish *Chicken Fiat*, a chicken is combined with steel ball bearings and cooked until 'the flesh has fully absorbed the flavour of the mild steel balls' (Marinetti 2014: 97). The taste of steel is taken to impart an essential quality of steel (as representative of the industrial, mechanised world), which is incorporated into the body of the diner, imbuing them with the qualities of the metallic world. This essentialist thinking renders metaphorical or symbolic qualities of the ingredient as a literal and material quality, which will be transferred into the body of the diner. But the same could be said of the technoemotional contemporary cuisine, when it suggests that there is something essential about seasonal, local or organic produce that is apparent in the final prepared dish; that it then imparts those qualities in the diner, connecting them to the land in which the ingredient was produced. Indeed, this is the overarching thinking at Noma, especially given their grounding in the

Nordic region, as though there is something essential about Nordic culture that is found in the ingredients and the preparations of food, which in turn makes the food essentially Nordic.

Perhaps the key distinction between the Italian Futurist cuisine and the contemporary technoemotional restaurant is the apparentness of political discourse surrounding the food. The Futurists had a complicated relationship with Fascism in Italy in the first half of the twentieth century. Marinetti began his work closely associated with Mussolini and the Italian fascists. Indeed, he was the first artist to be officially recognised by Mussolini. The Futurists played a key role in the establishment of the Fascist party. However, Cecilia Novero draws out the more complicated relationship between Futurism and Fascism, writing of *The Futurist Cookbook* that 'even when it endorses the same fascist vitalist views' as the Fascist party ('the cult of the body, the affirmation of biological life, and the view of existence as the survival of the fittest'), it did not fully submit to fascist politics because it advanced 'a Futurist cuisine that dispels boredom, weightiness, ugly cubic and static Italian bodies' (2010: 7). Nevertheless, in attempting to produce the modern Italian citizen, the Futurists explicitly engaged with the political construction of the body and made this apparent in their practice. A number of their dinners were overtly racist, such as the 'Dinner of White Desire' (formulated by the artist Fillìa), which sought to demonstrate White Italian dominance by preparing white-coloured food, served by Black waiters (Marinetti 2014: 186–87). The plan for the meal rests on utterly offensive notions of identity, taken to be essential qualities of bodies based on nationality and race, which overtly both continues and reiterates supposed White European 'superiority'.

By comparison, the work of technoemotional restaurants is seemingly less explicit in its politics. Helostosky argues that Modernist cooking offers a subtle and limited politics, encouraging engagement with concerns around the systems of global food production and the privileges of luxurious consumption (2017). While both of these are at work in the restaurants, to say they are subtle invokes a political positioning of the diner that is by no means absolute. While many diners may encounter this as an undercurrent of politics, for others, it can and does come to the fore. Technoemotional cuisine does contain a rhetoric around the politics of food production, but this is ultimately in service of a different politics: the commodification of experience. As explored in the final chapter of the book, the rhetoric of 'ethical production' can operate in such a way as to make the experience all the more enjoyable and therefore 'worth the cost'. While the Italian Futurists' political positions were a provocation, explicitly foregrounded in the work, the politics of technoemotional cuisine is a foundational, organisational principle that underlies and structures the practice.

In exploring these two realms of work in relation to one another, we can begin to identify the ways in which their practices implicate a particular kind of body (or body politic) and form part of the ideological world through which those bodies are produced. Novero observes of *The Futurist Cookbook* that the meals were 'nutritionally impractical, even when supposedly scientifically grounded' (2010: 12). The assumption that underscores this observation is that 'nutrition' is somehow self-evident, both in terms of what should be eaten and what purpose the food should play on, in and through the body. *The Futurist Cookbook* cites a number of scientists to substantiate its claims about the food and its properties. Heston Blumenthal does exactly the same in *The Fat Duck Cookbook*, including short scientific articles that outline and justify his approach to cooking and the diner. In both cases, the 'science' is a particular mode of revealing the body, its needs and workings, selectively deployed to substantiate a way of thinking about the body and experience. The body that is catered to in the restaurants and the Italian Futurist events is presented as a fixed and scientifically known entity, open to guidance and manipulation in order to bring about the desired experiences planned and executed by the artists and chefs.

The key distinction between them is the site of authority for disciplining the body; for Marinetti, it is the intervention of the artist and the state that is required, governing and shaping the body through external forces; for the contemporary restaurant, the governance of the body is produced as an individual, seemingly 'free' choice. Leda Cooks, in her article 'You Are What You (Don't) Eat', pursues this argument, writing that 'Bodies are no longer governed by the state but are surveyed and disciplined through self-observation' (2009: 97). Following the logic of neoliberalism, each individual is free to choose how to govern themselves, what food to eat and how their bodies ought to be formed. However, this apparent freedom is not free; rather, the individual is left to negotiate the various discourses surrounding the body, which are often in tension with one another (for instance, the drive to hedonistic pleasure and the drive to be healthy and eat 'well'). This mode of thinking frees the restaurant from the ethical and social responsibility of producing the body; they become merely an option amongst other options, for which the diner takes responsibility. The Italian Futurist artists took responsibility for and ownership of their explicit ways of forming the body and producing experience; the technoemotional chefs alleviate a level of responsibility by supposedly allowing for the agency of the diner to choose, while nevertheless utilising scientific and psychological knowledges to frame and form the experience.

Both the Futurists and the technoemotional restaurant cleave open the gap between food and nutrition. Barbara Kirshenblatt-Gimblett writes that 'While we eat to satisfy hunger and nourish our bodies, some of the most radical effects occur precisely when food is dissociated from eating and eating from nourishment. Such dissociations produce eating disorders, religious experiences, culinary feats, sensory epiphanies, and art' (1999: 3). The separation of food and nourishment or nutrition allows for a consideration of its other qualities, and these food practices (of Marinetti and the chefs of this book) play with how we understand, interact and engage with food. It is not about nutrition or the continuation of the body, but about the production and formation of the body through eating, with a focus on food's sensory, ritualistic and cultural properties. They each attempt to transform perception, to render sensible what might go unnoticed in the everyday world of food or to articulate sensory experiences that are not quotidian. By so doing, they offer a reflection on their context, making manifest the everyday world by making it strange and defamiliarising it. The work of both is grounded in inconsistencies, discontinuities and ruptures and there are similarities in the ways they enact this.

The overarching principle for a 'perfect meal' for the Futurists was a combination of harmony between the various elements of the experience (including the setting, the tableware and the flavours of the food) and 'originality in the food' (Marinetti 2014: 36). Alongside the drive towards creating a harmonious, continuous and immersive experience of a restaurant space, which places the food in a broader world and artistic context, there are a number of direct correspondences between the Italian Futurists' practice and that of the technoemotional restaurant:

- Restaurant space: The Holy Palate Restaurant, a key site for Futurist banquets, was designed to be an architectural and artistic rendering of the Futurist aesthetic, which both mirrored and framed the food. Like with the technoemotional restaurant, the space was designed and curated to house the food and performances as part of a coherent artistic site or world.
- Technologies: Like the technoemotional restaurant, the Italian Futurists advocated the use of new technologies in the kitchen, to explore ingredients and produce new sensations. Marinetti called for the use of 'ozonizers', 'ultra-violet ray lamps', 'electrolysers', 'colloidal mills', 'atmospheric and vacuum stills', 'centrifugal autoclaves', 'dialysers' and 'chemical indicators' as technologies to create new dining experiences, to assess with precision qualities of the food during production and to infuse ingredients with new properties (2014: 39–40).
- Unusual ingredients: both the Italian Futurists and technoemotional restaurants explore the use of unusual and unexpected ingredients in their preparations, including ingredients that push against cultural notions of what is considered edible.
- Tasting menu: *The Futurist Cookbook* details a number of dinners that are structured in a similar way to the tasting menu, often with a series of small, bold courses offered one after another, carefully timed and deploying various small and overarching narratives throughout the meal. For instance, the 'Autumn Musical Dinner' consisted of small courses: chickpeas (served for

two minutes), seven capers, 25 liqueur cherries, twelve fried potato chips, a sip of wine to be held in the mouth for one minute and finally a roast quail to smell but not eat (Marinetti 2014: 142).

- Sculptural forms: The Futurists explored ways of presenting the food as sculptural forms, such as the 'Network in the Sky' abstract sculptural dessert, designed by Mino Rosso, which consisted of a disc of cherry caramel, cylinders of puff pastry with tamarind and chocolate fondant, a cylinder of meringue with mandarin fondant and filled with whipped cream, tamarind and pistachios, topped with a shard of mandarin-flavoured caramel and all draped with green spun sugar (2014: 212). These abstract sculptural forms in dessert, where the dish employs abstract shapes and rises considerably from the surface of the plate, are commonplace in haute cuisine.

The similarities between *The Futurist Cookbook* and the technoemotional restaurant are numerous, with the former offering an aesthetic historical precedent for the latter. What is perhaps most compelling in this comparison is the shared attitude towards the senses and connections between them. Novero writes that the Holy Palate restaurant was 'made to function according to the Futurist poetic principles of synthesis, synesthesia, and analogical correspondences' and operated according to a multimedial logic combining different sensory experiences (2010: 19). Marinetti brought the idea of correspondences from his earlier work with the Symbolists in Paris and the idea, named for Charles Baudelaire's poem *Correspondences*, articulated mystical connections between different sensory experiences. The Futurists went further to categorise modes of correspondence with particular terms, some framing an 'affinity [...] with the flavour of a given food': Conprofumo (olfactory affinity), Contattile (tactile affinity), Conrumore (sonic affinity), Conmusica (acoustic or musical affinity), Conluce (optical affinity); and others framing 'the complementary nature [...] with a given food': Disprofumo, Distattile, Disrumore, Dismusica and Disluce (Marinetti 2014: 231–33). The Futurists deployed these correspondences in their practice, notably in the 'Extremist Banquet', which layered a series of smells over food sculptures (155–58) and the 'Tactile Dinner Party', where guests were given pyjamas to wear, made of or covered with materials including sponge, sandpaper, aluminium, cardboard, silk and velvet, to be touched by themselves throughout the meal and, in between courses, 'the guests must let their fingertips feast uninterruptedly on their neighbour's pyjamas' (170–71).

The connections and correspondences between the senses, as discrete, mutually reinforcing or sometimes discontinuous experiences have directly been employed by the technoemotional restaurant. Their work engages with the sensory experience of eating, considering the tactile qualities of the cutlery and crockery, the overlaying of sound to reinforce or disrupt the gastronomic experience and the spraying of smells around the table to accompany a particular dish. In doing this, the different sensory streams are exposed and explored, teased apart and put back together, defamiliarised and heightened, to transform the experience of eating from the quotidian to the aesthetic. Perception itself is deployed not as a medium, a means to an end, but as the site of the artistic experience.

The technoemotional restaurant continues the work instituted by the Italian Futurists, whose work in turn was influenced by the historical lineages of previous practice (directly the work of the Symbolists and the Dadaists, who in turn emerged as an engagement with their forerunners). Rather than making the case for the Futurists as a modernist counterpoint to postmodern cuisine, they seem to have engaged with similar ideas and practices, but within different contexts. While the impetus for the work is radically different, the work itself enacts similar processes and a similar positioning of the diner.

2

Presentation: Performances of the Restaurant

To consider the restaurant as a space of performance opens a perspective that moves away from merely considering its work in terms of feeding the body and satisfying appetites or, following the previous chapter, framing all of the activities as scientific manipulation and technological extraction. Ferran Adrià reflects on the restaurant by means of a theatrical simile: 'Every meal is a bit like a theatrical performance in which the waiters are actors playing the central characters, and they must know their lines perfectly' (Adrià et al. 2008: 144). In this, he begins to think about the performance qualities of the restaurant, specifically positioning the waiters and the front of house staff as actors performing character. However, to think about the restaurant as a space or site of performance goes much further than waiters adopting or performing some kind of character: the front of house staff do perform, but in ways that cannot convincingly be positioned merely as adopting a character; various objects in the space of the restaurant (and indeed the space of the restaurant itself) perform, both functionally and artistically; and the food itself performs, as an object that unfolds itself in time and experience and performs at the intersection of its material and graphic dimensions, its sensory qualities and its various framings.

This chapter turns to the presentation of the food in the restaurant, shifting focus from the overarching principles and practices of the world of the restaurant to the particular ways in which the food objects are presented to the diner. As such, the chapter has a primarily visual and aural focus, thinking about performances that are addressed to these sensory streams, though with the inevitable implication of the other senses. The chapter begins by addressing performances of the front of house staff, the waiters, in the restaurant, considering those performances as an integral part of the experience. In particular, this section considers the kind of performance personae adopted by the waiting staff, their performances around and with the food and how they frame, facilitate and activate the experience. This kind of framing, facilitating and activating is then pursued in a focused way, in the second section, through an examination of the construction of the menu, thinking about how this document both guides the experience and enters into the experience as a productive force, operating somewhere between script and theatrical programme. The final section of the chapter turns to the food itself, considering its formal construction and presentation as a performative sculpture or as installation art. A number of exemplary dishes are analysed in terms of their artistic and aesthetic qualities, the way the food objects perform and how they often play with ideas of appearances and revelation. Running throughout the chapter is a playful deferral between the 'frame' and the work itself, where the way the food is framed both facilitates or sets the coordinates for the experience and is a crucial aspect of the aesthetic experience itself.

Performing Front of House

The term 'front of house' is used both in the restaurant and in the theatre for those who are not overtly positioned as actors or performers but who are the public-facing side of the institution who nevertheless perform: explicitly performing functions and implicitly performing a particular persona. Playing versions of themselves and performing particular roles, the front of house staff are positioned as operating within the 'hospitality industry', often having undergone 'industry training' and working within particular coordinates of 'professional' behaviour and standards. However, like the front of house staff in the theatre, they perform crucial roles not only in facilitating the practicalities of an event but also in positioning, framing and facilitating a particular kind or mode of experience. Their role is not a 'neutral', pragmatic management, but the performance of practical functions in relation to the desired world of the restaurant. Like performers in certain kinds of immersive theatre, they straddle the line between artistic performance and management of the event.

The waiting staff in each of the four restaurants are performers in multiple senses of the word. They have particular tasks that they have to perform and carry out. They adopt a particular kind of persona that is somewhere between their 'everyday' self, the role of the waiter and the concept of the individual restaurant; as such, it is a complex action of triangulation. While the performance of one's everyday self and the performance of a role or function are often done in a way that is not especially self-aware, the performance of a particular aesthetic or concept is usually reserved for performers within a theatrical context and so is often done with a self-awareness of the adoption of the style or mode of performance. However, in the restaurant, there seems to be little self-awareness in the front of house staff of the extent to which they are adopting the aesthetic or style of the restaurant in which they work. A number of waiting staff at these restaurants are able to articulate a sense of the styles in which they have to perform certain tasks, as well as a general understanding of the ways in which they shift their persona in relation to the diner, but not how these individual moments of performance fit into the wider aesthetic or concept of the restaurant.

In reflecting on the waiters at elBulli, Adrià writes that 'their conduct should not be artificial or routine', but that nevertheless they must 'stay alert at all times and be sensitive to the needs of every guest' in such a way as to 'create maximum enjoyment for the diner' (Adrià et al. 2008: 144). The waiters are called to be responsive to the diner in a semi-improvisational manner, utilising their own readings of the needs of individual guests, within the coordinates of general expectations of the performance of a waiter and the codes, practices and expectations of the particular restaurant. This is an embodied practice, which, as noted above, the waiters are not necessarily able to easily articulate through reflection. Rather, they build on cultural expectations of how a waiter should perform: friendly, but not overly familiar; efficient, but not mechanised; a sense of individuality, but not becoming too personal or diverging too far from the ethos and aesthetic of the restaurant. These general principles, coupled with an understanding of the kind of experience the restaurants seek to offer, establish a framework for the waiters' actions and performances, which themselves are repeated so often so as to become habitual.

The performances of the waiters are semi-improvisational in that, while they do have a certain level of autonomy in their individual performance choices, they have a set of pre-established techniques and practices to draw on, a dictionary of practices that form the syntax of the performance. The waiters have techniques and texts to draw on, which they deploy based on their intuited understanding of the 'needs' of the diner. In other words, the front of house staff read the diner and make an immediate decision about the level of performance to enact. At The Fat Duck, each of the front of house staff is provided with a book of information about each of the dishes, which they are required to learn. This information includes from where individual ingredients have been sourced and the cooking processes for each dish. The waiter is then able to make use of this information when presenting the dish or in order to respond to questions. It is a choice made by the individual waiter as to how much information they provide and in what way it is to be expressed, although the strict temperatures of the food being served often restrict the amount of text delivered, so that the dish can be eaten as close to its 'optimum' temperature as possible. If the diner decides they would like to know more, the waiter has the information to hand and so at times the diner has some agency over the food before them in choosing not to eat at the moment when it is deemed by the chefs to be best. As the meal progresses, the waiters begin to judge each table, reading the diners in order to provide the 'right' amount of description without the diners needing to ask for more or less.

There are numerous correspondences between the performance of the waiter and contemporary devised or experimental performance. These traits of contemporary performance include the merging of the supposedly 'real' self with the fictional or explicitly created world of the performance; the modes of performance associated with participatory or immersive practices, where the inclusion of the audience-diner in the world of the piece requires a flexibility and responsiveness on the part of the waiter-performer; leading on from this, the direct address from the waiter-performer to the diner-audience, with the shifts between the acknowledgement of the audience's presence and the performances amongst the waiters that (re)introduce a metaphorical fourth wall; and the waiter's role as somewhere between performer and facilitator of the work, with the waiter both performing a persona and doing the work more conventionally associated with the backstage or stage management role. Finally, there is a certain self-reflexivity in the performances of the waiters. When visiting these restaurants, the waiters are receptive to discussing their own role within the frame of the performance. To ask them about their training, what they think of the restaurant, their favourite dish or about how they are required to work opens a space for the waiters to discuss themselves and their own performances within the frame of the performance itself.

All of these different modes of performance are at work in the performance of the waiter. At elBulli, Adrià gives a very succinct account of the role of the waiter. He writes that the waiter 'Creates a warm atmosphere during dinner', 'Conveys the philosophy behind the food', 'Serves the food to the table', 'Explains the dishes', 'Controls quality' and 'Controls timing' (Adrià et al. 2008: 320.2). This mapping of the waiter's role includes both functional and artistic qualities though these are not wholly separate spheres of activity. The service, explanation and timing operate as facilitation, guidance and framing for the experience of eating, and the manipulation of atmosphere and the 'philosophy' or conceptual drive of the restaurant form a background and organisational principle within which the functional service activities take place. The waiter has an apparently spontaneous freedom when choosing how to carry out these tasks, but what underscores it is a more general understanding of what kind of experience they are required to facilitate.

One of the key ways in which the waiter's persona is constructed is through presenting themselves as merely a facilitator, to make themselves as invisible as possible in order to foreground the experience of the diner and their encounter with the food. The food itself, rather than the staff, is the star of the performance. However, in adopting the mode of 'professional', with its accompanying assumptions of the inappropriateness of one's personal or private performances of self, the waiter is required to perform a level of emotional labour akin to that required of the professional performer. The waiters have to: always be available to the guests and their needs irrelevant of personal circumstances; perform a level of pleasant professionalism at all times; and maintain a level of deference to the diner, no matter what the diner might do or say (in an environment that includes a significant element of intoxication, with the sometimes accompanying behaviours from diners that do not hold up their side of the implied social contract). There is an attempt to performatively neutralise the waiters according to a logic that places the customers' comfort and experience above all else. There is an attempt to foreground the food in the attention of the diner, which inevitably involves an attempt to background the staff of the restaurants (both the front of house staff and those working in the kitchen). At The Fat Duck, one of the opening encounters with the front of house staff for me was being asked 'Are you excited?' While this may appear to be merely a conversation starter, a friendly introduction, it demonstrates very clearly that the focus is on the emotional experience of the diner, rather than, as one might get in other restaurants, an introduction to the space and the waiter ('Hello, my name is x and I will be your waiter this evening').

The uniforms, too, attempt to perform this neutralising function. As with any uniform, there is an attempt to reduce the individuality of the staff and to present a coherent image of the establishment and to maintain the divide between the professional and the guest. At The Fat Duck, the uniform is a white shirt with grey trousers and waistcoat with a pastel lilac tie. At Noma, the waiters wear a light grey shirt, darker grey trousers and a pastel grey apron, while at Alinea the uniform is a black suit with a black shirt and no tie. The colourless suits have both an air of authority and allow for the backgrounding of the staff in relation to the colourful and spectacular food. The pastel tie at The Fat Duck lifts the monotony of the attire slightly, without pulling focus. The aprons worn by the Noma waiters very clearly point the diner's attention towards the food, beginning to blur the lines between chef and waiter. In each of these, there is a considered attempt to flatten out the waiter, to force them towards adopting a role and to lead them towards an ensemble performance practice, where no individual steps forward as the protagonist from the chorus.

At Noma, Redzepi has stated that he does not 'care about great armies of waiters in dinner jackets and bow ties manoeuvring their way through luxurious surroundings'. He wants the diner to have a 'pure and unpretentious experience' facilitated by the staff greeting the guests 'on an equal footing' (in Skyum-Neilson 2010: 15–16). The mood that Redzepi aspires to is one without the conventional trappings of the fine-dining establishment. However, while the waiters are very relaxed, friendly and personable when one first enters the restaurant, as the meal progresses, they become more formal – a subtle shift in their performance style with a stiffening of the relaxed atmosphere and a delivery that is less about conversation and more about presentation of the food. The 'unpretentious' experience that Redzepi describes may, in the opening act of the work, be present but is then overtaken by similar attention to detail and finesse that is found in the other restaurants. This is perhaps most explicitly demonstrated through the attention to detail from the waiters, whereby if a diner leaves the table, their napkin is replaced with one that is freshly laundered. This small act is far from the relaxed, anti-fine-dining atmosphere that Redzepi claims to produce. In thinking about the waiters' attire and attitude, Redzepi sardonically asserted: 'Like the food would improve with a bow tie' (2013: 6). However, the bow tie (as a synecdoche for the more classical or conventional service of the fine-dining establishment) does produce an effect in the perception and appreciation of the food. It creates the mood or atmosphere, which is one of care, precision and professionalism, leading the diner to a more complex or intricate appreciation of the food. In the same way, the more relaxed attire of the Noma front of house (in)forms the experience. The uniform of an apron (with its associations of food preparation) over smart-casual attire (not the formality of a bow-tie but nevertheless not entirely casual or informal) suggests a level of authority from the waiters over the space and experience but also suggests that the experience is finished or completed by the diners' actions. Bringing the apron out of the kitchen and into the dining room interrupts the division between the two spaces and presents the food not as complete commodity, merely to be consumed, but as something unfinished, requiring the sensory, embodied, emotional and intellectual work of the diner for completion.

The waiters inevitably play a substantial role in framing the food and guiding the experience; they are not merely facilitators or functionaries but are intimately caught up in the production of aesthetic experience. In 2015, food artists Bompas & Parr created a project that drew out and drew attention to the intimacy of this role of the waiter (though, for the artists, it was not framed in these terms), entitled *Anatomical Whisky Tasting* (Figure 1). In this, fifty people drank whisky directly from the bodies of five people who were the same age as the whisky they were serving, from 25 to 39 years old. Each of the five bodies on offer became tableware. Before the tasting, each of the 'performers' gave an autobiographical performance, telling stories from their life, in order to elaborate the time of ageing of the whisky by mapping it onto the experiences of a life lived in that time. This project reveals a number of ideas concerning the performance of service in the restaurant. First, it highlights how the body of the waiter can be transformed to function as an extension of the hardware of the restaurant. Reduced to equipment, the waiter performs functions, absenting their own subjectivity and becoming a mere tool. It could be argued that this is critiqued in *Anatomical Whisky Tasting*, as the bodies of servers are explicitly reframed as subjects. Second, the project troubles any notion of distance between the body of the server and the food that is served. As such, it offers a challenge to the waiter as a sterile functionary; no longer positioned like a conveyer belt, the waiter's bodily contact with the food

FIGURE 1: *Anatomical Whisky Tasting* (2015), Bompas & Parr. Photo by Nathan Pask.

is drawn out and the work of the restaurant is positioned firmly as 'live experience', with its implications of the mixing of bodies, as opposed to the prepackaged world of mass-produced food. Finally, the project makes apparent how the waiter serves to frame and guide the experience and understanding of the food, heightening what is always at work in the restaurant space, as the life stories told by the performers are directly connected to the age of the whisky to be tasted, mirroring the narrative frames provided by waiters that linger over the food and inflect the diners' experience.

For each of the restaurants, there is an attempt at 'informality' in their performance of front of house and the dining room. Blumenthal wanted the diners' experience to be informal, without 'a reverential hush in the dining room' or diners arriving 'feeling nervous or, in fact, anything other than relaxed' (2009: 110). He argues that this is to reduce stress, which 'can affect our perception of taste and even the sensitivity of our senses' (2009: 110). Similarly, at elBulli, the restaurant manager, Juli Soler, 'had a clear idea that the dining room had to be informal', rejecting conventions of impeccably dressed diners and waiters in 'immaculate white jackets', so that diners would be treated 'in a way that made them feel at home' (Adrià et al. 2014g: 435). The rejection of a certain mode of formality in these restaurants could superficially be understood as an attempt to limit the performances of class and privilege, to make the space feel more welcoming to those not accustomed to the black-tie formality of traditional dining rooms. However, the cost and elite framing of the restaurants make this a moot point. There is a level of economic and cultural capital required to dine at a three-Michelin star creative restaurant, and the attempts to limit formality are not an opening-out but rather an aesthetic choice: a rejection of an aspect of tradition in order to consolidate the sense of being 'contemporary'. For Blumenthal, the primary focus is the enjoyment of the diner and so he conceives of the informality as heightening relaxation for the purposes of pleasure. The purported informality is part of the commodification of the experience, where the diner only needs to pay (a substantial sum) to the restaurant in order to have pleasure.

As an extension of the informality and attempt to provide a heightened pleasurable experience for each diner, there is an attempt to address each diner as an individual (rather than as a group of customers). Adrià writes that this attitude 'is characterized by generosity and cordiality, so that every guest feels like an old friend making a welcome return' (Adrià et al. 2008: 144). To address the diner as an individual is to attempt to make the experience seem like it has been designed and enacted for the particular tastes, expectations and pleasures of the particular diner. At each of the restaurants, the diner is greeted warmly by the front of house staff on entering. At Noma, each of the diners is greeted by name, and the front of house staff remember whether the guest has chosen the wine or juice flight through the meal (where a particularly chosen wine or juice is presented to complement the food). At The Fat Duck, a 'Nostalgia Card' is left on the table for the diners to encounter when they are first seated. This offers an opportunity for the diner to write down and reflect on their own personal memories of a previous, exciting experience with food (and they are not used in any other way during the meal). The 'Nostalgia Card' acts as an encouragement to the diner to make connections between the present experience and an exciting food memory – to find a personal, emotional resonance with the meal and to encourage a personal and individual reading. The restaurants offer a framework that approximates an individualised address, a series of performances that apparently address the diner as an individual, to encourage a sense that the experience is designed for each individual, despite it being a generalised approach.

The front of house staff operate as performers, within a particular register of performance, according to the overarching aims and principles of each of the restaurants. Not only is this manifested in the costumes or uniform of the staff and their mode of address to the diner but also in the embodied performance practice of the waiters. For instance, at The Fat Duck, the waiters have worked with a choreographer on the style of movement they adopt in the dining room. This is evident in the way they navigate the space, which is at once controlled and fluid. There is a formality in their presentation, but one that deviates from the conventions of the waiter. The movement style is an ensemble practice. Each of the waiters has been trained to be aware of one another. They move around the restaurant holding themselves upright, acknowledging one another as they pass. If a waiter is carrying something away from a table and is interrupted by a diner, seamlessly another waiter will take away what the first is holding, so that the work continues and diner is treated as the utmost priority. The choreographer who worked with the waiters advised them to see the spaces between tables as streets, and as the waiting staff are overwhelming not English, they move on the right. The waiters operate by balancing out the space. They do not bunch together but spread out around the space, aware of the diners in their vicinity and ensuring that no area of the restaurant is ever without a waiter to hand. Each movement is fluid and it does not pause or stutter. A movement can be started by one waiter and continued by another. There is a horizontal structure to the space, so that the staff presence is spread out and the ensemble works without an apparent director.

At Alinea, performances in the space of the restaurant are markedly different. They adopt a more vertical structure, whereby there is a central block in the restaurant around which the waiters congregate, a hub from whence the waiters move out to the various tables and to which they return. This vertical or hierarchical structure is evident not only in the return to this central hub but also in the waiters' focus as they move around the space. Each of the waiters seems secure in their job when they have a task to perform. When delivering or retrieving dishes or responding to the diners' call, they move with precision and care. However, at times they pass tables without a task, and, at this point, they seem more awkward and self-aware. They seem unsure whether to meet the diner's gaze, whether to acknowledge the co-presence in the space and whether to look or to turn away. It is also apparent that instructions are issued through a hierarchy: the front of house manager does not attempt to hide away the gestures beckoning a member of staff across the dining room. The difference in the level of detail in the training of the waiters at The Fat Duck and Alinea is apparent. For the latter, the waiters operate as task-based facilitators still caught in the trappings of the conventional restaurant space, whereas for the former, the waiters have been taught to go beyond these conventions through a self-aware construction of their own bodies. Both of these styles produce effects in the experience of the space and the food. At Alinea, the sense of control is not as secure as at The Fat Duck, which can produce an uneasy experience. At The Fat Duck, because of this fluidity and control in the performance style, it feels more like the experience has been carefully curated and the diner is being led through it. In both cases, the diner may not be consciously aware of the effect of this style, which gives it potentially more power in producing its effects and affects, precisely because it forms part of the horizon of the experience rather than being its central focus.

The front of house staff begin to complicate the front of house/backstage binary, in much the same way that experimental performance practices have drawn attention to processes of creating their work in the work itself. This can be seen most explicitly in the use of waiters to finish the construction and presentation of some of the dishes at the table. For Adrià, this role of the waiter was first and foremost a pragmatic one, given that some dishes were fragile and were best served if they were finished at the table (Adrià et al. 2014g: 405). But it also had an aesthetic role. Some of elBulli's dishes were finished at the table not because they were too fragile in their finished state to transport, but because it allowed the waiter 'to call attention to its beauty by doing it in front of the diner' (Adrià et al. 2014g: 405). The presentation of a dish will always implicitly reference the acts of its construction, making the dish performative in that it carries the trace of action. By finishing a dish at the table, attention is explicitly drawn to the constructedness of the dish. This can have an influence on the nature of the experience of eating on the part of the diner, given the more explicit awareness of construction and a subsequent suggestion to pay attention to how and why the dish has been constructed in this particular way.

When the dish is finished at the table, a different kind of performance is required by the waiter. The performance register shifts from a background role as functionary to a role that takes more of the stage and the spotlight. There is a common trait in each of the restaurants, given the kind of food being served, for the waiters to act in a way akin to a magician, performing seemingly impossible or illogical transformations of and with the food at the table. At elBulli, one of the dishes served in their later years was 'In-situ Spherification of a Cucumber Soup' (Dish Number 1262 in Adrià et al. 2014b: 236–37). For this dish, the waiter would take 30 seconds to spherify liquid cucumber in the soup in which it was to be served. Spherification is the process by which a liquid is encapsulated in a thin skin, turned into small balls known as caviar, created through a reaction between the liquid to be spherified and the liquid into which it is immersed. While this usually is done in a separate liquid and then added to a plate, with this dish at elBulli, the soup itself was used to spherify the cucumber. The effect of this is that the dish seemingly produces itself, transforming in front of the diner of its own accord into the final presentation. For this, the waiter adopts the role of a magician, facilitating a transformation that is, of course, possible, but seemingly impossible or counter to common sense for the diner.

At Alinea, there is a continuation of the magician's role in the dish 'Pork Belly (Parsnip, Black Trumpet, Kombu)'. For this, a fire is created in the centre of the table for the previous dish, where the diner cooks their own kebab on an open flame. After this dish is cleared away, and the fire has died down, the waiter approaches the table and reveals that the fire had actually been heating the pork belly for the next course, which had been encased by the coals for the fire. After this revelation, the waiter then reveals that one of the coals is actually a charred parsnip, which is then removed, trimmed and served on a plate. The magical transformation had already been at work, a misdirection created through the use of the fire for the previous course. The waiter's function is to reveal and to do so in a way that gives nothing away in advance and slowly reveals how the diner had been tricked.

At The Fat Duck, one of the opening courses in the taster menu, the 'Nitro-Poached Aperitifs', involves the waiter spraying a foam from a siphon onto a spoon, which comes out like whipped egg whites, before 'poaching' it in liquid nitrogen at the table. When it has been 'poached' (i.e. rapidly frozen), the waiter holds it next to a candle flame and squirts the juice from a fine slice of lemon or lime peel through the flame onto the frozen aperitif, before handing it to the diner to be consumed immediately. Once again, the magical transformation is performed at the table, from wet cloud to delicate meringue through the seemingly counter-intuitive poaching in something cold rather than with heat. For each of these dishes, the waiter is deputised by the chef to complete the process of cooking and presentation at the table. The waiter is required to precisely work through the mechanical stages of the magic trick in order to produce the transformation. Each of the dishes could be produced in the kitchen and brought to the table readymade, but the spectacular flourish at the table allows for an element of theatrical surprise (enacted, staged, performed). This can intensify the sense of the extraordinary in the meal, not just in the complexity or spectacle of the food as-eaten but also in the staging of its preparation. The magical quality contributes to the apparent 'worth' of the meal, as these are not performances easily replicable by the average domestic cook: the experience is magical.

Alongside their duties as a deputy for the chef, the waiter is also deputised by the diner in terms of the interpretative strategies for understanding the food. A clear example can be found in the dish, the 'Mad Hatter's Tea Party', served almost halfway through the tasting menu at The Fat Duck (Figure 2). For this dish, the waiter becomes a narrator, not merely explaining how the dish is to be eaten but also explaining the narrative of the dish and outlining the intertextual readership needed to understand in the way hoped for by the chef-creator. On the table is served a clear teacup, in which are mock eggs, made from swede and vinegar, cubes of ox tongue, pickled turnip, cucumber, enoki mushrooms, black mustard seeds, micro-parsley and diced black truffle. Resting on top of the tea cup is a clear teapot with hot water. As this is served, the waiter says,

> Are you familiar with the story of *Alice in Wonderland*? You know what it is? She went down the rabbit hole and she met a lot of crazy people. She met the Cheshire Cat, who led her towards the house of the Mad Hatter and the March Hare. And they were having a tea party, a mad tea party. And they tried to fix the watch of the Hatter, because the watch was late. So, they took the watch, buttered it and dipped it into tea.[1]

At this point, the waiter opens a wooden box revealing a number of golden pocket watches. With tweezers, one pocket watch is lifted out of the box and placed into the teapot, as the waiter says, 'I have for you some watches. They belong to the Hatter. I will dip the watch in the teapot. I will ask you then to lift up the teapot and to swirl it around'. As the watch dissolves, the water changes into a tea-coloured consommé with the gold leaf, which formed the outside of the watch, swirling around inside. Finally, the waiter says,

> As you swirl, the watch dissolves and it turns into a tea. What do you do when you have tea in a teapot? You can pour the tea into the cup in order to create the Mock Turtle Soup. A Victorian dish from the time when *Alice in Wonderland* was written and, as well, the time when the tea party was created. As you drink your tea, please enjoy the Victorian sandwiches. You are ready now, so you can pour them into the cup. Pour it all, don't be shy!

This performance leads the diner towards a specific reading of the dish, one that draws out the connection to the explorations and reconfigurations of sense in *Alice in Wonderland* and the historical grounding of the dish in Victoriana. Even without the waiter's performance and narrative, there is nevertheless the ability to legitimately read the dish in relation to *Alice in Wonderland*, though this operates as one potential interpretation amongst others. But the waiter's performance overlays the dish and provides a structure for understanding (though with the caveat that this understanding and experience would be different depending on the diner's familiarity with Carroll's story).

FIGURE 2: 'Tea Party including Mock Turtle Soup' (2013), The Fat Duck. Photo by Romas Foord.

The actions, behaviours and presentation of the front of house staff perform a number of functions: they facilitate the experience, as a useful functionary, they play a considerable role in producing the general atmosphere in the restaurant and they play a role in positioning the diner, in terms of how the diner is addressed and how the diners are encouraged to appreciate and understand the food. The latter is not just in the narrative framing of the dish (the explicit narrative offered for the 'Mad Hatter's Tea Party' is unusual), but more generally in the (sometimes subtle, sometimes less so) attempts to guide both the attention and mood of the diner. When I was served the dish 'Eggs in Verjus (c.1726), Verjus in Egg (c.2013)' at The Fat Duck, the waiters were notably playful, which changed how I experienced the dish. The dish itself looks like a chicken's egg and is made from painted chocolate egg shell, filled with a verjus yolk and a parfait and panna cotta egg white. The waiter gave no explanation of the dish as it was presented, but as he walked away from the table, he kept glancing back at me over his shoulder, with a grin. He did this three times and for the third was joined by another waiter and, together, they looked, grinning, at the table. The effect was intriguing, setting up an anticipatory excitement as to what I might find within what looked like a boiled egg and caused me to smile uncontrollably back at the waiter. While not operating within the conventions of 'professional service', this small moment from the waiter guided my experience, shifting me away from mundane confusion ('this just looks like an egg') into excited anticipation ('the waiter is waiting for my surprised delight'). Even a glance or a gesture from the waiter can frame and form part of the unfolding experience.

Reading the Menu

Just as the front of house staff straddle a functional and an artistic-aesthetic role in the enacting and realisation of the meal, so too does the menu. The menu has two distinct meanings: as a document, handed to the diner that provides information about the meal, and as a term for the organisation of a series of experiences, sensations and ideas through the meal (for instance, the tasting menu). These are connected, as the document conveys in (usually) written form what is anticipated as the experience. As a document handed to the diner before the meal unfolds, the menu document provides functional information about the tasting menu that is about to unfold (the number and order of dishes, titles of dishes, key ingredients, descriptions, sometimes details of the drinks pairing that can accompany dishes). But it also has a narrative quality, mapping out the journey(s) of the meal, drawing attention to coherencies, consistencies and connections across the meal, guiding the diner through the meal and drawing attention to particular sensations, qualities and ideas considered important by the chefs creating the individual dishes and their place in the unfolding meal.

Following the theatrical analogy for the restaurant, the menu works between two specific modes: script and programme. As a script, the menu lays out, in written form, the organisation of the sections of the meal: titles of sections, the ordering of the meal, key components; like a script, the text is not the same as the live(d) experience, but nevertheless organises it and enters into it as a component part. As a programme, the menu provides, sometimes implicitly and sometimes explicitly, a conceptual account of the meal, encouraging a particular perspective, approach and understanding from the diner. A copy of the menu is often given to the diner to take away after the meal, so, like a programme, becomes a memento of the work. As a document presented to the diner, the menu maps out the meal and forms a part of the experience itself. In this section, the menu is explored in terms of its modes of language and how it operates as both map and memento of the experience.

In the second volume of *The Practice of Everyday Life*, de Certeau et al. offer a taxonomy of modes of language around food and cooking, involving 'four distinct domains of objects or actions': (1) ingredients; (2) appliances and technologies for cooking; (3) 'the performance, actions words' describing the processes of creation; and (4) the name that furnishes the finished product (1998: 215). While the menu often foregrounds the last of these four, the name, it also references, to greater and lesser extents, the other realms of food language. Sometimes they are conflated, where a raw ingredient becomes the name (a common trait at Noma and Alinea). In this instance, the various transformations of cooking are backgrounded and some essentialised notion of the ingredient comes to the fore, as though the chefs merely allow the ingredient to come forth. To use an ingredient as the name for the dish tells the diner what the central, organising component is meant to be, implicitly referencing something of the chef's thinking and development of the dish. All four modes of language are at the disposal of and deployed by the front of house staff when delivering and describing a dish, though the third area of actions and processes of creation are often the least used. The occasional discussion of technologies enters as a way of drawing attention to the experimental dimension of cooking technologies, but to describe the act(ion)s of creation has the potential to interrupt the curated experience in two ways: first, it can undermine the encounter with the celebrity chef, given the inherently collaborative practice of developing and producing the dishes, and second, it can undermine that element of the magical when the process of creation is explained (the quality of magic is lost when the magician explains the mechanics and actions of the trick).

The name of the dish always articulates something of a concept, even when the name is just a key ingredient, and that concept enters into and guides the experience. At The Fat Duck and elBulli, there was and is more of a tendency to name the dish in a way that foregrounds a concept rather than key component parts. Nir Dudek notes that there has been a shift in the practice of menu writing; that the chef has moved from an executioner to a poet (2008: 51). This is echoed by de Certeau et al., who acknowledge the connection between the cultural status of a restaurant and the obscurity of names on the menu:

> the higher [the restaurant's] status, the more the menu proposes mysterious dishes with pompous names whose reading generally provides no information; one must humbly resort to the help of a maître d', who is a trifle condescending, to get an explanation [...]. Here the name is used to veil or theatricalize, thus to intrigue and cloud, and the customer must blindly order unknown words that will become dishes filling him or her with satisfaction.
>
> (1998: 221)

While the tasting menu does not provoke the same lack of sureness over ordering (the diner is invited only to make decisions on drinks and to provide any dietary requirements), there is nevertheless an imbalance of knowledge around the experience. With titles such as 'Mad Hatter's Tea Party', 'Sound of the Sea' and 'Like a Kid in a Sweet Shop' at The Fat Duck, 'Graffiti' and 'Balloon' at Alinea, 'Flavors of the Ocean' and 'Forest Flavors' at Noma and 'The Sea', 'Flower and Nectar' and 'Autumn Landscape' at elBulli, the diner has to remain intrigued, remain confused or ask the waiter for more direct explanations. As poetry, the dish titles do not stage a particular issue, but, as Dudek notes, in the restaurant the diner has to confront (or be confronted by) the material realisation of the poetic (2008: 53). Dudek argues that this poses a question of meaning and understanding: the poetic name can be left at the diner's discretion to understand; the actual dish requires that the name aligns with the experience of eating.

The more poetic or obscure name on the menu, according to de Certeau et al., veils and theatricalises the dish. While in their writing this is implied to be pejorative, it can also be understood as an opening of the complexity of the aesthetic experience. Precisely because the diner is encouraged to reconcile the name with the experience of eating, a space is opened for an unsettled experience that interrupts an easy continuity between the two modes (the dish as experienced and its name). In *The Logic of Sense*, Gilles Deleuze draws out the ways in which making sense is a process or series. In the chapter on the 'Series of Sense', in a discussion of the proliferation of meaning-making statements, he writes that there are two series of names: 'the name which denotes something and the name which denotes the sense of this name' (Deleuze 2004: 37). This leads to an indefinite proliferation of sense, given that the second statement, which denotes the sense of the name, may then become the former 'name which denotes something', itself subject to a further statement of explication and the denotation of its sense. The seeming stability of a conventional menu, whereby a more conventional narrative of sense is presented (the narrative of ingredients and preparation methodology), is destabilised in the more poetic menu. The diner is unable to rely on conventional, acquired narratives of sense to connect the name of the dish and its realisation as an object for sensory experience. The poetic name becomes a provocation to reflection, implicitly posing the question of in what way the name stands for, represents or encapsulates the experience of the realised object.

The menu offers a sense of the journey undertaken by the diner through the course of the meal. It provides a grounding for the diner, a way of keeping track of their place in the unfolding meal, an awareness of what has already gone and what is still to come. However, it is only at The Fat Duck that the menu is presented in advance of the meal. At The Fat Duck, the menu is presented to the diner before the meal begins, in a brown leather tome. This suggests that, despite the experimental nature of the cuisine, there is nevertheless a reassuring authority that has created and curated the meal. It also poses a tension between the somber quality of the brown leather tome and the playful and experimental food to come. There is then a smaller menu left on the table to allow the diner to track their way through the experience.

At elBulli, Noma and Alinea, the menu is only offered at the end of the meal, to take away as a memento. The Fat Duck also present the diner with a fresh and clean menu to leave with, rather than the one left on the table, which bears other traces of the experience (splashes from the food, finger prints, etc.). The common practice of gifting the diner with a memento assumes a connection between the writing, the experience and memory. Implicit in the 'gift' is a presupposition that the writing can somehow encapsulate or provoke an embodied memory of the experience.[2] However, there are tensions between the experience itself and the ways in which it is described on the menu, not only for individual dishes but in the temporal structure of the meal. Each of the menu documents is structured with an even space between the courses, suggesting a homogenous time, based on the balance of significance of each course (as though every course has the same significance). The experience cannot be like this. The courses are different sizes, take different amounts of time to eat and, even if they were evenly spaced in terms of clock time (which they are not), the experiential time of eating would thicken for different moments. There is an attempt towards a generalisation in the menu, as the restaurant cannot hope to offer an individual map for every diner of their personal experience. As such, there is a tension at work between the experience, the menu and the memory. But to go further, the menu may begin, as a memento, to become a palimpsestic overwriting of the experience in memory. It begins to resolve the tension between menu and experience in that it offers an arguably more stable representation of the meal. Or, in a more nuanced way, there is a reconciliation of memory and text through the use of the menu as memento. It is not the memory itself but acts as a prompt to memory.

The menu at Alinea is designed so as to address some of the insufficient qualities of the written menu to encapsulate the experience. Presented at the end of the meal in a black envelope for the diner to take away, the menu not only lists the courses served but also offers a graphic representation of the experience. As well as the names and key components of each of the dishes, the menu employs a graphic notation system. Each dish has a corresponding grey bubble on the page, with the size of the bubble indicating the relative size of each dish, the darker or lighter shades of grey reflecting the richness or lightness of the dish and the placement of the bubble on the page corresponding to its savouriness or sweetness (closer to the left of the page signaling a more savoury dish, the right sweeter). This menu attempts to go further than the conventional description through text of a menu to visually represent how the chef understands the qualities of the food and the sweet-savoury and intensity trajectories of the meal. This visual representation is not offered in advance of eating, to guide the experience of the meal, but rather is presented at the end to guide the diner's reflections on the meal. There may, of course, be differences in how the meal was perceived to how the chef intended it; the menu flattens these out and allows for the chef-creator's understanding of the meal to take precedence. The menu goes beyond memento as prompt to memory to become a more explicit guide to how the meal should be recalled. The same could be said, to greater and less degrees, of all the other menus. While they do not offer this same graphic documentation of the meal, they do provide descriptions that will lead the diner to remember those traits or qualities outlined in the menu over their own experience.

Food Forms

The final section of this chapter turns to the food itself, thinking about the forms of the presentation of various dishes at each of the restaurants. Addressed largely to an audio-visual sensory register, the first encounter with the food itself for the diner (rather than its name on the menu) is as a sculptural form, as performative installation art. The food is performative in a number of ways: it bears the traces of previous actions in its constructedness and createdness; it is activated and framed by the performances around and with it; and it becomes itself via a series or serialisation of appearances. In amongst the more superficial spectacle of unusual forms, smoke and panache, the dishes challenge conventions of food presentation, engage in conceptual artistry and raise self-referential questions of their own constitution.

Adrià writes that the conventional approach to food plating is from a French tradition of a main ingredient, a side and a sauce (Adrià et al. 2008: 464.7). This classic model of food presentation in haute cuisine has been challenged, particularly since the advent of *nouvelle cuisine*, with high-end restaurants explor-ing and experimenting with other forms of presentation on the plate. Christo-pher Styler, in his book *Working the Plate: The Art of Food Presentation* (2006), attempts to codify different styles of and approaches to plating (with categories such as 'The Minimalist', 'The Architect' and 'Dramatic Flair'). In this guide for chefs, Styler offers different principles for the arrangement of elements on the plate, considering shape, visual interest, height and concepts. However, *Working the Plate* takes the white plate as a basis and focuses on the arrangement of elements. Each of the experimental and creative restaurants goes further and moves the presentation of dishes more clearly into the realm of sculptural and installation art. They draw, both implicitly and explicitly, on practices from the plastic arts and conceptual art.

The restaurants do not mark an absolute break from traditions and conven-tions of restaurant practice. At times, they depart radically from them and at other times take them as a basis for exploration, reconfiguration and estrangement. For example, the dish 'Beetroot and Rhubarb' at Noma (Redzepi 2010: 150, 294) takes the tripartite structure of classical French presentation but changes the dynamic of the relation of elements on the plate. The dish consists of three bold colours: a white circle of powder (a yogurt granita), a dark and grainy red quenelle (a rhubarb mousse coated in dried rhubarb powder) and a vibrant red quenelle of smooth and glossy red sorbet (made from beetroot). The dish has the traditional structure of three parts, but balances the three so that it is not easy to identify what the 'main' and 'side' or supporting elements are meant to be. This is mirrored in the name of the dish, which marks an equivalency between beetroot and rhubarb (rather than marking one as supporting or accompanying the other). The white yogurt granita is perhaps closest to a sauce, accompanying the other two elements, but it is also the largest and most dominating element on the plate. None of the elements over-laps with the others and each can be eaten alone or in combination with one or both of the other elements. For a diner conversant with the dominant traditional approach to plating, the dish offers something of a challenge. It bears the traces of the traditional and is relatively simple in its plating, but it is more difficult to under-stand the relation of the elements to one another given that it does not conform to the hierarchy of the traditional plate of a 'main' element, an accompaniment and then a sauce that bridges them and holds them together.

The psychologist Charles Spence observes that the traditional practice of plat-ing a dish is 'typically based on the intuitions of the chef, guided, if anything, by a series of rules of thumb perhaps vaguely remembered from cookery school' (2018b: 238). The experimental restaurants, while inevitably making use of this intuitive sense of creativity in the plating of the food, do go further and attempt to both reflect upon, and make use of those reflections in, the principles and ideas for plating. They draw on principles, techniques and practices from the plastic and conceptual arts to move beyond the intuitive or principles learned from training or convention. For instance, particular attention is paid to the use and understanding of colour in the construction of a dish. At Noma, the chefs explored the colour green, not merely as a colour, but, as Redzepi states, 'the bright, tart flavour that green echoes, the transformation that sees young tendrils shoot for the sky and bushes glitter with unfolding lime-green leaves' (2013: 65). This slightly poetic articulation brings together a colour with some of its associations (appropriately, given Noma's focus on the 'natural'). The colour is not just a visual quality but has potential as an organising concept. At elBulli, the dish 'Red Variation' (Dish Number 1189 in Adrià et al. 2014a: 346–48) was variations of the colour red, including different preparations of raspberry, strawberry, watermelon, cherry and pink grapefruit. The fruit was placed around the edges of the plate, in a circle, with a red foam ('Strawberry Air') filling the centre. The colour red was an organising principle for the plate, not only as a visual design but also for the choice of ingredients. The logic of the dish was not a necessarily conventional combination of ingredients (beyond the vague notion of a fruit salad) nor ingredients that might be found together in nature; instead, it rested on this visual quality.

The use of colour as a conceptual tool with food was used by Erik Satie in his Dada white diet, described in 'The Day of a Musician', and was organised by the principle of whiteness, with Satie eating eggs, sugar, minced bones, fat from dead animals, veal, salt, coconuts, chicken, mould from fruit, rice, turnips, white cheese and skinless fish (in Novero 2010: 74). Independent of its nutritional value, the diet was organised according to an artistic principle. While conceptually similar to the restaurants' idea of colour as concept, elBulli's 'Red Variation' clearly operates closer to conventions of edibility than Satie's white diet. But in both cases, the idea of diets being constructed only according to a logic of nutritional value is challenged. In Marinetti's *Futurist Cookbook*, whiteness was deployed as an explicitly political and racist concept in the 'Dinner of White Desire',[3] but this is not to say that Satie's white diet is apolitical by comparison. Within a Dadaist context, Satie's diet can be understood as a rejection of bourgeois good taste. Colour is never purely abstract, as it has associations and significations within a given socio-political, cultural and historical context. For Redzepi and Noma, green is not merely a colour choice, but speaks to the broader politics of the 'natural' espoused by the restaurant.

The use of food as an artistic material in the arts forms a background to the various presentations explored and deployed in the restaurants. However, the framing of the restaurant limits the extent to which the food is explored as an artistic material, given that the restaurants always seek to appeal to pleasure and enjoyment. They do not use the food in a way that radically departs from conventionally edibility to the extent of slipping into the arena of the abject and disgust. In the restaurant the food needs to be, in some way, appetising. This involves operating broadly within cultural narratives of edibility, both in individual ingredients and in their combinations. The combinations of ingredients in experimental restaurants, no matter how 'experimental', never diverge completely from cultural tastes and the plating always maintains cultural principles of what is pleasing, including balance, harmony and orderliness (see Spence 2018b). In stark contrast to this, in the 1960s the Vienna Actionists made use of foodstuffs in their performance and art practice as a political challenge, drawing on the tradition of Duchamp's ready-mades and Dada attacks on bourgeois good taste. Hermann Nitsch's multiple actions with a lamb's carcass, often split open and presented in a bloody and raw state, troubled the cultural narratives that allow movement from live animal to raw ingredient (by so doing, making manifest in a visceral and violent way Christian theology and the connections between the sacrificial body of Christ, the image of the lamb and the consumption of the body of Christ in the Eucharist). This would be unthinkable in the high-end experimental restaurant, in part because of the overt religious and political framing of Nitsch's actions and in part because of the radical staging of the transformation from living being to raw ingredient or product.[4]

The Vienna Actionists engaged in practices that not only used food but also spoke directly to and of the table as a site of political and domestic organisation (and, indeed, the intersection of the domestic and political at and around the table). In the semi-public sphere of the restaurant, there is an attempt to depart from the gendered politics associated with the traditional table in the domestic sphere (traditions of the female-gendered labour of hospitality and feeding, as well as the patriarch's traditional position at the head of the table). The Vienna Actionists confronted this politics directly, rather than attempting to ignore or forget it, particularly in Otto Mühl's 1964 work, *Material Action No.9: Still Life with a Female, a Male, and a Cow's Head*. In this work, the artist used various foodstuffs and everyday objects to interact with the heads of a female model and a male model, which protruded through openings on a table. The table also included a cow's head with horns. During the performance, Mühl daubed the heads of the models with lettuce, flower, eggs, Nivea cream, talcum powder, oranges, jam, milk, flour, breadcrumbs, pickles, bread rolls, Persil and paint (Mühl cited in Schwarz 1998: 281–82). The performance used foods and the site of the dining table to unearth the chaos and mess that threatens to break through the ordered world of bourgeois domestic space. Eggs were cracked and milk was poured; both loaded symbols of the 'maternal', with the eggs cracked over the head of the male model in a way that could be read as protest. Persil, red paint and bread rolls were aggressively beaten together, reframing the traditionally female labours of cooking, feeding and cleaning, moving away from any image of contented and submissive care and hospitality to expose the weary labour required, which verged on the violent and disgusting (the red paint operating both as a reminder of bloody violence and as a contamination of the edible).

By way of comparison, contemporary Dutch food artist Marije Vogelzang's *Sharing Dinner* (2005, 2008) created a meal where the tablecloth extended from the table in front of the diners and they put their heads and arms through slits cut in the white cloth. For Vogelzang, the setting aimed to create 'a sense of equality' by covering the clothing of the diners. The meal was an attempt to materially and figuratively cut off from the rest of the world and engendered an attempt at a political manoeuvre: to isolate the diners from the world, from the identity markers carried by clothing and thereby create a sense of equality and sharing with the food. The experimental restaurants operate, conceptually, closer to Vogelzang than Mühl: an attempt to move away from or forget the material, economic and gendered circumstances of the world in order to sit around an idealised *tabula rasa* – not unearthing and exploring the broader politics that nevertheless linger on, around and through the table and its activities, but to create a space where food is disconnected from particularly problematic or troubling political practices and discourses. The crafted presentations and performances at the table (of both the waiters and the food) have an element of restraint, despite the spectacle often employed, because they do not confront directly the mess, chaos and potential violence that traditionally, and even now, pervades the production of food and dining. That said, no matter how much Vogelzang or the restaurants might conceive of their dining spaces and presentations as apolitical or an idealised space of sharing, comfort and pleasure (indeed, the drives towards an aesthetics of equity and towards pleasure themselves are intimately political), the works can never be entirely decontextualised, and discourses such as gender politics remain – sometimes in an implicit and sticky way and other times in a way that is more overt and explicit.

While the restaurants do not make use of the radical practices of Vienna Actionism, at Alinea, the chefs do serve a dessert that takes directly from Jackson Pollock's actionist painting. The dessert, 'Tropical Fruit', is presented by the chefs directly on the table in front of the diner.[5] A silicon cloth is laid over the table and chefs emerge from the kitchen to 'plate up' the dessert onto this cloth. Armed with various sauces and small pieces of prepared fruit, the chef seemingly throws the items onto the table, creating patterns and a painting for the diner to eat. The similarity to Jackson Pollock's work is apparent. The presentation of the dish is not a finished product that emerges, fully formed, from the kitchen. Instead, the actions of the chef are presented at the table and the final presentation is created on the table. Whereas all the dishes bear the traces of their own constructedness, this dish draws attention to that act of construction. In 'The "Pollockian Perform-ative" and the Revision of the Modernist Subject', Amelia Jones marks out how Pollock's Action Painting presents 'painting as an *act* rather than a final object' and, in so doing, shifts thinking to 'not only about "art" as an expression of indi-vidual subjects, but about subjectivity itself' (1998: 55, original emphasis). She argues that discourses surrounding Jackson's painting are a site of contradiction, moving between the artist as 'an extreme case of the modernist desire to unify the subject as a source of intentional meaning and a conduit of divine inspira-tions […] and a subjectivity that attempts to define itself in *opposition to* what is perceived to be mainstream, bourgeois culture' (57, original emphasis). The same can be said of Alinea's dessert action painting: the various elements and ingredients flung, splashed, placed, thrown and cracked on the table require the actions of the chef to index their meaning (as an action, as assemblage, only coming into being through the actions of the chef). But equally, in the counter to cultural norms of a dish in the restaurant emerging fully formed and plated from the kitchen, the dessert is more open to the bodies of the diner, whose spectatorship is positioned as part of the constitution of the work. It is a performance for the diners directly, not merely an act of preparation behind the scenes. The work of the dish encom-passes not only the performances of its production but also those of its consump-tion: the messy-but-ordered-and-beautiful construction on the table becomes the messy taking apart in consumption, as the diner scoops, dips, licks and blurs the ordered and pleasing mess, until mere messy traces remain.

Like Pollock's action painting, Alinea's dessert has a lingering exploration of subjectivity. For Jones, the performativity of Pollock's paintings is in the indexi-cality of the gesture: 'the gestural loops of paint first and foremost tell the "story" of Pollock's body in action. But they are still insistently iconic: they still narrate a previous temporal action after all; they *represent* and insist on being, in [Rich-ard] Shiff's terms, "organized pictures"' (84). The tension continues between the indexing of meaning through the gestures of the artist-subject and the organised, iconic image that is created. In Alinea's dessert, these two poles are intercon-nected. The performance of the dessert, dripped and placed and smeared on the table, superficially suggests some artistic agency on the part of the chef and the dessert on the table becomes primarily a document of the actions of these particu-lar chefs, here and now, for the diner. However, the dessert nevertheless follows contemporary conventions of plating: curved lines of thick sauces, which maintain their integrity; blobs of sauce, swiped elegantly with a spoon; space between the elements to avoid a cacophony of mess; elements placed to create coherencies and contrasts of colour and texture. Far from an individual and individualistic moment of expression, the dessert is a rehearsed action, repeated at each table for each service, following conventions of elegant and appealing fine dining plating. The dessert is performative: a particular action that is repeating something rehearsed, performed according to norms (including conventions of plating and the over-arching concept of the restaurant) and, instead of *expressing* the subjectivity of the chefs who perform, the performance itself constructs their subjectivity (both in the eyes of the diner and for the chefs in the focused moment of the actions). The organised picture on the table is both indexed by the actions and gestures of the chefs and becomes the index for their presentation of self in the moment of the action (they are chefs, preparing and serving a dish, with any other elements of their sense of self backgrounded or forgotten).

Each dish sets up its own world within the broader horizon of the world of the particular restaurant. Adrià et al. writes that 'The way a dish is arranged on a plate not only effects its visual appeal but also provides a guide as to how it should be eaten, and can radically affect the way the dish is experienced' (2008: 464.8). While they acknowledge that the form of the dish has an impact on and in the dining experience, there is a problem in the articulation here, as there is an assumption of an essence or ideal of the dish that can be thought as free from the form it takes. For each dish to set up a world (in the Heideggerian sense, from the 'Origin of the Work of Art'), the work sets itself up and produces itself. It is created, but the *work* of the world of the work of art is that it 'opens up a *world*', not a 'bare placing' of elements but 'a form in which what is essential gives guidance' (Heidegger 2011a: 108). While not explicitly framed in these terms by Heidegger, his understanding draws out a performative quality of the world of the work of art: that it becomes itself in its own articulation, taking on a world and life of its own in its being, separate from the intentions of the artist. The experience of the work is not an ideal that is modulated by the form, the experience of the work is guided by the work itself (its sensory qualities, what is available for experience and interpretation). The work *works*. As such, to understand a dish as art, then its form, as a setting up of a world, *is* the artwork, facilitating an aesthetic experience, not, as Adrià et al. suggest, an essence that is manipulated by the form.

The world for each dish is both material and conceptual and the two are structurally interconnected: the material construction of the dish, its material articulation, establishes the coordinates of understanding and experience. While any act of readership or understanding has the potential to follow unexpected, eccentric, unplanned and personal pathways (there is no absolute determination of understanding grounded in a text or object), for an experience or mode of understanding to be strictly *about* the work (rather than the wanderings of imagination), it needs to operate within the coordinates established by the material world of the work. In other words, to be legitimately about the work, the experience or interpretation needs to circulate around and be connected to the material dimensions of the work itself, rather than an eccentric meandering of the imagination tentatively evoked or provoked by the work. The world of the work is not infinite but rather is strictly delimited by its material dimensions.

According to Heidegger's conception of art, the world of the work rests upon the 'earth', the material and actual foundations of possibility that is given form in its particular articulation in the work of art. A key trope in the dishes designed and presented at each of the restaurants is a playful exploration of discovery, tantalising and teasing the diner with processes of revelation of the foundation or substance of a dish. In Heideggerian terms, from *Being and Time*, we can conceive of this as the playful exploration of a 'phenomenon', which Heidegger conceptualises as the structurally interconnected notions of 'is' and 'seems'. For Heidegger, 'is' signifies 'that which shows itself in itself, the manifest' and the 'seems' (or 'semblance') is that which 'looks like something or other' or shows 'itself as something which in itself it is *not*' (1962: 51–52, original emphasis). Heidegger establishes a tension between what something 'is' and how it 'seems', the latter he also terms an 'appearance': 'Appearing is a *not-showing-itself*' (1962: 51–52, original emphasis). The unfolding experience of eating many of the dishes at these restaurants is a process of discovery, of uncovering or unconcealment, but one that never reaches a point of absolute revelation of essences. Rather, the experience itself is constituted as one of a process of revelation and discovery (which is the foundation for the 'surprise' factor in many of the dishes). This marks a departure from Heidegger, who argues that, in art setting up a world, it 'moves the earth itself into the open region of a world and keeps it there. *The work lets the earth be an earth*' (2011a: 109–10, original emphasis). There is a lingering sense in both Heidegger's writing on art and his writing on the 'is' that an essential nature can be discovered or revealed. To avoid problematic essentialism, we might say instead that the imagined notions of an essential 'is' or 'earth' and 'seeming' or 'appearance', the seeking out of the 'true' substance underneath the surface, are constitutive of the experience, not a genuine discovery of an essence, but rather the *process* of discovery or unconcealment itself as constituting the work of the work of art. This also introduces a temporal element to aesthetics (the experience of art), which moves it away from the static, apparently self-evident presence of the work to a process of unfolding more akin to performance than fixed sculpture. The art becomes itself as a series of appearances, none of which is formally privileged as the essence, heart or truth of the work. There are two modes of the performative at work in this theorisation of art: first, the constitution of the work as a series of appearances, which come together to form the work, with the work not reducible to any 'one' of these appearances, and second, the idea of art as *aletheia* (truth as discovery, unconcealment, revelation) has a temporal dimension, an unfolding process where the unconcealment is experienced as discovery (finding what could be said to already be there or be at work) but is, in fact, productive (producing in the experience what it purports to merely find).

In reflecting on his cuisine, Blumenthal echoes Heideggerian language in articulating a 'gap between things-as-they-are and things-as-they-seem' (2009: 105). But this is a problematic distinction when considering the experience of the dishes because they 'are' what they 'seem': the serialisation of appearances, taken cumulatively. A dish is an unfolding event, becoming itself in the way that it appears. That appearance is not merely operating within a visual register (which the term 'appearance' suggests). It can encompass any number of ways in which the dish presents itself to the diner: through the visual, the aural, the haptic, the olfactory and the gustatory. The seemingly static food object, the dish, unfolds in time as a series of appearances, a series of sensory streams, with the cumulation of sensory 'information' furnished with the name of the dish to give it a sense of wholeness. Nevertheless, it is not an absolute presence; rather a process of unfolding and becoming itself in the experience. This has a number of implications for understanding the dishes presented. First, the dishes cannot be taken as a static and fixed object, both because they change over time (the temperature changes, they are broken apart and consumed) and because they are never experienced 'completely' in a single moment (there is sight from different angles and perspectives, the unfolding of smell, the addition of tasting, which then takes apart and reconfigures how the dish looks). Second, the work of the dish as art is not complete until it enters into the dynamic, destructive and consummatory relation with the body of the diner, given that it is the experience rather than the object that is foregrounded in the restaurants' practice. Finally, the logic or concept of an individual dish is revealed, unfolds itself and becomes itself through the dish's processual character. The dishes that play on surprise and revelation are not grounded in a revelation of a 'true' essence, but rather in the playful exploration of what might be 'logically' expected or possible.

The series of appearances, taken cumulatively, constitutes the dish through a process of exploration, experience and reflection. A dish only *is* how it *seems* or *appears*, and the series of appearances constitute both the material, experiential encounter with the dish and its concept. For example, the dish 'Milk Ice and Barley, Poached Egg and Liquorice' at Noma plays with the process of discovery and the tension between 'is' and 'seems'. The dish is presented as an egg cracked open onto a plate, where the yolk appears intact and the whites have been scrambled. On eating, the diner discovers that the egg white is actually made from milk ice and barley. The egg yolk is 'actually' egg yolk, but by virtue of the representational strategy of the egg white, played on the plate by something else, the yolk is called into question. It is no longer an egg yolk, but an egg yolk *played by* an egg yolk: a kind of autobiographical performance, where the 'real thing' stands in for itself. The concept for the dish, as experienced, takes the diner through a process of identification: egg – not egg – egg-as-egg. But to conceive of the dish, none of these stages can be taken as the definitive essence of the dish; it *is* its processes of appearing.

The element of surprise, which is a core part of the practice of each of the restaurants (encouraging delight in surprise from the diner), is only possible because of the unfolding becoming of each of the dishes. Any notion of absolute presence or a direct and complete encounter with the food by the diner would mean surprise could not occur, because surprise itself is predicated on the unusual and unexpected intervention in an imagined causal sequence. Sometimes this is found in the dish itself, such as in Alinea's 'Pork Belly (Parsnip, Black Trumpet, Kombu)', where what appeared to be charcoal was revealed to be parsnip, or in The Fat Duck's 'Apple Pie Caramel', where what appears to be a cellophane wrapper around a caramel is revealed to be edible, or in Noma's 'Vegetable Flower', which appears to be a vegetable leaf but is revealed to be made from ants. But it can also be found in the production of seemingly impossible dishes, where the surprise is found in the realisation of what might have been unthinkable. For instance, Noma's dessert, 'Forest Flavors', is a bowl of chocolates, served on moss, with one of the chocolates in the shape of a mushroom. The chocolate tastes of both mushroom and chocolate; bitter-sweet, chewy and slightly salty. The chocolate-mushroom seems to conflate its two constituent parts into a single experience, such that the diner, without specialist knowledge of the preparatory processes, is confronted with a seemingly impossible product. The surprise of the dish is not constrained to just the seemingly impossible merging of two elements into a single, homogenous experience, but also in the unfathomable logic of production.

The restaurant operates as a site of multiple modes of performance, including the performances of the front of house staff (what they say and what they do), the performance of the written menu (how the language performs a function of framing and guiding the experience) and the performances of the food itself (how it unfolds as a series of appearances). Each of these arenas of performance works in relation to one another in the production of the experience of the restaurant, at times conforming to the hedonistic logic of an economy of experiences and at times unsettling the experience, opening up artistic worlds and reflecting on its own materials (both food and the bodies that encounter it). This chapter has largely operated in the realm of the artistic production and deployment of the restaurant: the skills of producing the to-be-experienced, in terms of the waiters' performance practice, the writing of the menu and the construction of dishes (though inevitably with an implication of the experience for the diner). In the following interlude and chapter, the perspective shifts further from the artistic to the aesthetic: from the artistic production of the restaurant to the aesthetic experience, especially in terms of the interrelation of the senses.

NOTES

1. This is the verbatim description of the dish from when I dined at The Fat Duck. While the structure of the narrative remains largely the same for each service, there is not a definitive script for each of the waiters to follow.

2. While the menu is presented like a gift at the end of the meal, often in an envelope, it is nevertheless part of the experience for which money has been paid.

3. Discussed in the previous Interlude on Italian Futurism.

4. Indeed, as an aside, this was explored in the 'Christmas Feast' episode of *Heston's Feasts*, where as part of the development of a spectacular feast for a small group of celebrity diners, Blumenthal experimented with presenting a cooked venison carcass covered in the treated hide of the deer. The effect was an uncanny and unappetising creature that seemed to exist at the boundary between the edible and inedible, with the cooked meat too close to the idea (and skin) of the live animal.

5. 'Tropical Fruit' was the name of the dish when I dined at Alinea. However, they regularly offer a dessert served in this fashion, though with different ingredients and preparations.

Interlude 2

Produced: Mediated Dining

Each of the chefs under consideration in this book has their own position as a celebrity chef, but Heston Blumenthal has pursued this role to the greatest extent, given the number of television programmes he has presented and his broader marketing of his celebrity status. He began his televisual career with a series for the Discovery Channel entitled *Kitchen Chemistry with Heston Blumenthal* (2002), before solidifying his celebrity persona on British television with the series *In Search of Perfection* (BBC 2004–07) and *Heston's Feasts* (Channel 4 2009–10). He followed this with the Channel 4 series *Big Chef Takes on Little Chef* (2009), *Heston's Mission Impossible* (2011), *How to Cook Like Heston* (2012), *Heston's Fantastical Food* (2012) and *Heston's Great British Food* (2014). It was the series *Heston's Feasts* that cemented Blumenthal's celebrity persona, mixing his approach to science and cooking with the use of historical sources to produce spectacular and theatrical themed feasts for a group of celebrity diners. In this interlude, I look to the first episode of that series, 'Heston's Victorian Feast', as well as reflections on the position of the celebrity chef, to explore how the celebrity chef persona operates in a mediatised economy, how food operates on screen as an implied sensuality and how the concept-driven dishes are presented. This draws on, and deploys in a different way, some of the ideas from the last chapter around the presentation of the food, but in the context of the screened image. The ephemeral food object, which changes, disappears and is consumed in the live experience, is transformed into a fixed and repeatable image – a commodity that resists ephemerality and cannot satiate the appetites of the consumer. This interlude moves from the ways in which the food is presented, in the previous chapter, into the embodied nature of sensory perception, which is the focus of the next.

In *Heston's Feasts*, each one-hour episode explores Blumenthal's creation of a feast themed around a particular historical period, developing a four-course meal, which is then served to six celebrity diners, with different celebrities for each episode. The series moved between the Victorians, the Ancient Romans, the Medieval period and the 1970s and 1980s, as well as more focused meals exploring Roald Dahl's *Charlie and the Chocolate Factory*, Grimm's *Fairy Tales* and the Titanic. In each case, Blumenthal uses his received or intuitive knowledge of the particular period or theme, along with historical sources, to create a conceptual menu of extravagant and spectacular dishes, comprising an apéritif, an entrée, a main course and a pudding. The first episode, the Victorian feast, was appropriate as a first episode for the series, as it spoke to and of a number of facets of Blumenthal's celebrity persona: the use of technologies, the titillating use of elements of the sexual and the image of the maverick scientist or inventor. For this feast, Blumenthal moved between an exploration of Victorian Britain generally and Lewis Carroll's *Alice in Wonderland*, which he described as the quintessential Victorian novel. For Blumenthal, the return to history for inspiration offered a way of discovering new possibilities for future cuisine, which went on to be the driving principle for his restaurant in London, Dinner by Heston Blumenthal.

At the beginning of the episode, Blumenthal articulated his overarching understanding of the Victorians as 'split personalities', caught between the industrial innovations of the period and their predilections for sex and drugs. This tension became the overarching narrative of the episode and the meal, which shifted between his own innovations in methods for cooking (using new technologies in the kitchen) and the titillation of the sexual. Of course, in relying on his received understanding of the Victorians, Blumenthal simplifies a vast expanse of time and its various cultural practices and relations of labour engendered across the period; but for John Langer, in his writing on the 'Personality System' of television, this is Blumenthal's role. Langer writes that 'The "real" world may be unstable and unbalanced, but the world of the television news personality who *explains* that world is not' (2006: 188, original emphasis). Extrapolating from this, the television personality, as a perceived expert, takes on the role of stabilising the unstable, reducing complexities to clear statements, partly for educative reasons, but mostly for the purposes of entertainment. And the television programme itself stabilises the instability of the 'lower' senses of touch, taste and smell by fixing them in a document that conforms to the distanced, seemingly stable, repeatable and reproducible logic of the audio-visual.

Blumenthal's celebrity persona is, first and foremost, that of celebrity chef. His particular deployment of this celebrity status is a mixture of the 'mad scientist' and 'Willy Wonka' (the latter solidified in the *Feasts* episode on *Charlie and the Chocolate Factory*). His role sits within a generalised characterisation of the Victorian inventor, a maverick who discovers by unusual means, exploring the uncanny, unnerving, illicit and sexual. He has made use of this persona partly as a marketing ploy, as it allows an access point to his cuisine for the uninitiated. It requires no understanding of (technoemotional) cuisine, instead framing the work as eccentric, unusual and spectacular. His celebrity persona, in large part constructed and disseminated through his television work, frames his live practice. It constructs the image of the 'creative genius' that lingers behind and through the experience of his restaurants and holds it together as a coherent experience: not fragments of experimental cuisine, but an encounter with the cuisine of Heston Blumenthal. The persona lingers throughout his work on television and in his restaurants. It is playful, non-threatening and entertaining and frames his food in the same way.

The figure of the celebrity chef has political importance alongside facilitating the gluttonous gaze of the viewer. In Toby Miller's *Cultural Citizenship: Cosmopolitanism, Consumerism, and Television in a Neoliberal Age*, he argues that 'Food TV is a key site of risk and moral panic, a space that physically forms and maintains citizens, gives them pleasure, and makes them vulnerable to medical hazards' (2007: 121). Food television programmes present a space where food is explored in a highly politicised way: it marks out distinctions between the edible and inedible; it navigates, for the viewer, the line between pleasure and fear, especially in relation to unusual or experimental cuisine; and it contributes to local and national discourses of identity, in terms of constructing and deploying the ingredients and tastes of a particular community. The expertise of the celebrity chef guides the viewer through food preparation and consumption, both instructing and decoding, and by so doing enters into the political arena by revealing what should be pursued for pleasure, what should be avoided for fear of contamination and how ingredients and preparations should be conceived in terms of provenance.

In writing about television food programmes, Emma Govan and Dan Rebellato observe that the 1990s saw a proliferation of food-based television alongside an increase in publicly documented food scares. They argue that these are interrelated and that the celebrity chef navigates food scares in three key ways: first, through the 'hypertrophied personality' of the chef, which 'locates the food as coming from a recognizable source'; second, through the inability to actually eat the food, ensuring that the viewers' 'faith in the chefs need never be directly tested'; and finally in the 'safety factor' of the professionalism of the chef (Govan and Rebellato 1999: 36–37). The celebrity chef is presented on television as an expert, to be trusted. Despite Blumenthal's persona and work being characterised as experimental, he nevertheless appears as a trusted expert, opening space for fun, exciting and spectacular food with the reassurance that he draws on the ultimate marker of expertise in the public realm: scientific discourse. He works in a 'lab', makes use of scientific implements in his test kitchen, is exact in measurements and references scientific knowledges in explaining the processes of cooking. These tropes combine with the established figure of the celebrity chef to reassure the viewer that the food is edible and safe; the experiments with cuisine can be enjoyed without fear or anxiety. The enjoyment of the celebrity diners at the feast allows the audience to experience the food by proxy. The range of figures and expertise around the dining table (including journalists, academics, comedians and actors – familiar faces and voices) consolidates the trust in Blumenthal as an expert and makes use of vicarious tastes in two ways: observing the enjoyment experienced by others and utilising the viewers' tastes in the celebrity diners (if the viewer likes the celebrity diner and the celebrity diner likes the food, then the viewer likes the food).

Blumenthal engages directly with questions of the edible/inedible. Part of his celebrity chef persona is the exploration of the weird and wonderful, distinct from the everyday experience of cooking and eating. He models through the programme new forms of the edible, exploring those things usually considered inedible. In the Victorian Feast episode, there is a section of the programme dealing with the edibility of insects. In an attempt to produce an edible garden (reminiscent of Alicia Rios' *A Temperate Menu*), Blumenthal explores using insects in the garden. He visits an 'expert' in eating insects (although the expertise is never substantiated, beyond showing Blumenthal some edible insects and preparing them) and eats a number of different insects. Some he reacts to with disgust, and others he seems to enjoy. Blumenthal models for the home audience the edibility of the insects, but at a safe distance, so the television audience can watch and experience by proxy, kept at a safe distance by virtue of the mediation of the screen.

Food television programmes are often framed as instructional. Making use of the expertise of the celebrity chef, they teach the viewer, step by step, how to prepare various dishes and meals. However, while Blumenthal does demonstrate the process of creating the spectacular dishes, the instructional quality is by far a secondary concern. These are not dishes that can be made in a domestic kitchen.[1] Indeed, at the beginning of each episode in the *Feast* series, he explicitly tells the audience not to try this at home. In *Žižek's Jokes*, Slavoj Žižek offers a joke about cooking:

> Here is how anyone can make a good soup in one hour: prepare all the ingredients, cut the vegetables, etc., boil the water, put the ingredients into it, cook them at a simmer for half an hour, stirring occasionally; when, after three quarters of an hour, you discover that the soup is tasteless and unpalatable, throw it away, open up a good can of soup, and quickly warm it up in a microwave oven. This is how we humans make soup.
>
> (2014b: 50)

This is the same logic of Blumenthal's programmes: he 'teaches' the viewer how to prepare the wild, experimental and complex dishes, step-by-step, precisely in order to demonstrate the viewers' inability to do this in the domestic kitchen. Instead, to be able to experience this food, the viewer is solicited to purchase it: to buy a product that has been created or endorsed by Blumenthal (such as his range of products for the supermarket Waitrose) or, even better, to visit his restaurants. The programmes are not instructional but rather slightly overwhelming in terms of how much work goes into creating the dishes and so they become an extended advertisement for the restaurant, demonstrating the production process in order to sell the live experience. As McDonnell observes, 'gastropornography teases the line of unattainability, tantalizing the audience to believe that they could do that, have that' (2016: 242). Within the framing of hedonic instant gratification, the unattainability is countered not by the arduous and expensive process of learning skills and acquiring equipment, but by booking a table and paying for the live experience.[2]

The experience of watching the programmes mitigates the lack of tactile, olfactory and gustatory experience by providing other information to create an imaginative experience of eating for the viewer. For example, in the Victorian Feast, Blumenthal produces, as the apéritif for the meal, his version of the 'Drink Me' potion from *Alice in Wonderland*: a layered drink that moves through different flavours (toffee, toast, custard, cherry tart, turkey and pineapple), presented as a homogenous bright pink liquid in a test tube, with no discernible separation between the different flavours. The celebrity diners are shown tasting the drink, attempting to distinguish the different flavours and demonstrating surprise and excitement with each new taste that unfolds. The home viewer is, of course, denied the experience of actually tasting. But they are able to imaginatively follow the experience with the celebrity diners, by virtue of having seen Blumenthal develop the dish. Indeed, the programme includes shots of Blumenthal watching the celebrity diners taste the food, so the television viewer is positioned alongside Blumenthal, able to enjoy the diners discovering what the viewer already knows. The television viewer then straddles two positions in the programme: alongside Blumenthal, who has created the dish and watches his creation being experienced, and alongside the diners, who are given the dish to taste, discover and unravel. The oscillation between these two positions means that the viewer can vicariously and imaginatively experience the dish, because they know what it is, how it has been constructed and experience its consumption alongside the actual diners.

In seeing how the dishes are created, the viewer is given access to the conceptual drive of the food, marking out how it attempts to go beyond mere satiation of hunger. Indeed, by removing the possibility of the satisfaction of physiological hunger, the TV programmes could be said to foreground the conceptual work of the dish and allow it to be more apparent, through the distance it enacts from the direct experience of the incorporation of food, which itself can take precedence in the restaurant, backgrounding the conceptual-artistic qualities of the work. The entrée for the Victorian feast was a Mock Turtle Soup, inspired by a recipe from the *Encyclopaedia of Practical Cookery*, written by Theodore Francis Garrett and published in 1892, combined with the character of the Mock Turtle from *Alice in Wonderland*. The dish consisted of a beef consommé, condensed and compressed into the shape of a pocket watch, coated in gold leaf, which was then stirred into hot water in a tea cup and then poured over a bowl containing a turnip and swede jelly in the appearance of a poached egg with cubes of pickled turnip, black truffle, a terrine of ox tongue and pork fat, enoki mushrooms, mustard seeds and micro-herbs. Blumenthal goes through a (staged) process of making this dish, beginning with a trip to New Jersey to catch and eat real turtle, before exploring the mock turtle made from cow's head. Adrian Kear reflects on the nature of the food commodity in contemporary capitalism that 'In the cultural logic of late capitalism, cooking is conceived in terms of consumption rather than production, product rather than process. The commodity necessarily conceals the process of its production and rarely reveals the work put into its creation' (1999: 45). The television programme complicates this thinking because it relies on exposing that process precisely as the final creation. The labour of the work, including Blumenthal's research trips, is drawn out and placed directly before the viewer. The process itself becomes the consumable – not ignored, but incorporated into/as the commodity-form. The labour itself is reconfigured; it is not the exploited labour of the worker, but a labour of luxury. Indeed, luxury itself becomes a component part of the concept of the dish, given that Blumenthal states that the turtle was a luxurious ingredient for the Victorians.

Unlike the live experience of the restaurant, the television programme produces food so as to continue its existence, cut off from its transience. The food images do not rot and decay as the live food does. It does not go cold or become unappetising. It is a fixed image that is reproducible and to which one is able to return. The food programmes capitalise on this in a number of ways: first, it allows for continued profit from a single expenditure; second, it is open to a greater audience without the need for more primary resources; and finally, it can be presented time after time in exactly the same way. It is the same capitalising structures found in the translation from live performance to film, whether as performance documentation or acting directly for the camera. In that process of translation, the continuity of sensory experience is lost: it reduces the multisensory experience to a stream of information encoded as sight and sound and it reduces the potential for the shifts of attention given the direct focusing in the image by the camera. But this is not to say that all of the other senses are lost or obscured completely. To watch the screen is still an embodied experience and, as such, framed by the contingencies of the body in time and space, subject to the various sensory inputs surrounding the screen viewing experience. There is an implied sensuality at work in the images and sounds themselves, encouraging a series of associations and embodied memories on the part of the viewer in order to evoke a sense of the sensory.

In 'Playing to the Senses', Kirshenblatt-Gimblett writes of 'studio food' that it functions to draw out 'sensory experiences that are invisible' in and to the image;

that it provides 'visual cues that we associate with particular tastes and smells, even in the absence of gustatory and olfactory stimuli' (1999: 3). She continues by arguing that images of food are both mimetic, where 'the dish prepared for the camera must looks as if it could grace the table', and indexical, where 'the visual details must index qualities that we can know only from other sensory modalities' (1999: 3). This dual interplay of the mimetic and indexical is at work in the screened image. It not only attempts to present the food for the visual diner dislocated in time and space but also acts as a provocation to embodied memory and multisensory associative reading to produce an imaginary experience. In this regard, the screened image is not so different from the live encounter, in that it implicates an anticipatory reading, whereby the imaginative work of the diner is crucial in the experience of the dish. The psychologist Charles Spence observes that the brain is more engaged in thinking about or anticipating food than in the actual process of eating (2018a: 65) and that, when seeing images of food, the brain engages in 'embodied mental simulation', imagining what the various sensory qualities of the food might be (2018b: 249). The screened food, then, becomes an intervention into the everyday experience of eating, teasing out the purely virtual dimension of that experience, cleaving apart the gap between the material incorporation of the food (the physiological processes that allow us to feel the food enter our mouths, be swallowed and eventually trigger the embodied feeling of the satiation of hunger) and the virtual experience associated with anticipation and simulation, which is at work in both images and the live encounter with food.

The image of the dishes on screen in Blumenthal's *Feast* series evokes this anticipatory simulated imagining of the taste of the food and, by proxy, experiencing through the reactions of the screened diners. We watch the chefs try elements of the food in the process of its preparation and the diners eat the final dish, observing their reactions and vicariously experiencing with/alongside them. In the Victorian Feast episode of Blumenthal's series, when the diners eat the finished dishes, their descriptions of the food are not descriptive. Rather, they articulate the pleasure of the experience, using generalised adjectives such as 'nice', 'lovely', 'delicious', none of which speak of the actual qualities of the dishes. Instead, we are presented with a broad articulation of pleasure, perhaps itself an attempt to continue to whet the appetite of the potential diners amongst the viewers, an encouragement to visit the restaurant and pay for the experience directly. At the same time, however, we are presented with the dishes and an explanation of their component parts. In doing this, the programme allows for vicarious access to the experience, allowing the audience at home to imagine each of those component parts and mentally map out how they might be experienced together. In effect, the programme asks viewers to engage in what Adrià called the 'mental palate', requiring the largely non-expert audience to mentally combine the different parts (including not only tastes but textures and temperatures) and to imagine an experience of the final dish. As part of this imagining, the audience at home are brought into the collective aspect of the dining experience, implicating how the reactions of the others around the table in the live restaurant have a significant impact on our own experience of pleasure, disgust or the identification of the different parts of the dish.

Throughout the show, there are shots of the final dishes, taken out of the kitchen and not presented as they would be for the diner on the table. These shots are abstracted from the contexts in which they might be produced or eaten for the camera alone. This is the moment of consumption for the viewer at home: a rich, carefully constructed image, with the camera panning over the food, allowing the viewer to eat with their eyes. The camera does not function here solely as mediator, to relay the live moment to the home viewer, but intervenes into the event for the purposes of presenting the dish for those not bodily present. The aim of this shot is to allow the audience to gaze with lust at the food – to see it for themselves, directly, not just vicariously while others eat it. It is food porn.

NOTES

1.   Interestingly, Blumenthal did release a book entitled *Heston Blumenthal at Home* (2011), where he attempts to simplify some of his dishes for the domestic kitchen. The recipes are still far more labour intensive than most recipe books and still require a number of specialist ingredients. The book, like Blumenthal's television programmes, appears to be designed more for the consumption of the book itself (its images and descriptions) than as an instructional guide for the home cook.

2.   From the *Feasts* series, I have eaten the Mock Turtle Soup from the Victorian episode at The Fat Duck and the Meat Fruit from the Medieval episode at Dinner by Heston Blumenthal. In both cases, the dishes were framed by what I had seen on television, in terms of the preparatory processes and concepts. I was also struck by a sense of excitement at being able, finally, to actually taste something I had previously consumed as an image on screen.

3

Perception: Sensory and Sensual Experiences

In Michel Serres' *The Five Senses*, he writes that 'Taste is a kiss that our mouth gives itself through the intermediary of tasty foods. Suddenly it recognizes itself, becomes conscious of itself, exists for itself' (2016: 224). In this image of taste as a kiss, Serres draws attention to a number of things: that the experience of food of course requires a body; that there mediations in the act of eating that trouble an idea of a direct and unmediated encounter; that the body becomes aware of itself in an experience that is heightened or intensified; there is a connection between dining and the arena of the sensual and sexual; and there is an appeal to pleasure in dining. These are some of the key ideas that run through this chapter, which turns to the experience of actually eating. This chapter explores the aesthetic dimensions of that experience and how sensory perceptions are deployed in the restaurants both in service of pleasure and as a defamiliarisation of perceiving.

The focus of this chapter shifts from the work of the restaurant to the encounter between the diner and the food, considering how perception operates in aesthetic experience. It begins with an exploration of sensory experience as a challenge to immediacy. This section engages with perception that is experienced as ostensibly immediate (present and unmediated) and various conceptual and experiential challenges to that immediacy. These challenges are posed in the experience itself, calling into question the body, its sensory apparatus and ways of making sense of experience, and they constitute a core part of the experience of the restaurants' practice. In the second section, the chapter turns to language and its role in embodied, sensory experience, not just as description but as a force in perception, particularly in terms of language in consciousness and its place in constituting perceptual experience. The penultimate section of the chapter addresses the intimacy of the mouth as a site and some of the conceptual and experiential intersections of eating and sex. Finally, the chapter ends with some reflections on culinary deconstruction, the technique used in designing and plating dishes, considering how this frames and inflects the dining experience.

The underlying premise of this chapter is that sensory perceptions cannot be thought as a momentary, abstracted encounter between the body and the object of attention, where the perceiving body merely 'gathers information' about the object through the senses. Rather, the senses are always already implicated in-the-world. They are caught in structures and processes of making sense and sensory perceptions themselves are always already guided by, and carry the implications and associations of, Being-in-the-world. Sensory perceptions do not merely mediate between Being and the world, but are a site of the constitution of Being-in-the-world. The restaurant, as a site of relational art and performance, is not a self-contained artistic practice but rather comes to fruition in the experience of the diner. At elBulli, the chefs conceived of the diners as a 'receptor' for the experience who could have a 'gastronomic experience' across different modes, including experiencing ingredients and dishes, experiencing styles and characteristics of the work and implicating the diner's own previous memories and experiences (Adrià et al. 2008: 320.2). These modes of reception (of interpretation, understanding and judgment) are not merely processing after the moment of perception but are also frames for perception, guiding and constituting the experience. As such, the temporal separation of perception and reception is troubled. Ways of thinking and processing have a force in perception itself, guiding attention, suggesting in advance what might be significant and framing the diners' approach to the dishes. At the same time, the restaurants produce experiences that can re-sensitise the diner, offering new kinds of perceptual experience outside of the everyday and quotidian frames and guidance of perception. This chapter explores the ways that perception can be framed and guided in advance of experience, manifest in perceptual experience itself, and the ways that the restaurants re-sensitise the diner, encouraging an awareness of the aesthetic potential of sensory and sensual experience.

Immediacy

Famously, in *Unmarked*, Peggy Phelan defines performance's ontology as existing in the present (1993: 146). Her position emerges as a way of separating performance from the processes of reproduction – recording and documenting – which transform performance into becoming something other than itself. This statement has become a key definition of performance's liveness, its being in/of the present. This is echoed in Josephine Machon's *Immersive Theatres* in relation to the experience of performance, where Machon cites Elaine Scarry on the etymology of presence as *prae-sens*: 'that which stands before the senses' (2013: 44). Both of these definitions rest on a notion of immediacy: an unmediated experience of the world through the senses, where the presence of the present constitutes performance's liveness (or 'live(d)ness' for Machon [2013: 43], where there is a slippage between the live and lived). In this form of argument, the political power of performance, in the age of reproducibility, is grounded in its liveness and resisting transformation into a reproducible commodity.

However, following Heidegger, it can be argued that the very idea of presence, liveness or immediacy continues the fallenness of Dasein into the world of the *they*. Heidegger argues that Dasein, as Being-in-the-world, is always in a world, a 'totality of involvements' and that, in letting itself 'be involved', Dasein behaves 'circumspectively' (absorbed and lost in activity, where mediation becomes transparent) and 'this in turn is based upon one's previously understanding significance' (1962: 145). What is deemed 'significant' is derived from the world, from the *they* and cultural discourse, and the 'significance' has a force in determining not only the activities in which we engage but also how we are able to become absorbed in activities and experiences. It is only with the background reassurance of significance (which is not our own) that an activity or experience can take place without slipping into, or being interrupted by, anxiety. As such, to experience 'presence' is to give oneself over to the world. One behaves as if one is present with and to the world and time, becoming absorbed or lost in activity in such a way that one is not aware of the various mediations that allow that very experience of presence to take place. To assert presence, not just in language but also in experience, is to forget or ignore the mediating structures and discourses that allow one to be seemingly present (including the sensate body, language and understandings of time, presence, experience and significance).

In the contemporary economy of experiences in late capitalism (part of the current world of the *they*), where 'lived-experience' itself becomes a commodity, the purported immediacy of performance is transformed into the ultimate commodity, which cannot be maintained and must be purchased and repurchased. Live experience has significance and worth as something purchased, given a monetary value, and as something that furnishes one with cultural capital (the ability to say 'I went there, I did that'). Live experience does not resist capitalisation but rather has become its zenith. The fallenness into the world, argues Heidegger, is 'tempting' and 'tranquillizing', as one is given over to the 'self-certainty and decidedness' of the *they*, reassured that 'one is leading and sustaining a full and genuine "life"' (1962: 222). In a contemporary context, the tranquilising effects come from giving oneself over to the reassurance of purchasing live experience, of paying for the commodity of apparently immediate and fully present experience, which is both invigorating and calming in its invigoration. This is not a contradiction: the very attentiveness to invigorating, exciting or overwhelming experience is part of the soothing and calming operations of the experience economy. One

101

can rest assured that one is living (and paying for) a full and rich life. To partake in the apparently overwhelming immediacy of sensory experience, the heightened and powerful sense of sensation, to become absorbed in an experience, is what is offered by the experience economy in general and the high-end restaurant in particular. However, it is in that heightening of sensation, in that attempt to be *more* present and immediate, that immediacy itself is ruptured, by moving out of the everyday modes of experiencing. Challenges to immediacy appear in the experience itself. In this sense, we might return to Phelan: performance's power *is* in the present because, in its heightening of the experience of presence, it ruptures everyday notions of presence itself and can begin to resist the promise of immediacy offered to the customer paying for a truly live(d) experience.

The experience of dining in the restaurants encapsulates three key challenges to notions of immediacy and presence: the unfolding of time that resists pure presence; the fragmentation of the sensate body that counters immediate bodily presence to the world; and the mediations of ideology that frame and guide experience. In Hervé This' *Molecular Gastronomy*, he explores the first two of these in relation to a significant shift in psychological understandings of perception. He writes that the previous understanding of perception, whereby 'pieces of information obtained by the various sensory cells traveled upward from neuron to neuron until they reached the higher centers of the brain' is being replaced with an understanding of the joining of sensory information before 'it reaches the first neuronal relay station' (2006: 106). First, perception is acknowledged as unfolding over time (even though it might be minute amounts of time) and second, sensory streams are broken apart – not a holistic experience in the body, but the body combining different streams of 'information'. The body and experience are decentred, not a self-given whole, but fragmented from within and perception is enacted as a process across and through the body.

The seeming presence and immediacy of sensory perception is an illusion generated by the small passage of time. Edmund Husserl, in *The Phenomenology of Internal Time-Consciousness*, theorises that this fragmentation gives rise to the illusion of the continuity and presence of perception, arguing that live experience is the retention of perceptual encounters from moment to moment (1964: 44). This 'continuity of retensions' (52) gives rise to a 'flux of consciousness' (45), beginning with a 'primal impression' (50) – the material encounter, through the senses, between the sensate body and the world, which lingers in perception to allow for continuity of experience. Presence is, then, an emergent illusion, combining sensory streams in consciousness and, as such, has an imaginative quality, whereby ways of thinking (themselves produced and framed by past experience, fantasy and cultural and ideological discourse) constitute our experience of presence and the senses. Without necessarily being consciously attentive to it, we produce our perceptual experiences in a process of gathering together sensory encounters within schemas of understanding. This happens seemingly automatically but is nevertheless framed and mediated by those schemas and ways of thinking. The continuous experience of time is an illusion of the continuity of retensions. The continuous experience of the body is an illusion produced by the imaginative combinations of sensory streams and experiences. The experience of a direct encounter with the world is an illusion produced by the imaginative processing of consciousness, which is always already framed and mediated by past experience, language, culture and ideology.

At times, the sensory experiences offered in the restaurant conform to the spectacular logic of the everydayness of the experience economy, offering an intensified experience that is pleasurable and tranquilising. At other times, the experimental nature of the food and the heightened intensity of the experience can draw attention to, trouble and defamiliarise the easy continuity of perception. At The Fat Duck, the 'Nitro-Poached Aperitifs' offer an evanescent experience for the diner, which draws attention to the ephemerality of perception. A small meringue is placed in the diner's hand by the waiter and the diner is encouraged to put it straight into their mouth, and, seemingly instantaneously, it disappears in a wave of cold freshness, followed by cold smoke that issues from the mouth and nose (Figure 3). This dish disrupts the experience of eating by drawing attention to the mouth as a transitory space through which food passes, leaving a lingering mark on the taste buds. The disruption comes from the incompletion of the act of eating: the food disappears before it can be swallowed. Just as one registers the perceptive experience, it is over; there is no opportunity to savour the taste. It draws attention to the perceptive registering of an experience, which has always already slipped from the present to the past. This was also explored by elBulli's 'airs': a flavoured air or smoke that disappears in the moment of incorporation, vanishing as one becomes aware of it. This tension was teased out more carefully in elBulli's 'Frozen Parmesan Air with Muesli' (Dish Number 1009 in Hamilton and Todolí 2009: 124), where the foam 'air' was placed in contrast to more solid, substantial and lasting muesli. The swift disappearance of the air was set against the lingering solid, drawing out the different temporal modes of both.

The intensified attention on ephemerality and transience speaks to and of the supposed dematerialisation of contemporary capitalism and the experience economy. Notions of the virtual run through contemporary capitalist discourse, from the fleeting nature of experiences to be purchased through to the virtual nature of the stock market and circulation of capital across the surface of the globe. However, elBulli's 'airs' and The Fat Duck's 'Nitro-Poached Aperitifs' problematise this, revealing that the supposed dematerialisation is inevitably grounded in some kind of materiality. Maria Domene-Danés argues that the 'airs and foams' of elBulli 'are a perfect portrait of the transformation from material

FIGURE 3: 'Nitro-Poached Aperitif' (2001), The Fat Duck. Photo courtesy of The Fat Duck.

production [...] into immaterial finance capital [...]. Adrià's molecular gastronomy is another example of the general dematerialization of production under finance capitalism' (2013: 121). However, this is to confuse ephemerality and demateri-alisation. The former is about attentiveness to the quickening passage of time, the latter about the movement away from materials and materiality. Contemporary capital, in general, and technoemotional cuisine, in particular, are engaged with the quickening of time, enacted through the transience and transformations of materials; as such, they nevertheless have a material basis. Notions of demateri-alisation imbue contemporary capital with a pseudo-transcendental or spiritual dimension, furnishing it with a faith-based cultural narrative, but this narrative attempts to cover over the fact that it has a material basis (and an important one, given the reliance on the material processes of production and exploitation on which capitalism depends). To read the restaurants' practice as dematerialised (which is not confined to Domene-Danés – Jean-Paul Jouary does the same in reflecting on elBulli [2013: 83]) is to forget that it achieves the effect or illusion of dematerialisation by means of a material practice. Again, it offers a comforting or tranquilising narrative for the experience, suggesting the existence of a reassur-ing higher power (the operations of capital as a pseudo-spiritual and comforting guarantee of meaning) rather than the far more disturbing notions of ephemeral-ity and the fast, destructive transformation of materials (which can extend from the material encounter in experience to the material existence of the body itself).

Food artists Blanch & Shock explored a similar idea, but instead of drawing attention to the transience of experience through quickening its disappearance, they created a work that dwelt in that moment of disappearance, fixing it in a material sculpture made from food. In 2011, Blanch & Shock created the work *Exploding Cake*, which used fishing lines and 100 clear perspex disks to create a three-dimensional edible sculpture of a cake paused in the moment of being exploded. They crafted the work in 'a shape that would suggest a dense "epicenter", leading outwards to smaller fragments, as if an explosion had been freeze-framed' (Blanch & Shock 2018). Not only did the sculpture play with the pausing of time to tease out notions of ephemerality, but in using the image of an explosion, it became a simile for the experience of tasting: an 'epicentre' of an explosion being the evental moment when the body meets the food, with perceptual experience rippling out in time and space from that conceptual centre. As an articulation of experience, the work troubles any notion of an absolute moment of experience, as it demonstrates the contact between body and object (the epicentre), which ripples out across the body while the event continues. The ephemerality of the tasting experience was rendered as a fixed and static object, though one that also spoke to and of the 'continuity of retensions' in experience, articulating in the sculptural image how a 'moment' of experience is constituted by an imaginary process of holding together fragments of 'sensory information'.

We can begin to conceive of perception not as a flat continuity of the world spread out before us, but as a fluctuating landscape, with epicentres, ripples and areas of flatness. Our experience of the world, space and perception is not a smooth surface but one that has fluctuating densities: intense, heated up areas and cooler, lighter and softer areas, intermingled with each other across time and space. This is not a reflection of the density of objects in the world although this can have an influence on our perception, but rather the ways in which our perception and attention are experienced. Attention is not deployed uniformly towards everything that lies before us, but shifts, focuses and fluctuates. Attention is, in part, conditioned in advance of perception. Attention is directed as a result of the production of the sensible: learning what is worthy of notice and attention, which manifests itself seemingly immediately in how our attention wanders around and across our perceptual environments. Heidegger writes of this in relation to hearing: that 'it requires a very artificial and complicated frame of mind to "hear" a "pure noise"' because 'What we "first" hear is never noises or complexes of sounds, but the creaking wagon, the motor-cycle [...], the fire crackling' (1962: 207). The experience of perception is not 'pure' sensory data, but an experience always already (and seemingly apparently) infused with meaning. We experience through personal and cultural frames that mark out particular elements as worthy of attention, precisely because those objects of attentive perception are congruous with a schema of the world, of worthiness of attention and of (potential) meaning.

As such, even an apparently singular mouthful of food is not a singular, homogenous experience. It is a mass of potential that is experienced as meaningful sensation. The spherification technique, used for a number of dishes in the restaurants, plays with this shifting of attention and the heated density of the moment of perception. Using the reactions between sodium alginate and calcium, intensely flavoured liquids are turned into bubbles (sometimes resembling caviar, other times as large as a golf ball) as the reaction causes a flexible skin to form. When eaten, these allow for bursts of flavour to be released in the mouth. At Alinea, the dish 'Lily Bulb (rambutan, distillation of caviar lime)' is served as a palate cleanser and is presented as petals and leaves seemingly floating in a bowl of water. This dish includes spherified Australian lime. While eating it, the spherified lime bursts in the mouth, layering in intense explosions of sharp citrus on top of the light, floral and fragrant jellied liquid. By including the spherified lime, rather than mixing the citric acidity into the dish, the eating experience is not homogenous, but unfolds in waves. The inclusion of the spherified lime caviar allows the chefs to modulate the experience. It not only introduces new bursts of sharpness but also changes the experience of the jelly within which they float, which initially seems sharp, but mellows in contrast to the intense acidity of the spherified lime. The bursts of flavour from the spherification are noticeable because of their intensity, but they also speak of the broader framing of the world of the restaurant, which directs attention towards the intense, the interesting and the unusual, rather than those things that otherwise go unnoticed (for example, the seasoning of the dish, which is nevertheless present).

Perception is not immediate (fully present and unmediated) because perception is always already memory, conscious thought catching up to sensory stimulation. There is an infinitesimal gap of time that cleaves apart the material contact of the body with the sensed object and the recognition and processing of that experience. Heidegger writes that perception is 'consummated' and made 'determinate' when 'one *addresses* oneself to something as something and *discusses* it as such' (1962: 89, original emphasis). Heidegger builds on Husserl, who marked as distinction between 'presentification' (the material sensory encounter) and perception (1964: 57), though for Husserl the presentification can exist without perception, which Heidegger refutes. In other words, for Heidegger, perception is constituted in positioning oneself in relation to a sensory experience, recognising it *as* perception. This is echoed in Maurice Merleau-Ponty's *Phenomenology of Perception*, where he writes that 'Judgement is often introduced as *what sensation lacks to make perception possible*' (2002: 37, original emphasis). Perception unfolds in time with consciousness catching up to, recognising and positioning itself in relation to what is perceived. It is in this process that the imaginative quality of perception becomes apparent: there is no neutral encounter with objects of perception. It is always already mediated by consciousness, which itself is not and never neutral, but formed and framed by past experience, culture and ideology.

To illustrate this, we can turn to one of Blumenthal's more famous dishes – 'Sound of the Sea'. This dish is served with an iPod in a conch shell. The iPod and conch with headphones are delivered to the table before the food is served and the diner is able to listen to sounds recorded at a British seaside: waves, seagulls and the wind. The food that is then served is a sheet of glass, through which one can see a layer of sand and on top of which is an edible tapioca sand, along with seaweeds, sea herbs, razor clams, oysters and a fish stock broth foamed to look like the crashing surf. The sounds go beyond being an installation art device and seem to intensify the flavours of the food. By tapping into a shared cultural memory that associates the seaside with particular textures, scents and flavours (graininess, saltiness, seaweed, fishiness), memories are recalled, relived and folded into the present experience. The site of the experience is dislocated: from the present and across the senses, the latter as the different streams of sensory information (sound, sight, taste, touch and smell) combine to reinforce one another and thicken the experience. While the inclusion of the sound does this, both elBulli and Noma have also made dishes that circulate around the concept of the sea/seaside and draw on those cultural associations, implicitly rather than explicitly. Noma's 'Sliced Raw Squid and Cabbage Stems' is presented as small cubes of squid in a bowl made of smooth ice with a roughened rim, which for my meal there was followed by 'Langoustine and Flavors of the Ocean', which was a langoustine tail served with an oyster emulsion and Icelandic seaweed powder. In bringing these different items together, each of which is reminiscent of or taken directly from the sea, there emerges an oceanic motif that intensifies those flavours and sensations associated with the sea. Indeed, the langoustine was to be eaten with the fingers, directly engaging the haptic and recalling a certain childish playfulness of picking things up and tasting them. The imaginary quality of perception is fundamental to the experience of experience itself.

Perception is multisensory, with each of the senses operating in relation to and alongside the other senses, building an imaginatively coherent experience out of the fragments. Charles Spence has observed that 'the presentation of familiar, or congruent, combinations of olfactory and gustatory stimuli leads to an enhanced neural response in those parts of the brain that code for the hedonic [...]' (2018a: 61). When different sensory stimuli mutually reinforce one another, operating within a framework that allows them to be understood as relating to one another and part of the same experience, pleasure is intensified. In the above dishes, the connections between ingredients, smells, sounds and the idea of the sea or seaside allow for a coherent and pleasant experience to be manifest. A cultural narrative brings together the different sensory stimuli and organises them as a coherent experience. In that coherency, elements that might interrupt or disrupt the continuity are overlooked or ignored, as attention focuses on those things that are congruous. What is understood as 'sensible', as making sense, frames and directs the senses themselves.

In *The Sublime Object of Ideology*, Žižek elucidates this connection between the internal-experiential and the orders of sense that structure and maintain that experience. He frames this in terms of thought in relation to the cultural unconscious, the latter being

> *the form of thought whose ontological status is not that of thought*, that is to say, the form of thought external to the thought itself – in short, some Other Scene external to the thought whereby the form of the thought is already articulated in advance.
>
> (2008: 12, original emphasis)

For Žižek, the cultural unconscious frames, forms and orders thought. He continues that this ordering 'disrupts the dual relationship of "external" factual reality and "internal" subjective experience' (2008: 12). In Heideggerian terms, the world comes into being as world(hood), as sensible, as opposed to earth, through its reliance on, interaction with and infusing of Being. For a sensory experience to have substance as sensible, it requires this background understanding, this paradigm of sensibility, which troubles any distinction between internal and external. There is no pure, unmediated experience of the world because it is within the epistemological, conceptual and material horizons of the world that any experience can be said to take place.

For the restaurants' practice to be coherent, sensible and enjoyable, it must in some way conform to this background that allows the sensed to be experienced as sensible. Indeed, the appeal to pleasure itself becomes a core part of the sensible rendering of the meal, given its position in the economy of experiences and the hedonic logic of capitalist consumption. By comparison, Blanch & Shock's 2011 work, *A Feast to Cure Melancholy*, unsettled the relation between the experience of eating and the background frame of the sensible and pleasurable. The work was presented at The Wellcome Collection in London as part of a series of events exploring Robert Burton's *Anatomy of Melancholy* (1621). The construction of the menu for the meal was to counter an imbalance in the humours, following the logic of the four humours approach to the body. The menu was a four-course meal of potted wild boar with hay squash and pea shoots; grey mullet with wheat beer, spiced potatoes and spring onions; wild duck with wheat raisins and dittander; and cheese with prunes, medlars and endives. While the food can and did offer some pleasure, the unusual combinations of elements and ingredients, devised according to the logic of balancing the humours, drew attention to its own construction. It was experimental because it did not conform to everyday combinations of ingredients and required a different kind of organisational principle to understand and experience.

Part of the pleasure of dining, and the completion of perception in taking a position, is in the process of finding or producing sense in and from the experience. The rendering of sensory stimuli as sensible is particularly of note in the experimental restaurants because of their unusual and experimental practice with food. In his reading of Lacan, Žižek discusses enjoyment as *jouis-sense*: enjoyment-in-sense. He writes that the way that subjects 'avoid madness' and find substance is 'through the binding of our enjoyment to a certain signifying, symbolic formation which assures a minimum of consistency to our being-in-the-world' (2008: 81). It is the process of discovering or producing sense, of making sense, that allows enjoyment to emerge. This enjoyment is experienced against the backdrop of the disturbing potential of an absence of sense. Indeed, in the contemporary restaurant, given the focus on serving a pleasurable experience for the diner, *jouis-sense* could be said to work equally in reverse: not just enjoyment-in-sense but also sense-in-enjoyment.

Enjoyment or pleasure, as the primary goal or purpose of the experience, becomes a foundation for making sense of the experimental cuisine, which in turn allows the diner to enjoy because there is a foundation of sense. For example, Alinea's 'Salad' (in Achatz 2008: 200–01) is a small dish containing a small mound of green granita, topped with a smaller amount of red granita. The green is made from various lettuce leaves, the red from red wine vinegar. The premise of this dish rests on the confusion and subsequent pleasure of discovering-by-eating the underlying concept: that the dish is attempting to heighten the refreshing qualities of a salad. Pleasure emerges as the ice melts on the tongue and the sensations are released in the mouth and the food is transformed from an abstract form in the bowl to an understandable perception in the mouth (the known combination of salad leaves and vinaigrette). The ability to recognise the dish as a 'salad' requires a cultural knowledge of what constitutes a salad (perhaps, at the very least, a mixture of leaves with a vinaigrette). That cultural knowledge is at work in the perceptive experience, which allows pleasure to emerge in recognising the sense that makes sense of the senses.

The pleasure (or displeasure, or disgust) experienced in tasting the food manifests a broader structure or culture of sense. In Pierre Bourdieu's *Distinction*, he marks how taste (as judgement) manifests a preference that naturalises a social and class-based distinction (2010: 49). While Bourdieu is writing about tastes for things and events, this mode of thinking can be applied to pleasure in taste perception.

The diner's social and class worlds impact upon what is experienced as pleasurable, mediating the experience of tasting. The restaurants operate within broader cultures of taste (of what is likely to be considered a pleasurable taste experience), though in their range of ingredients, they depart from a strict cultural hierarchy of ingredients. For instance, Alinea's 'Hot Potato' combines potato and truffle: the potato is a staple of cuisine, served as a hot potato and a cold potato soup and associated with lower tastes and subsistence; the truffle is an expensive ingredient with a strong musty and earthy flavour, the taste for which can only be cultivated by those for whom it is an affordable ingredient. The combination of potato and truffle might appear to be an attempt to challenge a class determination of the dish. However, it actually co-opts the traditionally lower-class ingredient, the potato, and transforms it into a luxurious experience. The mediations of class-based tastes continue and the apparently 'humble' potato is combined with truffle in order to appeal to a more privileged sensory palate. The potato is not a bland staple, but part of a sensorially rich perceptual experience. To those unfamiliar with truffle, the simple and satisfying pleasure of the taste of potato is interrupted by the potentially unpleasant musty quality of the truffle. The perceptual experience itself, in terms of pleasure, is mediated by the previous experiences and tastes of the diner, which are a marker of class and socio-economic position and privilege.

Cultural frames mediate perceptual experience and furnish different sensory stimuli with continuity in relation to one another. At times, this is seemingly immediate, as with Blumenthal's 'Sounds of the Sea', where the sounds, tastes and form of the dish mutually reinforce one another to heighten the experience of perceiving salty and fishy flavours. With other dishes, the process of perception is drawn out and the experience of coalescing different sensations into a coherent and apparently singular perception takes longer. Alinea's 'Wild Turbot' combines the fish with the smell of hyacinths by pouring boiling water over hyacinth leaves at the table to release their fragrance as the diner eats (Achatz 2008: 102–03). While superficially this seems to clash two distinct and unconnected sensory experiences (fish and flowers), it actually conforms to the culinary convention of 'surf and turf', which is not unusual. Rather than teasing apart the sensory experiences to trouble the connections between taste and smell, to cleave open experience from within, it reiterates a cultural and culinary convention in a slightly altered way (though it requires this previous understanding of 'surf and turf' as a culinary concept). The idea of 'surf and turf' transforms the at first fragmented sensation of flowers and fish into a single, coherent perceptual experience.

While at times relying on cultural narratives of sense to frame the experience of the dishes, to mediate perception and to furnish the experience with a sense of the sensible, the restaurants also construct experiences for the diner that challenge those narratives. There are dishes that rely on sensory discontinuities, which challenge the coherency of experience. The Fat Duck's 'Hot and Iced Tea' and elBulli's 'Pea Soup 60°/4°' (Dish Number 552 in Hamilton and Todolí 2009: 300–01) both interrupt narratives of sense and use temperature to provoke the diner into reflecting on their own sensory apparatus. 'Pea Soup 60°/4°' is a pea soup served at two separate temperatures, one hot and one cold, in the same glass and all the same colour. 'Hot and Iced Tea' is a sweet black tea served in a shot glass, where the liquid is experienced as two temperatures simultaneously: hot on one side of the glass, cold on the other, with no other apparent differences and nothing in the glass to maintain the separation. Both dishes provoke a shock of defamiliarisation: the notion that two distinctly different liquids could maintain their separation with no barriers between them, without mixing and without either heating or cooling in relation to one another, and not just as an optical illusion but continued through tasting (indeed, the 'Hot and Iced Tea' can be felt keeping the same two distinct temperatures as it is swallowed), seems to be impossible. Yet it has been made possible. The experience is unsettling, running counter to common sense. The mediation of forms of thinking in perception comes to the fore through a challenge: this is an unusual, seemingly impossible perceptual experience.

What appears to be immediate in sensory perception – fully present and unmediated – is rather an illusion. The experimental food served in the restaurants often provides a heightened and intensified sensory experience, which trades on the promise of a lively, rich and immediate series of sensations. However, in that heightening, intensification and experimentation, the dishes can also begin to fragment and to at least question if not undo the idea of immediacy in experience. As such, the perceptual experiences can operate both as an experimentation for the sake of spectacle and as an experimentation exploring the body, sensation and sensory perception itself. In the examples of 'Pea Soup 60°/4°' and 'Hot and Iced Tea', there are two modes of experience that could be at work: a challenge to common sense and a defamiliarising of immediacy (an aesthetic experience) as well as a novel and sensational experience, merely for the sake of amusing spectacle. The dishes themselves are not absolutely determined by either one of these frames. They contain the potential to be experienced both as commodified sensationalism and as a more troubling and unsettling aesthetic experience.

Orality: Language

There is a tension inherent to the mouth, as the site of speaking and eating. It is a transitory location in the body, the site of incorporation, where internal experience is externalised and external objects are internalised. This first section on 'orality' explores the role of language in perceptual experience, not just as a description but as a core part of embodied, sensory experience. It explores how language is layered into and through experience, with an ability to both stabilise and unsettle perception. It examines how systems of signification are bound up with the live(d) experience of the body, as a process of consciousness. Notions of sense-making and signification are intimately bound up with the phenomenal and experiential processes of the body, entering into a symbiotic and relational system. Language is at work within perception and experience. It both compounds and produces sensations and perceptions.

Language and sensation are not absolutely separate as both are woven together in perceptual experience. Language operates around and through sensation, guiding it and producing it. Sensation does not operate in a vacuum, ripped out from all contexts. Indeed, Spence has observed that language can *produce* sensations. He notes that 'even reading the word salt has been shown to activate many of the same brain areas as when a salty taste is actually experienced in the mouth' (2018a: 65). The productive force of language in perceptual experience is particularly evident in the title of dishes, which carry the weight of cultural associations and personal memories, playing an anticipatory role that is either confirmed or confounded in sensation. For instance, Blumenthal reflects on The Fat Duck's 'Crab Ice Cream' dish in observing that diners found it more acceptable and less sweet when it was named 'Frozen Crab Bisque' (2009: 111). The name not only positioned the diner in a particular way in relation to the food, but it also changed what they tasted in it ('ice cream' being sweeter, 'bisque' being saltier). The same performative function was explored by Noma in their dish 'Ice Cream of Jerusalem Artichokes' (Redzepi 2013: 184). Perception is not just the material entering the body (light waves, sound waves, food stuffs, smell particles), but the imaginative quality that both anticipates and experiences them. The imaginary quality allows language itself to produce sensation, which is no less 'real' than other sensations.

In perception, language has four key functions: it has a productive function, creating the experience of sensations in an imaginary yet experiential way; it has a dissecting function, teasing apart component parts of experience; it has a combinatory function, bringing together different sensations (flavours, tastes, textures, temperatures) as a singular perception; and it has a liminal function, marking out the boundaries of what constitutes one perception as separate from another. Language can produce, separate, conjoin and discriminate. Noma's dish 'Curdled Milk and the First Garlic of 2015' manifested each of these; some in ways that are applicable to many dishes, some particular to this dish. Presented in a ceramic bowl, the dish was a globule of freshly made cheese with a quenelle of garlic and a fan of baby sorrel leaves, all surrounded by a fermented barley oil. First, the naming of the dish as 'Curdled Milk' rather than as 'cheese' and framing the garlic as the 'First Garlic of 2015' produced an experience that was not of deep and mature flavours but rather something young, fresh and light. Second, the conjunction splits the dish into two major parts, dissecting the experience of eating into curdled milk *and* garlic (even though these were only two of four major elements). Third, the name of the dish nevertheless brought the whole dish together, giving it coherence as a singular dish despite the parts being presented separately on the plate (this is complemented by the plate itself, which also serves the function of bringing together and arranging elements as a single dish). Finally, as with the name of any dish or course in the restaurants, the name sets the limits of the experience, marking it as something to be considered as a whole and as distinct from the course that came before and the one to come after.

Language enters into perception and can both stabilise and disrupt it. It can direct attention in experience and furnish it with significance or meaning. In 2009, elBulli served a series of 'mimetic' nut dishes: 'Mimetic Peanuts', 'Mimetic Almonds' and 'Mimetic Pistachios' (Dish Numbers 1572, 1605 and 1606 in Adrià et al. 2014e: 154, 197–201). For each of these dishes, they used the particular nut as the basis of a number of preparations (including pralines, creams, frozen milks and jellies), which were then recombined in the shape of the nut from which they were derived. Had any of these dishes been described merely as the name of the nut, the encounter with the dish would be relatively stable: the particular nut, prepared in different ways, presented as looking like the nut that formed its core element. However, the inclusion of 'mimetic' in each of the titles troubles the experience because the nut is treated as an imitation of itself.

The ways in which language is used in the naming and description of a dish, at the table as it is served to the diner, can set the coordinates for what is to be experienced and frame the perception in advance. Blumenthal acknowledges this in writing 'The phrasing of a menu creates expectations and perhaps plants in the diner's mind certain words whose importance only later becomes apparent' (2009: 120). It determines the legibility of the oncoming sensations and marks their significance in advance. elBulli's 'Snails *à la llauna*' (Dish Number 1391 in Adrià et al. 2014c: 253–54) is a bowl of spherified herb oils and snail jus served as pearlescent and greenish-brown caviar balls. Without the name, the difference between the two colours of spherified flavour would be less apparent and it would not be clear which of the two was the main feature of the dish and which the garnish. The name creates expectations of sensory experience, constituting experience itself and, as Spence has noted, this often goes unnoticed when the expectation and the material encounter are largely congruous with one another (2018a: 59). Language prioritises sensations in perception, establishing the foreground and background of attention, the 'main feature' and the 'supporting acts', in advance of and alongside sensation. Indeed, Alinea name each of their dishes according to the 'main' ingredient, drawing attention on both the plate and in tasting to that central focus, relegating the other elements to complementary or supportive roles.

Appropriately for a discussion of food, Foucault's discussion of language in his seminal *The Order of Things* uses the analogy of a table, in the sense of both the site for the meeting of things and as tabula, the ordering and organising table (2002: xviii–xix). Language is the ordering principle, where things are placed together, examined and sorted, labelled and categorised. Foucault goes on to write, 'Where else could they [certain linguistic categories] be juxtaposed except in the non-place of language? Yet, though language can spread them before us, it can do so only in an unthinkable space' (2002: xviii). Language takes on a double function: it contains within itself the ideological-symbolic ordering principle, whereby the *possible* is articulated in advance through its potentiality for articulation, and in its ability to model the new or the seemingly impossible by forcing together the incommensurate. Both of these modes are found in the specific and individual deployment of language because of its potential to operate in these ways. In experience and consciousness, language is either congruous or in tension with experience. In the former, there is an easy sliding back and forth between language and experience, where previous descriptions continue to function for the present experience. In the latter, language is somehow lacking, unable to fully account for the experience in a 'logical' manner, and so it moves into the realms of the impossible, bringing together in its 'non-place' those things that go against the continuity of the symbolic system. In a final stage, it can lead to the ineffable, where language itself ceases to function to account for experience, though at this stage, the name ascribed can start to function as both noun and adjective. For instance, elBulli's 'Hot Frozen Gin Fizz' (Dish Number 621 in Hamilton and Todolí 2009: 111) is a hot and cold cocktail, much like The Fat Duck's 'Hot and Iced Tea'. There is no word for the simultaneity of hot *and* cold, so the language seems to enact a non-place of their conjoining, as a way of articulating the seeming impossibility of the experience. The title of the dish holds in place the seemingly impossible conjunction of hot and cold, where the common sensibility that denies their simultaneity is rendered as an apparent contradiction, 'Hot Frozen'. This enacts a reversal of Foucault's observation: it is experience rather than language that articulates the seemingly impossible. The language falls short.

The language used by the front of house staff to describe a dish as it is presented at the table lingers through the experience, guiding the attention of the diner and, in some ways, produces in advance what the diner will experience. The Fat Duck's 'Jelly of Quail, Crayfish Cream' offers both an example and a visual metaphor of this process. The dish includes a white ceramic bowl with layers of pea purée, quail jelly, crayfish cream and chicken liver parfait. Alongside this is served a rectangle of toast toppled with black truffle, presented on a small wooden board. In the centre of the table is placed a wooden block covered in moss, on top of which are small, rectangular and plastic containers. As the dish is served, the diner is encouraged to take one of the small plastic boxes and to remove from it what appears to be a translucent square of plastic. The waiter then pours a liquid onto the moss from a small teapot, which causes a flavoured dry-ice smoke to pour across the table. As the waiter goes through this process of serving the dish, they say

> So, we're going for a walk in the forest. We start from here, from the moss. You can take the little plastic packet and open it up at the top. Pick up the film inside with your fingers and pop it on your tongue. It will start to dissolve and you can taste the flavours of oak moss; like mushroom and wood. You can find similar flavours in the truffle in front of you. […] At the same time, like in the forest, you can see the fog and you can smell the same things.[1]

There are a number of things of note here. First, the description of the dish functions to guide the attention of the diner in advance. The language used at the very least aids the diner's perceptual experience, if not beginning to determine it. On hearing the description, the diner's experience will incorporate this language (oak moss, mushroom, wood) and be inflected by those terms, either using them as a frame for the experience and seeking those sensations or experienced as a disjunction between the language and the sensation. In both cases, the language has a force in the perception, as constitutive or unsettling. Second, given that the flavour of oak moss is not especially part of everyday experiences of flavour, the diner is furnished with a name, a description, to make sense of and understand the perceptual experience. The unsettling experience of the unfamiliar is mitigated through providing a name, which gathers together the sensory qualities and holds them together as a name. This is extended to include both the dissolving film and the smoke, so that they are experienced as the same (the same flavour, the same experience), as well as connecting it to the truffle toast. Language lingers through the experience to forge connections between the component parts. Finally, the smoke itself forms a visual metaphor for the way that language lingers through the dish: it pours across the table, over each of the other parts of the dish and into and over the diner. The smoke lingers and, while it does not necessarily fragrance the parts to be eaten, it seems as though it has because of the connections made between the different elements by the waiter's description. Like the smoke, language lingers over and through the experience, 'fragrancing' each part, bringing them together as one dish and one experience. Language operates like a final seasoning for the dish, not merely a description, but a productive force, guiding the experience and producing continuities.

Language can come before sensation, anticipating what is to be experienced and, in so doing, guiding that experience. With some of the dishes in the restaurants, the idea for a dish can sometimes be a linguistic conceit: word-play as the conceptual frame for the dish. Here the language is more markedly an organisational frame for the experience. However, the language can be insufficient and a gap can be cleaved open between how a dish is named or described and the actual perceptual experience. At this point, the language fails to provide continuity to hold together the sensations. For example, The Fat Duck's 'Whisk(e)y Wine Gums' is presented as a framed map of Scotland, Ireland and areas of the United States, with jellied whiskies placed on the map at the site of their origin. The dish was developed from the idea of making wine gums with actual wine and then shifted to using whiskies. As they are not in the shape of mass-produced wine gums, nor presented in a wine gums packet, the only connection to the idea of wine gums is in the name. Once the diner begins to peel off and taste the whisk(e)y jellies, the initial word play ceases to have much force in perception and attention shifts to teasing out the tasting qualities of the different whiskies. In the same way, elBulli's 'Black Truffle Mini-Truffles' (Dish Number 1533 in Adrià et al. 2014d: 276) rests on the double meaning of truffle: a chocolate dessert and a luxury edible fungus. It introduces the flavour of black truffle to a chocolate truffle. In so doing, the initial linguistic concept is overtaken, in sensation, by teasing apart the pungent qualities of the fungus from the sweet, bitter and rich qualities of the chocolate. In both cases, the wordplay that forms the concept for each of the dishes is merely a game, a spectacle, rather than speaking to and of a concept running through the experience. For language to function as a concept or as a framework for a coherent experience (and to achieve the 'wit' that seems to have been the aim of 'Whisk(e)y Wine Gums' and 'Black Truffle Mini-Truffles), it needs to still be grounded in a conventional relationship between word and sensation; otherwise there is an unsettling discontinuity of language and sensing. The language does not have a witty function in the experience.

In terms of perceptual experience, language plays a role both in how a dish is named or described and through the language of consciousness (with the former entering into experience through the latter). Language can produce sensations, dissect mixtures, combine elements and mark out the boundaries of an experience. Language seems to move through the body as a constitutive element of perceptual experience – sometimes as a major element and at other times as a seasoning. When there is a learned connection between language and a sensation, they can mutually reinforce and even heighten one another. But when the language and sensation are incongruous or in an unstable relationship, an unsettling gap can be cleaved apart. There is potential for this to be deployed as an aesthetic experience, where the language is unsettling in such a way as to defamiliarise perceptual experience, to make it strange and encourage reflection upon the diners' processes of perceiving, though it can also operate at superficial level, as a game or joke that operates apart from the main substance of the experience.

Orality: Sex

As a transitory site of incorporation, the mouth is one of the most intimate areas of the body. In its intimacy, the mouth is bound up with sexual pleasure and desire. The mouth is used for kissing, licking, nibbling, biting and oral sex. The sexual act and the act of eating can be considered analogous and shed light upon one another. They both invoke the mouth as an intimate site and deal with desire, pleasure and satiation. For Ferran Adrià, 'Together with sex, [food is] the most multisensory event that exists' (Adrià et al. 2014g: 94). Both eating and sex appeal to the body, have the potential for pleasure, are often understood on a scale from the animalistic to the sublime and unfold in order to lead to satiation, though often fall short or go past this moment. This section turns to the intersection of food and sex or the erotic, considering how positioning dining as a pseudo-sexual experience inflects the perceptual experience in particular ways, foregrounding pleasure, sensuality, enjoyment and relations with others.

While ostensibly located at a particular site in the body, eating and sex extend beyond the mouth and genitalia to implicate and appeal to the whole body. The whole body is implicated in the experience of sex and in the experience of eating. In *Phenomenology of Perception*, Merleau-Ponty argues that what constitutes the erotic or the sexual is something presented to the body, to which the body adapts itself in a sexual mode (2002: 181). The sexual is not located merely in relation to the genitals but in opening out one's body in a sexual manner to an experience. What marks an experience as sexual or erotic is not an appeal to the genitals but to a mode of appeal to the body; one that operates generally within the coordinates of desire, appetite and pleasure and specifically through perceptual modes connected to ideas of the sexual (sexualised imagery, sensual and titillating sensations). These modes of appeal to the body are a relatively common trope in a number of dishes presented in the restaurants, which then combine the general intersection of food and sex with a more explicit sexualised framing.

If we take eroticism as an attitude rather than inherently contained within any given object, then the erotic sensibility charges perception and guides it in a particular way. To say that it is a sensibility or attitude, a position, rather than in the object itself, is not to say that the object does not contain traits that might stimulate erotic desire. It becomes a process of negotiation, whereby anything might provoke an erotic attitude, but there are conventions more often associated with eroticism and that are perhaps more likely to elicit this attitude. Di Benedetto observes that 'Sexual attractiveness, bodily functioning, and emotion are known to have a direct affect on our olfactory system' (2010: 96). In other words, to be 'turned on' changes our sensorial positioning in relation to the world and objects, drawing attention to particular qualities of the encounter.

To provoke an erotic reading changes the qualities the diner might focus on in the experience of eating and moves them towards a sensory-sensual understanding of the experience. Michael Portnoy's *WANDBISS* ('biting room', 2007) did just this. In the work, diners were offered small bites of food served through holes in the wall. The diners were not allowed to use their hands and had to have the food bites placed directly in their mouths, sometimes with the food being pulled back and re-served, tempting and titillating the diner (in Howells and Hayman 2014: 133). The menu, designed by Portnoy and chef Christina Ramseier, was an eight-course meal served in ten minutes and sometimes forced the diner to get down on all-fours to reach a hole lower in the wall. There was a clear reference in the work to the 'glory-hole', slang for a mode of sexual activity and pornography where penises are presented through a hole in the wall to engage in sexual activity while maintaining a level of anonymity between the participants. There was a similar use of anonymity, though to different ends, in Marije Vogelzang's 2016 work, *One Bite*. In this, the participants were blindfolded, in pairs and fed each other fruit. The final moment of the work included both participants taking a bite from an apple, biting into the apple simultaneously so that the apple was held, for a moment, between their two mouths. In *WANDBISS*, the anonymity focused the experience on the sensations of the food; in *One Bite*, the food became a mediator between two bodies. The restaurants seem to straddle these two modes of sexualised intimacy in their work: a mixture of a sexualised and sensual encounter with the food, cut off from the chef, which encourages attentiveness to the sensual qualities of the food, and establishing a sense of an intimate connection with the chef through the medium of the food.

Portnoy's *WANDBISS* has a clearly pornographic quality, though it was not designed to be watched from a third-person perspective. The intersection of food and pornography has its own term in common parlance – 'food porn' – and is designed to appeal to a desiring-consuming gaze that is unable to be fulfilled by actually eating.[2] For Erin Metz McDonnell, food porn is 'a set of visual aesthetics that emphasizes the pleasurable, sensual dimensions of food, derived from (but not actually employed in) human sexuality' (2016: 239). It is not that the food in food porn necessarily resembles the human body, the genitals or sexual acts, but that it attempts to provoke the desiring, sexual gaze. McDonnell continues that food porn is a 'voyeuristic practice', which combines 'food as an object worthy of gazing' with 'the long-standing social intimacy associated with food' (2016: 240–41). Food porn presents the food as something worthy of the desiring gaze and operates in relation to the implied intimacy with others that historically surrounds the sharing of a meal.

Food porn often constructs images with an implied sensual dimension. McDonnell offers a number of common traits of the food porn image, including material that appears sexual, the implied intimacy of extreme close-up shots, teasing with what is or is not in the frame of the image and a short depth of field to draw attention to the food rather than the background (2016: 251–62). Food porn speaks of the connection between food, sex and sensuality, representing food in a sexualised mode in order to heighten a particular erotically charged attitude or approach. elBulli's 'Banana' (Dish Number 1420 in Adrià et al. 2014c: 313–15) plays on the association of a banana and a phallus, presenting a banana made from banana sorbet, passion fruit pulp jelly and coffee on a plate with syrups of vanilla toffee and sweetcorn. The joke of the dish is that it looks as though the banana has just ejaculated. The dish has some elements of food porn but in a live experience: it is not a fixed image, but nevertheless utilises an image that connects food and genitalia. Similarly, The Fat Duck's 'Pine Sherbet Fountain' (in Blumenthal 2009: 242–49), which resembles a Sherbet Fountain sweet, references the phallus and male orgasm. The dish is a cylinder containing pine-flavoured sherbet with a vodka-infused vanilla straw. The dish looks phallic and the sherbet that erupts from the top of it is something that fizzes and explodes in the mouth. In both of these dishes, there is a humorous titillation that attempts to provoke excited giggling, but without being too realistic a representation of genitalia, which would shift the food porn experience from titillation and whetting the appetite to something direct, crude and potentially confrontational.

Bompas & Parr's *Funland: Pleasures & Perils of the Erotic Fairground* (2015) revelled in the sexualisation of food, though in a way that was more direct, more explicit and operating in a way that was closer to fun and humour than the excited titillation of the body and its appetites. *Funland* was an installation at the Museum of Sex in New York City, including a bouncy castle of cartoon breasts ('Jump for Joy') and a climbing wall of genitalia ('Grope Mountain') with 'edible treats' served along the way. It also launched Bompas & Parr's 'Snake Oil', a fairground-flavoured sexual lubricant, with flavours of candy floss, caramel, toffee apples, salty sweat, flowers, metals, worn paint and wood. Rather than soliciting a sensual and sexually infused approach to and appreciation of the food, the cartoon aesthetic of the installation encourages a playful rather than passionate experience, reflecting on the connections between food and sex rather than staging that connection experientially. The lubricant began to stage how sexuality is not a thing unto itself, but always already a bi-product; it requires a level of fantasy beyond itself to operate. In the lubricant, the frivolity of the fairground is used as analogous to a mode of sex: playful, fun, lighthearted, raising the heartbeat and raising a sweat. There are various mediations at work: the fun of the fairground is experienced through candy floss, caramel, sweat, the smells of paint and wood; sex is presented as mediated by means of analogy, like the fun of a fairground. In the lubricant, sex is understood as mediated by, and analogous to, something else. In the same way, the pleasures and desires of food can be thought as mediated. It is not a direct pleasure of the sensory encounter with the food object but rather implicating other pleasures and desires: the diner's inherited and produced tastes, the implied encounter with the celebrity chef through the food, the references to sex in eating. These fantasies frame and produce the pleasure of dining and, like in sex, shift the experience away from a direct encounter with materials and the body. The pleasures of dining and sex are reliant on these fantasies, without which the experience slides from pleasure into a direct confrontation with materiality (no longer the desirable image of the other, but a body consisting of material parts; no longer an enjoyable experience of food, but ingredients that implicate death and destruction). Both food and sex avoid the direct and unsettling confrontation with the materiality of the other (be it a body, an object or a body-as-object) by imagining layers of fantasy and meaning, which then allows pleasure to be experienced.

Pleasure and desire are never free of this layer of fantasy, because it is the fantastic layer that allows pleasure and desire to function. Without the fantastical imaginary, we are confronted with base materiality. Some of these fantasies are eccentric or individual and others are more common. The more common fantasies constitute part of Heidegger's everyday mode of Dasein, where we do not own ourselves but give ourselves over to modes of experience of the *they*. In 'everydayness', Heidegger writes, 'We take pleasure and enjoy ourselves as *they* take pleasure' (1962: 164). Indeed, the very desire for and drive to pleasure itself is a considerable element of contemporary ideological discourse, which is predicated on the hedonistic search for pleasure, positioning the everyday self as always already a potential consumer, continually in search of the next experience of pleasure. However, as Žižek argues, the seeking of pleasure as an ideological duty of the subject of late capitalism is not a simple permissive solicitation of pure pleasure but rather works in relation to prohibition.

In *Event*, Žižek argues that the Father (symbolic of patriarchal ideological authority) is constitutive of enjoyment through a process of prohibition; that pleasure and enjoyment are experienced as an illicit transgression of prohibition. Žižek writes that contemporary, hedonistic and supposedly permissive capitalism institutes a deadlock, 'where the master-expert no longer prohibits enjoyment but enjoins it ("sex is healthy", etc.), thereby effectively sabotaging it' (2013: 128). As such, the ideological framing of the experience economy has the potential to undermine the pleasures of the restaurant because it solicits rather than prohibits pleasure. But there are nevertheless cultural forms of prohibition that are at work in the restaurant that allow pleasure to function as a transgression. The pleasures of the restaurant could be said to emerge from health discourse that positions luxurious consumption as an excess, as something unhealthy and not to be pursued. There is also a sense of the prohibition against sensual intimacy in public. To take a concrete example, elBulli's 'Flower and Nectar' (Dish Number 1584 in Adrià et al. 2014e: 166) is an orange trumpet flower from which the diner sucks out a sunflower and jasmine honey. Eating the dish forces the diner into a pseudo-sexual act, slurping a thick and sticky substance from a drooping phallic cylinder. The dish is constructed so as to make this a pleasurable experience: defying the injunctions to keep sexual activities private and the injunction to stay away from sugar (in service of decency and health, respectively).

The presentation of food to resemble genitals is a feature of a number of dishes at the restaurants. This mode of presentation is designed to amuse and titillate and suggests a sensual and sexual pleasure in eating. However, where the restaurants implicate genitalia in the presentations of the food, it is always as analogy or suggestion, never a realistic representation. A realistic representation, or indeed serving genitalia directly, slips over from playful titillation into a more direct confrontation with cultural codes around sex and sexuality.

In Mao Sugiyama's 2012 work, *Genital Banquet*, the artist took this representational trope literally. For the work, Sugiyama auctioned the opportunity for five diners to eat his surgically removed penis, testicles and scrotum, cooked with button mushrooms and Italian parsley. This provocative work posed a number of questions, including around the difference between animal and human flesh for consumption, ownership of one's own body (and its subsequent potential as capital), the selling of genitals for consumption conceptually connecting the restaurant and the brothel, the violence inherent to the construction of sexual difference and the logic of oral sex as a mode of consumption. Sugiyama questioned the extent to which our gendered identities are located in the genitals and, by implication, whether those gendered qualities are imbibed and incorporated through the act of eating. This level of provocation is unthinkable in the restaurants. They are not willing or able to engage in a radical form of conceptual art in and through food, because the experience is predicated on playfulness, easy spectacle and pleasure. The experience may be unsettling or defamiliarising but shies away from the kind of explicit challenge of Sugiyama's *Genital Banquet*.

The presentation of food to resemble (but not to directly and realistically represent) the genitals is at work in a number of dishes offered by each of the restaurants. The resemblance is deployed to elicit a particular perceptual mode from the diner: aroused, excited, seeking pleasure and sensually attuned to the dining experience. Each of the restaurants offers a dish that uses oysters as a sexualised ingredient: presented in a way that can appear vulvic and playing on the supposed aphrodisiac qualities of an oyster. Indeed, these two things are connected, given that aphrodisiac foods are often thought as such because of their visual resemblance to genitalia. Noma's 'Oysters Steamed in Seawater with Condiments' (in Redzepi 2013: 190–91) is an oyster presented with vinegar pearls surrounded by seaweeds and shells. Alinea's 'Oyster Cream' (in Achatz 2008: 184–85) is a cream flavoured with oysters served as two soft mounds with lychees and caviar in the centre. The Fat Duck's 'Jelly of Oyster and Passion Fruit with Lavender' (in Blumenthal 2009: 144–49) consists of oysters served in the shell with an oyster and passion fruit jelly, horseradish cream and lavender. Across each of these dishes is an attempt to draw out the vaginal qualities of the oyster, using soft folds of textures and flavours coupled with salty and warm ingredients. For elBulli's 'Shanghai Abalone' (Dish Number 1526 in Adrià et al. 2014d: 258–60), the resemblance to a vulva in the presentation is even more apparent, with the abalones served in an oval shape with pork, mock golden enoki mushrooms and yuzu and ginger jelly, surrounded by velvet horn seaweed shoots arranged like small black hairs around a vaginal opening.

These dishes raise issues of both class and gender. For Bourdieu, the distinction between pornography and eroticism is a class-based hypocrisy (2010: 199); that it is a class distinction between them rather than an inherent quality of the image. A similar distinction can be seen in the phallic and vulvic dishes at the restaurants: they are not considered pornographic, despite coming very close to overt representations of genitalia, because they are framed by the Michelin-starred, *haute cuisine* context. In terms of gender, there is a potential equivalence between the phallic and vulvic dishes, in that dishes resembling both are served in the restaurant. However, this is not a genuine equivalence because of the histories of violence enacted on women's bodies and the cultural positioning of a woman's body as something to be consumed (see Adams 2015: 27). To consume a vulvic dish implicates this historical context, making their consumption a more disturbing experience than the playfulness of the phallic dishes. In terms of both class and gender, the broader contexts surrounding sex and gender make a significant difference in terms of how the dishes are experienced and understood.

The relationship between food and sex can be further elucidated by considering the relationship between sex and love, particularly in terms of modes of pleasure. In Žižek's *Event*, he considers the connection between love and sex. He writes that there are four potential intersections of sex and love:

> (1) the celebration of asexual 'pure' love, as if the sexual desire for the beloved demonstrates the love's inauthenticity; (2) the opposite assertion of intense sex as 'the only real thing', which reduces love to a mere imaginary lure; (3) the division of these two aspects, their allocation to two different persons [...]; or (4) their false immediate merger, in which intense sex is supposed to demonstrate that one 'truly loves' one's partner, as if, in order to prove that our love is a true one, every sexual act has to be the proverbial 'fuck of the century'.
>
> (2014a: 133–34)

We could use this model to characterise the pleasures of the restaurant in examining the distinction between the seemingly 'lower' pleasures of sex and 'higher' pleasures of love: (1) not to demonstrate hunger, desire or any 'base' bodily experience so as to assert the 'higher' dimensions of aesthetic pleasure; (2) to focus entirely on the embodied 'pleasures of the body'; (3) to divide oneself between 'high' and 'low' culture, to maintain a separation between them; or (4) to demonstrate loudly the pleasure in order to demonstrate (publicly) one's appreciation of the work. However, Žižek continues by arguing for a fifth position: that 'love is enough in itself', that sex therefore does not matter and sex can be enjoyed without the pressure of a connection to love (2014a: 133–34). In an analogous way, in the expensive, Michelin-starred, *haute cuisine* restaurant, the diner fulfils the cultural duty of acquiring cultural capital simply by paying for the experience. Dining in the restaurants is performed as a way of demonstrating one's refinement and 'good taste'. As such, the diner is freed to enjoy the sensory and sensual pleasures of the meal; to revel in the 'base' pleasures of sensation and the satisfaction of hunger, without worrying that their public display of good taste is undermined by showing this level of embodied and sensual enjoyment. For the restaurants to encourage or solicit enjoyment in the sensory, sensual or even sexual qualities of the meal, they have to explicitly stage themselves as refined, cultured and elite. Otherwise they risk sliding into a different class culture that is positioned as primitive, crude and too close to the pleasures of the body.

Culinary Deconstruction

Deconstruction is the term for a common approach to creating dishes used in high-end restaurants. It broadly refers to the process of taking apart a dish in both the process of development and in the final presentation. The term originated at elBulli, where it was suggested as a way of describing how they were reimagining conventional and classic dishes (Adrià et al. 2008: 136.3). Before this, terms such as 'decomposition' and 'reconversion' were considered. elBulli conceived of deconstruction as a mode of adaptation, where there is an 'original' dish, which is subjected to various modes of exploration and experimentation, and the final dish relies on 'the guest's memory of the original' (Adrià et al. 2008: 240.3). In the restaurant, deconstruction is largely an aesthetic rather than philosophical strategy, perhaps better described as de-structuring or re-composition to avoid confusion with Derrida's philosophical process of deconstruction. This final section of the chapter turns to culinary deconstruction, to consider where it might overlap with its philosophical usage and how ideas of immediacy and the force of language in experience are brought to the fore and explored in a deconstructed dish.

A number of scholars, both in the arts and in gastronomy, have engaged with deconstruction as a culinary approach and form, often making comparisons between the culinary and philosophical use of the term. Clark and Peterson (2017) argue that where philosophical deconstruction 'sought to reveal the metaphysical presence that gave meaning to seemingly material certainties', culinary deconstruction reveals the 'materiality of human hunger' that is at work even in the consumption of foams and airs. However, this seems insufficient as a bridge between the philosophical and gastronomic uses of deconstruction because it still posits an absolute substrate of experience (the material, hungering body) as a given and self-sufficient 'reality' underlying the experience. Domene-Danés, writing about elBulli, argues that, while aesthetically culinary deconstruction favours 'simulation and pastiche', it nevertheless 'emphasizes originality, authorship, and uniqueness' in the work of the chef, creating a tension between the production of the new and the thrust to dismantle 'the inherited knowledge that structures our food' (2013: 117). Indeed, the food scientist Hervé This argues that 'culinary constructivism' is a more appropriate term, given the drive to construct and create – not just dishes but also creating an emotional experience for the diner (2009: 113–14).

In the philosophical usage, it is not appropriate to talk of a dish that is deconstructed, but rather to talk of a dish that encourages and engages in a deconstructive investigation. This can be explicated by way of Heidegger's writing on *destruktion* and being-historical thinking.[3] Heidegger writes that 'Tradition takes what has come down to us and delivers it over to self-evidence [...]. Indeed it makes us forget that they have had such an origin [...]' (1962: 43). The task of *destruktion* is to unearth (reveal or disclose) these inherited traditions that organise and structure being and experience (1962: 44). The task of 'self-mindfulness' and being-historical thinking is a becoming-aware of the 'history of thinking' as the 'history of be-ing' (Heidegger 2016: 52); these histories bear down on thinking (and by extension experience) as an organising force, suggesting the self-evidence of presence and meaning. For a dish to be deconstructive in the philosophical sense, rather than an art of de-structuring, it needs to encourage an investigative, revealing experience, which problematises the self-evidence of meaning and understanding.[4] Both of these modes are at work in the restaurants.

In describing elBulli's approach to deconstruction, Adrià et al. write that it modifies every part of an original dish (in 'appearance, form [and] texture'), leading to an unrecognisable appearance but retaining 'the essence of the original' (2008: 240.4). What is at work here is not deconstruction but de-structuring. It continues to rely on the notion of an *a priori* essence, which is maintained in the new presentation. It does not offer an engagement with notions of origin(al)s nor begin to take apart its own position as a cultural product with inherited narratives of sense. Rather, it is a gimmick: a superficial process of taking apart and putting back together the components that still suggests an original or originary narrative. This framing is not unique to elBulli. For instance, Noma's 'Walnuts and Dried Berries' (in Redzepi 2010: 168, 302) is a plate of walnut ice, walnut powder, dried berries and frozen milk, served as piles of powder on a black plate. This dish operates not as a deconstruction but instead its opposite: an affirmation of essences and essential qualities by attempting to present an intense version of the 'original' ingredients. In a similar way, food designer and artist Elsa Lambi-net's *Sweet Play*, while described as a 'deconstruction' (in Howells and Hayman 2014: 82), presents chocolates with removable and swappable fillings in a way that does not take apart their status as edible nor the connections between choc-olate and the flavoured fillings. Instead, it is a de-structuring; a new presentation of chocolates that does not engage with the production processes or combinations of chocolate and fillings.

In Nir Dudek's 'Reading a Plate', the article offers a 'postmodern' reading of contemporary cuisine, arguing that there is no canon of Western gastronomy *per se*, but rather that there are dominant narratives that mark out particular ideas and preparations of food (2008: 54). These narratives might refer to particular modes of preparation (the preparation, presentation and sensory profile of a 'classic' dish) or to ideas of an ingredient (its purported 'essential' qualities, its connection to a particular national cuisine, whether it is 'inherently' sweet or savoury). The extent to which a dish can be considered deconstructive, as opposed to de-structured, is found in whether it takes these narratives for granted and continues them or whether it encourages a deconstruction by defamiliarising these narratives, ques-tioning and drawing attention to them through estrangement.

There are dishes in the restaurants that engage in this deconstructive process, where the dishes challenge the supposedly self-evident, essential and stable identity of an ingredient. Alinea's 'Rhubarb: Seven Different Textures' (in Achatz 2008: 170–77) presents on the plate seven different preparations of rhubarb, includ-ing juiced with a beetroot sphere, dried, compressed and coupled with gin, as a sponge on a bay leaf, poached with lavender on a goat's milk custard, as a sorbet and jellied. In exploring a single ingredient through various preparatory methods, different qualities and flavours of the rhubarb are drawn out and any notion of its 'essence' is troubled through its combination with other flavours. Different flavours and textural qualities of the rhubarb are drawn out through the different methods and combinations, taking it apart as a stable and whole ingredient. Likewise, The Fat Duck's 'Best End of Lamb' (in Blumenthal 2009: 356–63) is an ice-filtered lamb jelly, braised lamb tongue with cucumber salad, a chop from a rack of lamb and a lamb hotpot made with lamb sweetbreads. As with Alinea's rhubarb, the lamb is taken apart and not treated as a holistic animal. Its body is broken apart and different qualities and textures are drawn out through different preparations.

The totality of the thing, the lamb, is nothing but the manifold construction of its qualities and appearances. The 'Best End of Lamb' ruptures that totality, exposes it as a construction of various parts, themselves subject to shifts and changes based on their preparation. This becomes a deconstruction precisely because it acknowledges the rupture as always already at work in the animal.

In the above dishes, the name of the ingredient functions as a quilting point for the dish: that which holds together the various elements and provides the potential for their deconstruction (it is only by presenting them as somehow 'the same' that they are available for deconstruction). For Žižek, in *The Sublime Object*, the Lacanian *point de capiton* performs this function: 'The "quilting" performs the totalization by means of which this free floating of ideological elements is halted, fixes – that is to say, by means of which they become parts of the structured network of meaning' (2008: 95–96). Under this quilting, the object or thing is unified as a set of qualities. Deconstruction becomes a performative act that changes the nature of the thing itself by interrogating the process of quilting and, importantly, exposing that the (meaning of the) dish could have been otherwise. Adrià et al. acknowledge this in the operations of some of their deconstructivist work in discussing the importance of the name of a dish, citing their dish 'Two Ways of Presenting Chicken Curry' as an example (2008: 240.4). For this dish, the curry was presented as an ice cream with apple jelly, coconut soup and chicken juice. They acknowledged that 'If the dish had been named *Curry ice cream with apple jelly and coconut soup* the gastronomic game would not have worked' (2008: 240.4). The potential for deconstruction emerges as a tension between the name and the fragmentation of the dish as presented – the question of in what ways the presentations can be understood as curry and how the different elements of the dish might relate to and work with one another under the same name. However, the name can also pull against the deconstructive drive. As with 'Two Ways of Presenting Chicken Curry', the name stabilises the dish once more: it does not dwell in the tension between the name and the experience, rupturing their unity. Instead, it provides a new, stable narrative.

A deconstructive dish is not merely the taking apart of elements or a game played with cultural narratives. Rather, it is an experiential process, unfolding in time, through the perceptual encounter with the food object. This experience draws attention to the historical contingencies of cultural narratives of particular preparations and the instability of language in relation to experience. A deconstructive dish prevents the experience from appearing as self-evidently and purely present and inherently containing sense and meaning. In *Writing and Difference*, Derrida critiques the phenomenologist as 'the "true positivist" who returns to things themselves, and who is self-effacing before the originality and primordiality of meanings' (2001: 194). As discussed in the first section of this chapter, experience is never immediate (absolutely present and unmediated). Deconstructive dishes draw attention to the discourses, structures and mediations that organise and make sense of experience. As such, the deconstructivist quality of the restaurants' practice is not only at work in dishes presented in the *style* of deconstruction. When the restaurants do engage in a deconstructive practice, the experience itself is defamiliarised or made strange. The diners' attention is drawn to those very discourses and structures (cultural narratives, inherited ideas, the seemingly continuous and immediate practice of the sensate body) that allow experience to be experienced as ostensibly continuous and present. This does not work as merely abstract argument but is manifested in the experience itself, rupturing continuity, understanding and presence. It is an experience that is defamiliarising and disclosive and, as such, it moves into the realm of the Heideggerian sense of the artistic and aesthetic.

NOTES

1. As with the 'Mad Hatter's Tea Party', discussed in Chapter 2, this is a verbatim description from my own experience of dining at The Fat Duck. The waiters do not follow a definitive script, but know the key things they are supposed to say.

2. While we might think of food porn as something connected to and facilitated by contemporary social media platforms, it has a longer history. Mary Douglas uses the term to describe an exhibition in her book *In the Active Voice* (1982: 114), though the term is inflected differently in terms of class when applied to an exhibition than when it is used in contemporary social media contexts.

3. Indeed, Heidegger's writing on *destruktion* and being-historical thinking can be thought as a key context for Derrida's deconstruction.

4. I draw here on Adrian Heathfield's reflections on Live Art practice: 'artists can create fissures or holes in perception and interpretation, *de-structuring* thought [...]. For many Live artists this is a means to critique cultural norms, fixed perceptions and sedimented values as they pertain to the body, identity and society' (2004: 9, emphasis added). There is a distinction between the aesthetics of de-structuring, the open question of taking apart, and the process of deconstruction, which is not merely an open question or fissure, but an attempt to interrogate, historicise and understand. The de-structured dish takes apart; the deconstructed dish actively provokes an investigative and interrogative, self-reflective and mindful (in the Heideggerian sense) experience.

Interlude 3

Pop-Up: Food, Performance, Philosophy

In Michel Serres' *The Five Senses*, he asks 'How can it be that for the last two thousand years we have commemorated the Last Supper, but merely studied divine Plato's *Symposium?*' (2016: 175). Serres draws attention to the meal as a ritualistic act of commemoration – a performance replaying a scene from the past, bearing the traces of its past articulations, becoming more and more suffused with meaning and memory with each enactment. The Last Supper, continually reenacted in the Eucharist, is a theological performance, staging for the communicants, through the consumption of bread and wine, a belief in the redemptive sacrifice of Christ by consuming his body and blood (for some believers figuratively, for others literally). Theological beliefs and ideas permeate the act of eating. Since 2015, Zuppa Theatre Company have been staging an immersive dining performance of Plato's *Symposium*, entitled *Pop-Up Love Party*. In the performance, they commemorate Plato's work, combining food and performance in a philosophical practice that, like the Eucharist, allows the ideas to permeate the experience of eating. This interlude examines *Pop-Up Love Party* as a particular example of the intersection of performance, philosophy and experimental cuisine, taking food practices from the experimental restaurant and explicitly weaving them into an immersive performance. The interlude draws on ideas of love, sex, language and experience from the previous chapter, as well as reflections on the presentation of food from Chapter two, and lays the ground for ideas in the following chapter, particularly around narratives of sense and the structure of the tasting menu.

Pop-Up Love Party is presented as a seven-course tasting menu, designed in collaboration with executive chef Daniel Burns and head chef Dennis Johnston.[1] The performance works through seven speeches on love from Plato's *Symposium*, coupling each speech with a different tasting course. Rather than performance being woven through, and operating as a frame for, the restaurant, here the tasting menu from the experimental restaurant becomes the basis for performance. In the performance, the speeches from Plato's *Symposium* are translated into a contemporary vernacular and the foodstuffs are transformed, much like in the Eucharist, into representations of each of the speakers. The performance begins with 'The Socialite', 'The Lawyer' and 'The Comedian', rendering Phaedrus, Pausanias and Aristophanes, respectively, as a caramelised onion chip flavoured with burnt hay; a parsnip and yogurt mousse served on a dark malt cookie; and a sandwich served in a plastic wrapper with an image of the globe. Alongside this is served 'The Doctor', a beetroot tea representing Eryximachus. The central course of the meal is 'The Poet', representing Agathon through a braised cabbage, cauliflower and fried oyster (or, for vegetarians, a mushroom) and the meal ends with 'The Philosopher', Socrates, and 'The Drunk Beloved', Alcibiades, presented as a ginger sorbet with lemon and mulled wine gums.

The performance is an energetic and raucous party, with guests sitting around tables, talking, eating and drinking, as each of the performers offers their speech on love from the *Symposium*. The performance brings together the food and the speeches in such a way that they speak to one another, with the text of the performers framing the food and the food inflecting one's understanding of the speeches. Each of the courses is a creative adaptation of the particular speech from Plato, using that source text as inspiration for the food, so that the two elements might work in tandem with one another. Alex McLean, artistic director of Zuppa Theatre, writes that the performance 'attempts to create–within Plato's own dramatic structure–experiences that are simultaneously visceral and intellectual' (2018: 21). The performance attempts, in other words, to take the idea and weave it through different sensory engagements with performance: sight, sound, taste, smell and touch. There is the potential to read this as a mimicking of the Platonic approach (exemplified in Plato's analogy of the cave) of the realm of the eternal Idea and its shadowy rendering in the world of shadows; the particular ideas of love extolled in each of the speeches are brought into a tangible arena through the text of the speech itself, its mode of delivery and the food forms presented to the diner. However, *Pop-Up Love Party* works in ways that are distinctly pulling against Platonic philosophy and, by so doing, enter into a dialogue with the *Symposium*, especially through the food, rather than merely repeating the ideas set down by Plato.

In rendering the characters as a dish in a tasting menu, *Pop-Up Love Party* takes the concept-driven food of the restaurant in a new direction. None of the restaurants under consideration in this book have explicitly framed any of their dishes as a character. There are a number of instances where the chefs discuss the autobiographical provenance of particular dishes and how the food offers a kind of self-portrait, but to transform a character into food and then overlay details of that character via performance onto it has not been done in the restaurants. This is where the food in the explicit setting of performance is transformed from that of the restaurant. The restaurant accommodates various ideas and narratives through the process of a meal. Even though there are motifs and themes that recur throughout a tasting menu, they do not follow so carefully a text-driven dramaturgical structure. The food itself is changed by virtue of being housed in an explicitly marked performance or theatre space. It becomes another element of the scenography or *mise en scène*, an actor or player in the work, with its own sensory functions in relation to the dramaturgy. We can then read the food itself in relation to the characters performing, not merely as illustrative of the text, but entering into dialogue with it, each framing the other.

To take a particular example, Agathon from the *Symposium* is presented as a dish entitled 'The Poet' (Figure 4). Agathon's speech in the *Symposium* continues the anthropomorphisation of love established earlier in the work, presenting it as a human-like god (Plato 1994: 32–36). The figure of the god, Love, is used to extoll the virtues and qualities of the idea, allowing the qualities of the idea to emerge as similes. There are aspects of the dish that are illustrative of the text and can be read as merely translating from the text into the food, just as the god itself is imagined as a tangible figure with particular qualities. Throughout Agathon's speech, he makes reference to flowers and this is added to the dish as a velvety petal placed on top of the food. For Agathon, Love has six children (hedonism, luxury, sensualism, delight, desire and eroticism), with the dish comprised six elements: a record (LP) and piece of greaseproof paper, on which it is served, a braised cabbage leaf, cauliflower, a fried oyster or mushroom and a petal. These are fairly simple ways in which the dish illustrates Agathon's speech, which add little in terms of understanding the text. But there are ways in which the dish begins to engage with Agathon's speech, to provoke questions, to develop ideas and to complicate the experience.

Near the beginning of Agathon's speech, he remarks that Love 'is the youngest of the gods. He […] takes evasive action in the face of old age – and the speed of old age is notorious […]. He is a constant companion of young men and […] he is therefore young himself' (Plato 1994: 32). Agathon is unambiguous in attributing to love the quality of youth. Yet the dish 'The Poet' in *Pop-Up Love Party* is presented on a vinyl record. This establishes an interesting tension between the food object and the text. On the one hand, it can be read as a contradiction of Agathon's remarks, incorporating the 'older' into the work of love by using a cultural symbol of the technologically archaic. But equally, the record as plate speaks to contemporary 'hipster' restaurant culture, which deploys found objects as plates, making the work perhaps even more 'youthful'. There is a tension in using an LP as a plate in relation to youthfulness, because it oscillates between different positions, questioning the connection between youth and love that Agathon so clearly promulgates.

Agathon also says of love that it is 'fluid in form. Otherwise, if he were inflexible, he wouldn't have the ability to adapt himself completely to his environment or to pass through minds and remain imperceptible on his original entry and on his departure' (Plato 1994: 33). For Agathon, love is not solid or substantial; it flows as liquid. There is a potential irony, then, in locating this notion of love in the solid food object (rather than, say, using the 'airs' process from elBulli). The object, though, is not homogenous but is rather a set of distinct parts presented

FIGURE 4: 'Agathon: The Poet' (2015), Zuppa Theatre Company. Photo by Mel Hattie.

together, one on top of another. This begins to mirror the breaking apart of love as a homogenous experience and presents it instead as that which lingers across and between various aspects. The dish has components that are fresh, floral and fried; it appeals to different appetites through including this component parts, which come together into one experience yet nevertheless remain separate. To 'enjoy' the dish, to take pleasure from it, to experience something analogous to the sensations of love (as described by Agathon), is to allow one's sense of pleasure to linger across the experience of the separate parts, in their mixture. Rather than reading the *dish* as a representation of Agathon's Love (the figure of the god), we can understand the *experience* as representative: fleeting, lingering, unable to be pinned down to a particular element or quality, disappearing if we investigate too closely.

While it can be interesting to consider food as (representative of) a character and can provide creative potential in performance and, by implication, in the restaurant, there is a fundamental issue in attempting to translate Plato's work into food, in that the form itself, food, begins to work against the principles of Plato's philosophy. In 'Cooking Time with Gertrude Stein', Adrian Kear discusses the role of food in relation to rhetoric for Plato. He writes that, for Plato, cooking 'forms "part of the same activity" as rhetoric [...] to the extent that it flatters to deceive' (1999: 47). He continues that they imitate 'outward appearances without knowledge of the essential properties. Their appeal, according to Plato, is to epicurean pleasure [...] and their gratification is the effect of "flattery" rather than "truth"' (1999: 47). Like Plato's rhetoric, the food in *Pop-Up Love Party* aims to 'flatter': it is designed first and foremost to be pleasurable, continuing the cultural framing of edibility and never straying from that. None of the dishes presented goes beyond what is generally considered pleasurable and edible, with all of them presented in a way that conforms to standard principles of presentation and plating. However, the performance also explores whether the ideas of the speeches can be manifested in the food, not as analogous, but experienced. In bringing together the food and the ideas, the work has the potential to go beyond mere rhetoric, but relies on the audience-diner to make the connections, for them to see past the flattery to the substance. As in the restaurants, the appeal to pleasure and flattery does not preclude the potential for an experience that is artistic and aesthetic. Indeed, the spirit of Plato's *Symposium*, carried through into *Pop-Up Love Party*, suggests that 'serious' thinking and ideas can be explored and articulated in the context of frivolity and fun.

Pop-Up Love Party is a lively and raucous event and encourages the audience to participate in the production and experience of the work. McLean reflects on the experience of the show that

> there's always a level of chaos as we encourage people to flag down servers (who take orders throughout the show), to drink, and to go to the bathroom when they please. They sit at bar tables together; they flirt; and sometimes they chat and ignore us completely. Occasionally someone gets belligerent. In a way, the ambient threat of derailment underpins the show (the main action of *Symposium* concludes with the arrival of drunken partiers).
>
> (2018: 21)

McLean et al. call this 'Ambient Drama', where the show happens *alongside* rather than *for* the audience. Indeed, their very participation in the action and atmosphere becomes part of the work itself, enlivening the space to produce the scenography, which is both the physical site or place and the actions of the performers and audience. All of this changes the way the food is experienced, as well as the food itself forming part of the world of the work. In other words, each element of the work, including the food, the audience-diners and the performers, enter into a network of interaction. It attempts to be a 'pleasurable' experience: one of fun, liveliness and inebriation. In this, the scene of the *Symposium* is re-enacted, not as a serious event, where complex ideas are discussed with somber reverence, but as a party: a place where ideas, actions and relations intermingle, just as the food, ideas and bodies intermingle, dislocating the site of the work.

Pop-Up Love Party triangulates food, performance(s) and philosophy, to allow them to bring life to one another, to speak to and about one another. It counters Plato's philosophy of the eternal, universal world of idea(l)s and instead posits philosophy, thinking, relationships and experiences as utterly contingent and reliant upon the bodies that think, enact and experience. The show relies on the performances of the diners/guests/audience, without whom the show itself ceases to work. In the same way as the restaurant, the audience-diners complete the work, bring their own bodies to it, which then become the site of the work (on and in the body, as well as between bodies). The work troubles the distinction between 'feeling' and 'understanding', conflating them and teasing out their reliance on one another. To 'understand' the work is to be present in/to it. To 'feel' the work is, in a way, to understand its focus (on love and feelings). Experience, feeling and thinking are brought into a single arena, and the boundaries between them are blurred.

NOTE

1. I draw on my own experience of *Pop-Up Love Party* presented during Mayfest in Bristol (24 May 2015) at The Kitchen. At the time of writing, the company is still performing the show and has toured it in Canada and the United Kingdom.

4

Processing: Making Sense

The tasting menu offered at each of the restaurants unfolds over a significant amount of time (around three to four hours, sometimes longer). Each present a series of courses, one after the other and carefully timed. We can follow a certain theatrical simile for understanding the meal: individual dishes like scenes, with their component parts like characters or actions, built into broader sections (acts) and, taken cumulatively, understood as the whole play or event. The event unfolds in time, moving through various experiences, tempos, textures and rhythms. Sense becomes an emergent property of the experience, arising not only across the whole event, the entire meal, but between sections, courses and mouthfuls.

Widening out from the apparently immediate perception of eating, this chapter broadens the conceptual lens to explore the relation between elements in the experience of the tasting menu meal. It considers how the ideas, motifs and narratives of the whole meal are built from the relation of its individual parts and how those narratives then frame individual dishes. The chapter begins with an exploration of the production of sense and, as such, engages with the double meaning of sense (articulated by Josephine Machon in *(Syn)aesthetics* as the doubling of 'making-sense/*sense*-making': the fusion of 'semantic "meaning making"' and 'feeling, both sensation and emotion' [2011: 14]). This section deals with how we might understand the activities of making sense, the active process of producing the sensible; how sense is made of sensing. The second section broadens the perspective further, considering the various narratives at work in the tasting menu (such as themes, motifs, correspondences and stories) and how these are implicated in, hold together and frame the experience. The chapter ends by addressing explicitly how the event of dining in experimental, creative restaurants can be understood as aesthetic: not merely an experience of spectacular pleasure, but one that defamiliarises and reveals, operating within a Heideggerian mode of art as opening up a world that takes itself as an issue.

To be able to conceptualise the sense that emerges from the meal (the meal entire or between small parts of it) requires an understanding of presence, time and the relationship(s) between a subject and object. If sense is not immediately given then it requires embodied and cognitive activity. As no object can give itself entirely to us, in its entirety, it must unfold in time, space and experience, then fundamental to an understanding of sense is how we engage with the object, how its various qualities are presented to us, how those qualities are brought together in the production of sense. In *The Phenomenology of Internal Time-Consciousness*, Husserl writes that 'in reflection we immerse ourselves in the unity of a structured process' (1964: 47). In other words, it is the (conscious) process of sense-making that provides us with wholeness and unity. It allows us to map out the object in its wholeness as the combination of its various qualities that are presented to us through sensory experience. Language intervenes in the constitution of the object. In consciousness, speech and writing, language forges the world of objects by cleaving apart one group of sensory qualities and attributes from another, ascribing to them a sense of identity. This is the fundamental gesture of sense. It furnishes an experience with an identity, a name, by grouping together a series of sensory qualities and wrapping and sealing them in a linguistic package: a noun.

However, this is not to say that an experience of wholeness is a linguistic trick. It is clear from our own experience that things seem to us to have an identity, to be experienced in their wholeness *qua* object. They seem to have an immediate sense in the act of perception. Following on from the argument of the previous chapter, I contend that this apparent immediacy of perception (sensing the object) implicates processes of understanding (the sense of the object). The two are inextricably bound together and reception is folded into perception. For something to appear, in experience, as a whole object, we require a certain fundamental level of continuity from one moment to the next (not that a 'moment' is in any way a fixed or given unit of time), joining together different sensory information in a way that coalesces as a single experience. While this might seem more apparent in building sense over the course of a meal, given that the experience stretches out and explicitly requires memory to make connections across the meal, it is also at work in individual 'moments' of perception. As attention shifts, even in a mouthful, noticing different things, memory is required to give consistency to the experience, to make connections between the elements. This chapter deals with the unfolding of experience, its processing and the sense that emerges from, and that is constructed between, the different elements, qualities and traits of the experience.

Making Sense

Sense is bound up with our sensory experience. Our making sense of the world, its objects and activities, is reliant on that which is available to the senses. If something is not available to the senses, it cannot form part of the schema or frame that allows something to be understandable (taking sense as the continuity between conscious mapping of the world and what we actually experience). This is the double meaning of the 'sensible': that which is available to be sensed by the senses and that of which is sense is able to be made. Making sense, understanding and intelligibility are bound up with the body that senses. The body and consciousness make sense of sensory experience, building continuities of sense that hold together different sensory information as a sensory perception or experience.

The manner in which sensory impressions are built into making sense can be thought in a way analogous to language. Individual units have connotations of their own, which are then built into larger and larger structures of sense. Individual letters can and do have connotative meanings, but a word is not reducible to the collection of meanings of its letters and the sense of a sentence emerges through the interplay of words. In a similar way, the individual sensations of a dish might each have their own connotations, but the experience of sense of the whole dish is not reducible to its constituent parts. The dish 'THE SOUP' from elBulli (Dish Number 1504 in Adrià et al. 2014d: 214–15) works according to the analogous relationship between sensations and language. The dish is a platter consisting of the shape of letters THE SOUP made from an elderflower infusion, constructed in the same way as spherification (i.e. a skin formed to contain a liquid). The letters are drizzled with ginger oil, interspersed with cocoa pulp and macadamia nut cream, drops of balsamic vinegar, glazed ginger cubes and nasturtium leaves. This dish exposes how food operates as a kind of language in relation to sense: the letters themselves are eaten one by one, interspersed with the other elements of the dish, as though each element forms a word, unfolding in time in its own grammar to produce a sense of the whole. The letters themselves furnish a particular kind of sense experience: the shape felt in the mouth, which bursts to reveal its content. But the letters themselves only contribute part of the sense of the dish, which relies on the other elements (which form the syntax of the dish – different 'words' to produce a more complex statement) and the retention of the various elements long enough for sense to emerge across the constituent parts. Like any language, the parts themselves do not contain, inherently, their own meaning; they require a body to consume and absorb them, to bring with it the ideological conditioning and social history of language, as well as personal experience and connections, to make sense of the language; in short, an ability to 'read' the work.

In reflection on how sense is made in and of eating, Blumenthal writes that it depends on 'memory and contrast', arguing that 'Memory provides us with a range of references – flavours, tastes, smells, sights, sounds, emotions – that we draw on continually as we eat' and that contrast provides 'a scale of comparison: hot is only hot in relation to cold; smooth is only smooth in relation to rough' (2009: 111–12). This is not only Blumenthal's understanding of the process of making sense in the dining experience. It also functions as an explicit part of the development of his cuisine, where he attempts to deploy this understanding in the creation of the event. While Blumenthal does not draw this out, the *connection* between memory and contrast is a core part of making sense of eating. Memory itself is defined in contrast to the present, that which is no longer before the senses but remains in consciousness. Contrast relies on memory to make distinctions (given that no perceptual experience is ever fully present but rather unfolds in time). Blumenthal also notes that the diner brings a 'range of references' to the experience of the meal in order to make sense of it. The processes of making sense implicate the position and experiences of the particular diner (personal memories and associations) and the more general connotations, implications, associations and significances that might be said to be shared with others: those modes of thinking and processing that are grounded in the world of the *they*, which can guide the process of making sense. The individual experience of dining then manifests these two positions, the personal and the *they*, though of course they are not completely separate, given that previous personal experiences themselves are equally open to being guided in sense-making by the modes of thinking of the *they*.

What is considered sensible plays a role in guide perceptual experience. In *Phenomenology of Perception*, Merleau-Ponty uses the image of a 'searchlight's beam' to conceptualise how attention is directed in experience to particular elements of one's environment (2002: 31). Merleau-Ponty argues that attention in perception can wander across an environment and pick out different elements on which to focus. While this is a visual analogy, conceptually it can be applied to the directing of attention of any of the senses. However, this searchlight of attention is not neutral. It does not freely wander but rather tends to focus on those things, traits or elements that are imaginatively marked as worthy of attention and therefore significant. Our attention is drawn and guided by those things that we imagine to be meaningful or significant. We are conditioned and trained to focus on those things that have the potentiality for some kind of meaningful experience and to background and ignore the rest. It is the same for the act of eating; what enters the mouth is a cacophony of various flavour and taste molecules. From this, we tease out those aspects that are sensible, partly based on what we recognise (those things we have eaten before, experienced before or know how to name) and partly based on the form of the dish itself (how it is framed, both as an object and by the language surrounding it). Perhaps the clearest way to demonstrate this is to think of an expert wine taster: the one who can pick out the region the grapes are from, citrus fruits, green apples, blackberries, etc., compared to the amateur, who merely tastes wine. The fundamental gesture of sense is identification and, in that identification, past sense is always already implicated in the experience. As such, memories, knowledge and modes of understanding (frames of sense) are core to the constitution of perceptual experience, by encountering an object through these frames of the sensible.

Given the documented, historical neglect of the aesthetic qualities of the 'lower' senses of touch, taste and smell in the Occidental tradition (see Howes and Classen 2014: 67), these senses become easier to ignore. It is not that they are implicitly less full of potential for rich, complex aesthetic experiences, but that we are not encouraged to be attendant to those dimensions of these senses, except in particular circumstances. This is in part because of the ubiquity of sight and sound as the dominant modes of both sensation and of making sense or the sensible. In the visual logic of the spectacle or spectacular, these haptic, gustatory and olfactory senses could be said to retreat even further as modes of sensing and making sense. The restaurant, then, as a site, is caught between the overwhelmingly visual logic of the spectacle and an attempt to draw out modes of sense through smell, taste and touch, as determined by the trained, expert body of the chef-producer.

At The Fat Duck, a means of achieving this is to co-opt the visual and aural in service of heightening the gustatory and olfactory; specifically in the reservation video that is sent out to all customers when they have booked to visit the restaurant. The reservation video is accessed via an online link and the just over seven and a half minute video is split into two distinct sections. The first is an animated visualisation of the tasting menu at The Fat Duck, accompanied by Gene Wilder singing 'Pure Imagination' from the film *Willy Wonka and the Chocolate Factory* (1971, dir. Mel Stuart). The animation begins with the words 'Like a Kid in a Sweet Shop' spelled out, word by word, in sweets on a white plate. This is followed by a series of images, which flow from one to the next, visually rendering various dishes from the meal. The reservation video includes:

- a steam engine, followed by growing lime green ice, a growing lime tree and a dance of slices of lime, referencing the 'Nitro-Poached Aperitifs';
- blowing green and red-brown leaves and a large tree, with a snail and a shot panning through neon pink mushrooms growing from the ground, referencing the 'Jelly of Quail' dish, which recreates a forest environment, and The Fat Duck's infamous 'Snail Porridge';
- black and white turtles swimming through the air and around a tree, from which pocket watches drop, referencing the 'Mad Hatter's Tea Party';
- a conch shell with headphones wriggling out of it, followed by small waves lapping a beach and shells dancing in the sand, referencing 'Sound of the Sea';
- a section of animation moving through a breakfast table, including tea poured from a pot into cups and saucers and on either side of the screen, the Black Forest Gateau served at The Fat Duck, referencing the 'Hot & Iced Tea', the 'Eggs in Verjus (*c.*1726), Verjus in Egg (*c.*2013)' and 'The "BFG"' (Black Forest Gateau); and

- ending the section with the card guards from *Alice in Wonderland* holding lollipops and candy canes and the Queen of Hearts holding the pink and white striped bag, in which, at the restaurant, the final dessert, 'Like a Kid in a Sweet Shop' is served.

The second half of the reservation video moves into a sweet shop, where the screen fades to black and John Hurt (who provides the voice of the narrator) talks through the process of putting together a bag of sweets. The voice provides a list of overlapping words (of ingredients and flavours) and the text is reminiscent of Willy Wonka's descriptions of his creations in the eponymous film.

The reservation video functions in two distinct ways: first, it frames the sensory experiences of the meal in advance, and second, it reveals something about the narrative construction of the meal. Watching the video in advance of eating the meal, various elements are marked as significant. Whether consciously or not, in introducing particular images and sounds to the diner, the video begins to frame what should be teased out of the meal; those aspects of the meal that are significant enough to be presented in advance, in order to stimulate the diners' excitement (as Blumenthal says of the video in a complementary short documentary about making the reservation video: the video's primary purpose is to generate excitement from the moment of reserving a table at The Fat Duck). In offering a précis of the meal in advance, it summarises the main themes and motifs of the meal (here, the tropes of *Alice in Wonderland*, the references to 'natural' environments, the implication of a quaint Britishness and the simile of 'like a kid in a sweet shop'). In doing so, it encourages the diner to find these aspects in the meal, to make sense of it in advance. Indeed, the reservation video also serves to solidify its reading of the meal after the fact, as it is again sent to the diner after eating at The Fat Duck. At this point it operates as a memento to be read alongside the menu to aid the recall and retrospective understanding of the meal.

What the video reveals about the narrative structure of the meal is less clear. It seems to give as much weight to the final course of the meal – the sweet shop bag – as to the rest of the meal combined. It also renders the experience of the meal as a series of seemingly unconnected images – a surreal journey that moves from railway to forest to ocean to breakfast table to abstract world of walking playing cards before landing in a sweet shop and darkness. But what this then encourages is for the diner to find other trajectories through the meal, not a journey through concrete places, but a more poetic and artistic attitude, more in tune with the ideas and aesthetics of the meal than a mimetic representation of a journey. By doing this, it encourages the diner to discover the sensory pathways, correspondences and motifs through the meal instead of attempting to discover a spatialised expedition. The 'narrative' of the meal is closer to that of *Alice in Wonderland*: a series of seemingly nonsensical images and experiences that, nevertheless, when taken cumulatively, produce their own kind of sense. The diner is positioned in advance of the meal to be like Alice: looking for different kinds of sense, perhaps wordplay made literal, perhaps eating that makes them feel physically and emotionally different (indeed, 'EAT ME' appears prominently in the video). The meal will play with the distinctions between sense and non-sense. Relying on the visual representations in/of each dish will not be sufficient to understand them.

The reservation video at The Fat Duck begins to articulate the operations of sense as always already being conditioned in advance, both in what is noticed by the senses and of what sense can be made. Ideologically, we are conditioned in the same way, but through a much more complex set of processes than one video, determining what we are able to sense and how we are to make sense of it. It is in this way that the senses are performative: they do not exist in and of themselves as a neutral substrate of the body and the self, an indeterminate and open mediator of the world. Rather, they are always already conditioned in advance through a number of social, historical, political (i.e. ideological) discourses. It is tempting to follow Michel Serres' writing on the senses: 'I taste; existence for my mouth. I feel; and a piece of me thus comes to exist. There was a blank void in the place which was just born of the sensible. Being settles in my body, a tunic of nothingness' (2016: 231). While it is tempting to follow this logic of the emergence of the self via sensation, which provides us with our subjective content, Serres' remarks assume a neutrality of the senses. As Judith Butler argues in *Senses of the Subject*, 'To say that I am affected prior to ever becoming an "I" is to deliver the news by using the very pronoun that was not yet put into play, confounding this temporality with that one' (2015: 4). The personal pronoun, the means by which we give continuity to experience and to posit meaning and sense at all, is not merely a result of experience, for that 'I' must precede the experience in order for it to be experienced. 'I' both precede and am a result of experience. And 'I' forge sense from the experience by virtue of its significance for me and 'I' am only what my previous experiences have allowed me to be.

In Heidegger's writing on 'meaning' in *Being and Time*, he argues that 'Meaning is the "upon-which" of a projection in terms of which something becomes intelligible as something' (1962: 193). For Heidegger, meaning is a projection from and by Dasein, where anything other than Dasein (Being-there) 'must be conceived as *unmeaning*, essentially devoid of any meaning at all' (1962: 193). Heidegger's notion of meaning or sense is a projection across Being-in-the-world, produced in relation to the world and projected onto the world; there is not inherent meaning to what is encountered in the world (in other words, meaning is broadly anthropomorphic). This operates as part of Dasein's everydayness, where we operate as though we discover or find rather than project and create meaning. This is because the notion of a world, for Heidegger, is a totality of significance, an interrelated network of signification, where Dasein operates according to the principle of equipment: able to inhabit a continuous, meaningful world as long as the objects and equipment with which we interact continue to function. Sense emerges and continues when individual objects, items of utility and perhaps even experiences are continuous and uninterrupted. But there are times when the latent *unmeaning* of the world can rupture continuous sense and sensory experience – when our interaction with an object fails to conform to the structure of meaning and action of the world. For Heidegger, this is the 'un-ready-to-hand'; the object that fails to be useful or, in this reading of Heidegger, fails to operate continuously within a totality of meaning, a world of sense. The un-ready-to-hand is unable to be used or encountered unthinkingly and '"stands in the way" of our concern', our care, engagement and investment in the continuous experience of a meaningful world (Heidegger 1962: 103). The encounter with the un-ready-to-hand exposes the constructed projection of sense onto the world, revealing objects in the world as essentially unmeaning, devoid of inherent sense. The object in experience becomes conspicuous, obtrusive and obstinate.

This idea of meaning is projective and performative, produced via an interaction with and experience of an object in the world and, in the everyday mode of making sense and meaning, framed by narratives of sense. Things have significance and signify themselves as being worthy of attention by virtue of the symbolic networks and structures within which they are encountered. This masks the inherent lack of meaning in the object itself. Heidegger goes on to write that significance always operates as a 'for-the-sake-of-which' (1962: 182). It is only within a structure of significance, a structure of meaning, that the meaning or sense of the object can be produced. Projected meaning is never an isolated projection but operates within a referential context of significance. Within the world of the restaurant, there are dominant narratives that form the background 'for-the-sake-of-which' that provide the coordinates of sense-making for the experience. There are regional and national narratives, which present food as bound with a particular land (e.g. the ingredient that is grown in this particular land); there are social and historical narratives, which present certain foods within a historical lineage or tradition of developments (e.g. the English roast); and there are sensory narratives, which make connections between the various parts of a dish or a meal and provide them with sense through reference to other sensory experiences (e.g. contrasts of textures in a dish or a flavour introduced in a starter and brought back in a dessert). These are not the only ways by which we make sense of the food being eaten, but they are encouraged as the dominant ways.

With the dishes served at the restaurants, there is often a dominant 'for-the-sake-of-which' that organises the dominant meanings to be found in (or rather projected upon) the food (though this does not preclude more personal or idiosyncratic readings). But the experimental nature of the cuisine can also mean a rupturing of this meaning, which can lead either to confusion on the part of the diner or a reading of the dish that resists being overdetermined by a single narrative of sense. For example, elBulli's 'Easter Coconut' (Dish Number 1474 in Adrià et al. 2014d: 159) is a sphere of frozen coconut milk served with a sprinkling of Madras curry powder. With 'Easter' in the title and being served as a hollow sphere, the dish seems to be a reference to Easter eggs; in bringing together coconut with spices, the dish seems to be a reference to curry; in bringing the freezing cold shell together with spices, the dish seems to have a narrative of hot and cold, using the contrasts between them to mutually highlight one another. These are the three dominant narratives for making sense of the dish, referencing places, traditions and sensory contrasts. But the dish does not hold together, because these different narratives compete with one another. What is required to make sense of this dish is a further leap into a meta-narrative: this is the work of elBulli, who pull together various smaller narratives in service of a more complex eating experience.

The fragmentary narratives are subsumed within the grand meta-narrative, where smaller narratives are exposed as just that – narratives – but covered by the meta-narrative that makes sense of the experience. In 'Reading a Plate', Nir Dudek reflects on a postmodern approach to contemporary cuisine, writing that where 'the modernist perspective acknowledges a canon of Western gastronomy', postmodern cuisine 'questions the very existence of such a canon' (2008: 54). He continues that there is no essential idea of a particular dish (Dudek gives the example of Boeuf Bourguignon) but rather that 'There are just narratives, one of them (due to historical reasons) overly popular' (2008: 54). Here, Dudek acknowledges how the sense-making process with food is bound in various cultural and historical narratives, which produce the sense made when a dish is cooked or placed in front of the diner. The attitude of 'classical' cooking or gastronomy is an absolute belief in a particular historical narrative, one that naturalises a particular preparation or dish as absolute. In the experimental restaurant, classical narratives may be de-structured or questioned, but they are replaced with a new overarching narrative of the 'experimental', itself a historically contingent narrative, and one that contains (both holds and withholds) the full force of the undermining or de-structuring of other historical narratives.

In writing on creative adaptation as a method for designing new dishes, Adrià et al. write, 'In order to be fully effective as a creative method, adaptation depends on the guest's visually recognizing the original dish. It requires a degree of interpretation on the guest's part to appreciate fully the chef's intention' (2008: 240.3). They recognise, here, the background knowledge or cultural position required to make sense of a particular dish or experience. As a counter to Dudek's postmodern reading of food, we can acknowledge the historical contingency of narratives while acknowledging their force in the interpretative act, because all meaning is, in some way, a historically contingent act. The narrative itself has reality in so far as it is the meaning-relation between the object and its observer/audience/diner.

The construction of sense does not merely happen in cognitive reflections but is also at work in experience itself. Continuing his thinking on significance, Heidegger writes that 'Existentially, a state-of-mind implies a disclosive submission to the world, out of which we can encounter something that matters to us. Indeed from the ontological point of view we must as a general principle leave the primary discovery of the world to "bare mood"' (1962: 177). The Heideggerian mood or 'state-of-mind' is the 'colouring' of our engagement with the world. We can conceive, then, of a 'mood' or 'state-of-mind' of understanding, whereby our seemingly immediate experience is able to operate in a continuous fashion; that our cognitive mapping of and assumptions about the workings of the world are congruous with our experience of it. Heidegger reiterates this in writing that 'even the purest [theory] has not left all moods behind it' (1962: 177) and that 'Understanding always has its mood' (182). The projection of sense or meaning manifests itself not only in a cognitive processing of experience but also in a seemingly intuitive, continuous and uninterrupted experience.

Each of the restaurants, in playing with the presentation of food and novel combinations of ingredients, engages with this mood of understanding. At times they rely on a quotidian sense of sense, a mood of uninterrupted and easy experience and pleasure, while at other times the mood is constructed to be unsettling or an interruption to easy sensing. It could be argued that in this shift from an everyday, unthinking appreciation and acceptance of eating, these restaurants are most clearly marked as engaging with the aesthetic and the conceptual in food preparation. It is a complex operation, as the restaurants play with the quotidian understanding of food and eating while providing a level of protection from absolute non-sense by covering the experience with the 'experimental' identity of the restaurant itself. The whole thing then becomes a game, something pleasurable and to be enjoyed, rather than a confrontation with our own historical conditioning and contingency.

If we remove the comfort of the restaurant's identity to frame the work, a more radical and unnerving experience can emerge. For instance, Dutch artist and 'Eating Designer', Marije Vogelzang, has created a number of installations, exhibitions and performances that engage with the easy, common sense processes of making sense of food and eating in order to trouble and interrupt them. Vogelzang's work is not encapsulated by the overarching narrative of 'fun' and 'pleasure' used by the restaurants. There is an element of playfulness in her work, but it is also more politically efficacious because it is not framed as merely a novel experience.

In *Feed Love Tokyo* (2014), Vogelzang curated a performance whereby participants feed each other and, at the same time, tell stories of childhood memories related to the food being served. The feeder tells their stories while the 'feedee' (Fogelzang's term) wears a white sheet that covers them completely, with a small opening at the mouth. The tablecloth, which is used to protect the table from falling food and spillages, is extended to cover the eater, serving as both tablecloth and extended napkin. Acts of sharing around food are made explicit, as one person places food in the mouth of another, while sharing their personal stories of the food – not merely sublimating the autobiography in the production of the food. The means of personally making sense of the food via the mediation of past experience is made manifest and troubled as the memories that mediate the experience are externalised, not my own, but those of another, spoken as I eat and overlaid on the food experience.

Moving further away from the experience at the table, Vogelzang's *Teardrop* (2013), made in collaboration with Robin van Der Werff, was an installation in which twenty-four glass pipettes were arranged in a circle pointing down to a fixed point. Surrounding this set up were ropes suspended from above enclosing the central pipettes. Some of the ropes were connected to the pipettes and could be pulled to release a flavour, dropped into the mouth of a participant standing underneath the pipettes. The connected ropes contained tags with short texts, such as 'I will always be there for you' and 'I'm so tired of myself!' For Vogelzang, the installation 'plays with childlike emotions; the sensation of being fed by someone else. You can read the tags but you don't know which flavor is connected. [...] a tool for human interaction and play' (Vogelzang 2018). Again, the installation works by making strange the experience of sensing flavour, encouraging a reconfiguration of how sense is made: it relies on the agency of another to deliver the flavour; it triangulates the diner, the server and the mysterious other, who constructed the installation and made the creative decisions about the flavours and texts, in the process of making meaning; and it reiterates Vogelzang's understanding of sense-making and the construction of personal taste as connected to childhood.

All of these ideas are at work in the restaurants, but in a way that is less overt and partially hidden by the comforting identity of the restaurants as places of pleasurable spectacle. Nevertheless, the restaurants engage in a problematising of the process of sense making. They engage with how sense works as a process of serialisation: the placing of things in a temporal order, with sense emerging in the relations between the elements placed in temporal and spatial sequence. There is a phenomenological continuity of sense in our quotidian experience of eating. Through ideological training and conditioning, we take for granted the unfolding of sensory experience when eating and are not attendant to the serialisation that makes sense of things placed in sequence. In Deleuze's *The Logic of Sense*, he writes of the process of sense-making that

> Sense is never only one of the two terms of the duality which contrasts things and propositions [...]; it is also the frontier, the cutting edge, or the articulation of the difference between the two terms, since it has at its disposal an impenetrability which is its own and within which it is reflected. [...] I never state the sense of what I am saying. But on the other hand, I can always take the sense of what I say as the object of another proposition whose sense, in turn, I cannot state. I thus enter into the infinite regress of that which is presupposed.
>
> (2004: 35)

Deleuze conceptualises sense as a frontier between two terms or things – an in-between space at the edge of things where their relation to, and reflection upon, one another is made manifest. While Deleuze writes of objects and words, or words and words, we can equally triangulate this as the relations between objects or experiences, where the sense is articulated in, by and through words or in embodied experience. We can conceive of this in the food event in the various parts that constitute a whole dish or in the unfolding of a menu, between one dish and the next and across a whole meal. In each case, sense is not given absolutely, but emerges in the relations between the various parts. Indeed, in 1998 elBulli introduced 'Parallel dishes', which were designed to present '[...] a repeated elaboration, the first one to bring an element of surprise and to enable an understanding of the harmony of textures and tastes, and the second to confirm it' (Serrano and Pinto 2013: 38). The more parts that are brought together, the greater the potential for both complexity and sense, finding those things that speak to one another across multiple parts.

This process of sense making is what is at work in every experience, in academic discourse and critical writing. A greater range of experiences and constituent parts leads to greater potential for sense, discovering and articulating those things that emerge across and between multiple experiences. This way of considering the sense-making processes of experience is equally applicable to any art: teasing out those things that are at work in multiple experiences; finding the way that two or more constituent parts speak to and reflect upon one another; being aware of those things that are drawn attention to and those things that form the background to experience; finding those things that are taken for granted as part of the background horizon of experience or paradigm of thought, without which sense would be reconfigured or, indeed, would cease to operate. One's embodied knowledge, through experience and encounters and training, becomes part of the expertise of sense making, in both what we are attendant to in our sensory experience and how our understanding is framed, always already in advance.

Consider the background knowledge required to make sense of a dish from elBulli: 'Three Suckling Pig Tails with Fermented Tofu and Ham Consommé with Jasmine' (dish number 1529 in Adrià et al. 2014d: 266–67). Three fried pigs' tails are served with tofu cubes in an Ibérico ham consommé with tofu sauce and Cantaloupe melon cubes, coriander shoots, mini-carnation petals and jasmine oil. For these various parts to coalesce into a single, understandable dish, one needs to be aware of the 'Three Little Pigs' fairytale; to know that Ibérico ham and Chinese tofu bring together two distinctly different culinary traditions; that there are various flavours from different cuts and preparations of the same animal. These offer access points to the dish, but none of them is enough to quilt the entire experience; they remain separate strands. Indeed, it is complicated further given the place of this dish in an unfolding meal that has included the 'Easter Coconut' and 'Shanghai Abalone', neither of which seem to offer an obvious connection to this dish. The conceptual working of the dish is fragmented, but it is by means of that fragmentation that it appears as a complex, rich, multilayered and inventive dish. If the diner manages to lock onto one or two of those narratives underscoring the dish, then they are able to gain some control over the experience, a semblance of understanding while nevertheless acknowledging that they fall short in their reading, that the sense of the dish is not singular, and by virtue of that take pleasure in the expertise of the chef in resisting a totalising, easy narrative.

To take pleasure from this kind of food could also be proposed as the universalising narrative that holds a dish or meal together. But the pleasure is never going to be the same for all diners – diners who visit with different expectations, different past experiences, different food preferences, in different moods and from different contexts. How, then, is the restaurant able to cater for this multiplicity of tastes, especially through a tasting menu that has no options (beyond a basic acknowledgement of specific food requirements: veganism, vegetarianism, gluten intolerance, etc.)? The personal tastes of the chef are utilised in the construction of a dish, but those tastes are not absolutely individualised. They contain within them some of the shared cultural conditioning brought by the diner. There is no universalised 'good taste', but there are shared tastes. The Latin *sapio* has the same double meaning as the English 'taste': taste as in the sensory experience and discernment. We might then read the *Homo Sapien* as a rendering of the human as a group that shares or has the same taste: a group whose individual taste preferences are conditioned by particular contexts and circumstances, with similarities in what they like, furnishing the group with a foundation for a shared group identity. Good taste is not *a priori*, but that is not to say it does not exist. It is part of the cultural context and identity of a particular group. It is porous and open to development and change, but nevertheless operates at the level of individual food preferences. It forms a background to cooking and eating that can be drawn on by chef and diner alike in producing and consuming 'good tasting' food and food in 'good taste'.

It is the possibility of those things that do not fit the shared ground of sense or the potential overarching and unifying narratives that allows for the pleasure of sense itself (any one of the pleasures of sense in Adrià's hierarchy). Deleuze writes that 'Sense is always a double sense and excludes the possibility that there may be a "good sense" in the relation' (2004: 39). Good sense and good taste could be used equally here, and they both implicate that which they are not, so to have good sense or good taste is equally to have an awareness of bad sense and bad taste, because their opposite, their difference, is always already at work within them. At the same time, there is a remainder: something in experience that is not covered by good or bad sense or taste, those outliers that have the potential to disrupt totalising sense or taste and, by virtue of being outside, give consistency to sense or taste itself.

In *The Sublime Object of Ideology*, Žižek writes about ideological interpella-tion in Althusser and Pascal that

> this 'internalization', by structural necessity, never fully succeeds, that there is always a residue, a leftover, a stain of traumatic irrationality and senselessness sticking to it, and that *this leftover, far from hindering the full submission of the subject to the ideological command, is the very condition of it:* [...] in other words, which – in so far as it escapes ideological sense – sustains what we might call the ideological *jouis-sense*, enjoyment-in-sense (enjoy-meant), proper to ideology.
>
> (2008: 43, original emphasis)

It is the very potentiality of (the disruption of) non-sense that makes space for sense and its enjoyment, of taking pleasure in the discovery-construction of understand-ing and meaning. To make sense requires for the thing, the object or the experi-ence to be congruous with the horizon of meaning, the contextual state-of-affairs, the ideological and epistemological paradigm. It is that horizon that furnishes us with the sensible: able to be sensed and of which sense is able to be made sense. Sense is always a triangulation of the world, ideology and individual experience. It might be sense in language or embodied and felt comprehension, but it is never a direct experience; it is always already mediated by the *they*, by the ideological paradigmatic worldhood within which we are presented with the possibility of meaning. Enjoyment in that sense is co-opted to support the ideological structure, to maintain it through giving consistency and substance to experience.

The double rendering of 'sense' as both sensory experience and meaning are intimately connected, symbiotic. The ideological sphere, the cultural, historical and political conditioning that allows us to emerge as a seemingly individual subject, determine what we are able to sense, and sensory experience is the means and mediator of that ideological sphere, which forms us as a subject. The possibility of the non-sensical (that which is unable to be sensed or incorporated into a system of meaning) gives consistency to, and allows us to take pleasure in, sense. Given that a restaurant is a site that prioritises and foregrounds the senses and their interactions, and that the experimental restaurant in particular raises questions of the making of sense (meaning), the questions of sense and the boundaries between sense and non-sense come to the fore of the experience.

Food Narratives

In elBulli's 'philosophy', the penultimate part of the 23-point document states that 'The tasting menu is the finest expression of avant-garde cooking. The structure is alive and subject to changes' (2008: 281). Perhaps the most significant and far-spread development from elBulli was that of the experimental tasting menu (or '*menu dégustation*', which emerged from nouvelle cuisine [Adrià et al. 2008: 240.6]).[1] As a development of the *table d'hôte* or fixed menu, the tasting menu allows the restaurant to carefully curate a meal experience, deciding on the progression of ideas and flavours, structuring the meal in such a way as to allow contrasts, correspondences and narratives to emerge. Unlike dining *à la carte*, the diner has little to no choice over the food to be served (beyond particular dietary requirements). The tasting menu, as that 'finest expression of avant-garde cooking', allows the chef more creative freedom and greater control over the diners' experience and, in serving smaller courses, offers an opportunity for greater experimentation because the diner is presented with a fixed menu.

The tasting menu allows for a rapid succession of flavours and textures, greater control over the diner's experience and a greater display of the range of work of the restaurant. It also functions to increase the creativity of the restaurant in two key ways: first, it encourages experimentation to produce multiple, distinctive courses (beyond the standard three or four of the à la carte menu), and second, each course is given less significance within the whole meal because of its relative size, allowing for greater risks to be taken with individual courses. The tasting menu allows for the restaurant and chefs to have greater creative control in planning the meal, and it alleviates the diner from the tyranny of choice. In a way, these two things work hand in hand in shifting the meal into an artistic and aesthetic frame. The curation of the meal, its constructedness as an artistic event, emerges because the work is given as an artistic product rather than a selection of choices that appeal to the diners' already existing sense of their own tastes and pleasures. The art is given integrity, both in terms of its wholeness and in the creative and conceptual principles of the chef-as-artist. The lack of choice counters the prevailing neoliberal dominance of (apparent) choice (though in an artistic rather than economic sphere).

However, the tasting menu experience is also offered as a commodity – an experience to be purchased, in which the diner pays for the comfort of not having to make decisions. The tasting menu experience is one that has a dual politics: it is both communal and exclusive. Clark and Peterson (2017) argue that, in being served the same meal, the diners in the restaurant are 'not simply isolated individual consumer-spectators, but intra-connected partaker-*audiences* whose experiences are in a significant sense shared and mutually dependent'. There is a sense that the diners share the experience and that the ways they experience the meal, make sense of it and enjoy it are grounded in the communality of the event. However, the diners are nevertheless individual consumers and the communality of the event is not egalitarian; it is only available to those who can afford it and who are able to book a table. As such, there *is* a sharing and co-production of meaning in the experience, but one that circulates around a particular demographic. To be able to partake in the experience, there is a level of economic capital required. With this economic capital comes an implication of a certain level of cultural capital, too, which will then manifest itself in modes of making sense of the experience. The narratives of the tasting menu are designed for those familiar with fine dining and an aesthetic appreciation of dining.

At elBulli, artistic comparisons were used to conceptualise the construction and functioning of a tasting menu. Adrià et al. write that the menu is '[...] choreographed as a whole experience' (2008: 240.7). The menu

> [...] should be planned in the same way that the narrative of a film or short story might be structured. The menu should set out a coherent culinary philosophy [...]. Portion sizes, the order and timing of dishes and the preferences of the guest should all be considered, and the menu should have several themes running through it [...].
>
> (2008: 240.6)

However, this is an analogy, because the narratives of the tasting menu are often articulated as olfactory and gustatory rather than imagistic. Particular tastes, flavours and sensations are sequenced and become motifs in a similar way to images and languages in a written or filmic narrative. Below I offer the gustatory narratives that appeared through the meals I had at The Fat Duck, Noma and Alinea. In identifying them, I present a way of thinking about the construction of the tasting menu and the correspondences and connections across the meal, the narratives of food as opposed to the textual narratives of films, stories and plays.

At The Fat Duck, the meal opened with aerated beetroot with a horseradish cream, which had an earthy note from the beetroot and a mixture of fieriness and softer creaminess from the horseradish. This was placed in direct contrast with the next course, the 'Nitro-Poached Aperitifs', which were light, cold and sharp. This was followed by 'Red Cabbage Gazpacho', served with mustard ice cream. Here, elements of the previous two courses were brought together: the coldness of the aperitifs in the ice cream and gazpacho with the pepperiness of the horseradish in the mustard; the dark purple of the aerated beetroot lingering in the dark purple of red cabbage, coupled with the lighter colours of the cream and aperitifs. The opening three courses worked as a short progression of a sensory thesis, antithesis and synthesis. This fiery and sharp opening was followed by two dishes that dwelt in an earthier and meatier flavour palette: 'Jelly of Quail, Crayfish Cream', including the richness of chicken liver and the deep earthiness of moss and truffle, followed by 'Snail Porridge', with braised snails, Iberico Bellota Ham and fennel. This felt like an altogether more mellow, rich, earthy, subdued and sophisticated section, which was then coupled with and developed by 'Roast Foie Gras', served with barberry, combo and crab; the luxurious richness of liver, established in 'Jelly of Quail', returned (as did the 'surf and turf' combination – liver with shellfish then crab), with the sharpness from the barberry connecting back to the zesty and light tone of the 'Nitro Poached Aperitifs'.

These were the first six of a fifteen-course tasting menu. It begins to give an impression of the care and attention given to the curation of the tasting menu. Sensory motifs are established, returned and transformed, re-contextualised and woven throughout the meal in a way that holds the tasting menu together. What is of particular note is that the 'narratives' established and deployed are not grounded in character or story but are sensory, gustatory, haptic and olfactory. Blumenthal writes that the key principle of his construction of the tasting menu is 'contrast' (2009: 81), but what becomes apparent in the eating is that contrast is in relation with similarity and continuity. At The Fat Duck, the abiding principle may be contrast between and within courses, but it also weaves together a particular set of sensory characteristics that bind the meal together as a singular event. For the meal I ate, the key characteristics were earthiness, the oceanic and rich sweetness. Of the huge range of qualities a dish or meal might have, these were the dominant and recurring set of gustatory qualities.

The distinctiveness of this flavour and sensation palette at The Fat Duck perhaps becomes more apparent in relation to those of other restaurants and menus. At Noma, the meal I ate included a different constellation of sensory qualities, including the sharp vinegariness of pickles: a dominant flavour in the first two courses (pickled elderflower, blackcurrant and cherries, followed by fermented wild plums transformed into a circular crisp disk), which returned in a sharp broth served with shrimps five courses later, where it was no longer the dominant sensation, and then once more in a thick, black garlic leather leaf with a sharp paste made from ants. There were also recurrences of the bitterness of leafy vegetables, established in the third course with barbecued leaves and returned to with fresh baby sorrel two courses later, followed by raw damson leaves (which wrapped the shrimp and brought together the acidic and bitter narratives, while introducing the sweetness of shellfish, which again returned later in a langoustine tail) and later barbecued cabbage leaves served with roasted bone marrow, bringing back the barbecued note from an earlier course. The final dessert at Noma, 'Forest flavors, chocolate and egg liqueur', was a bowl lined with salty and crisp moss, with a dark choc-olate-coated mushroom, a dark chocolate leaf with a light garlic note, a choco-late cube, which released a cold cherry liquid when bitten and a leaf coated in red glitter, which was rather sour. This final course brought together a number of the elements introduced and explored earlier in the meal and reconfigured them as a dessert and brought them into direct contact with one another. The various motifs established throughout culminated in this final dish that allowed them to work with one another but again transformed them to become something new.

While there were identifiable flavour and ingredient traits and motifs at Alinea, the prominent constructive principle of their menu was in broader strokes of tastes (tastes of sweet, sour, bitter, salt and umami, rather than the more complex and nuanced experience of flavour). This is reflected in the menu presented to the diner: a sheet of paper that attributes to each course a circle. This operates as a guiding key for the diner of the journey through the meal, progressing with each course in order from top to bottom, with smaller circles representing smaller courses (and larger ones larger or more substantial courses); sweeter courses as a circle moving to the right of the page, savoury courses to the left; and the darker and lighter shades of the circle standing in for the relative richness of each course. While of course this graph-ical notation system is grounded in the experience and expectations of the chef (as opposed to what the diner will themselves experience), it nevertheless articulates a tasting journey, broadly moving from savoury to sweet, though with fluctuations throughout the meal and with denser and lighter moments. This graphical notation highlights how the Alinea menu does not subscribe to an easy shift from savoury to sweet, nor a dense and heavy main course, which is built to and receded from in terms of the substance of each course of the meal. For Achatz, the inclusion of sweet courses interspersed within savoury broke 'the monotony of the savory to sweet progression' (2008: 45). However, this dramaturgical construction of the meal goes further and engenders a two-fold challenge: first, it challenges the conventions of the split of a meal into savoury then sweet, and second, it acknowledges that the categorisation of a dish as savoury *or* sweet is misleading and then the place of a dish in the course of a meal can encourage us to experience it as predominantly savoury or sweet.

In Carol J. Adams' *The Sexual Politics of Meat*, she cites the anthropologist Mary Douglas on the ordering and structuring of the meal, writing that Douglas

'[…] suggests that the order in which we serve food, and the foods we insist on being present at a meal, reflect a taxonomy of classification that mirrors and reinforces our larger culture' (2015: 16). For Adams, the key is 'meat' – that meat is culturally significant in producing closure in a meal and that the political power of vegetarianism is that it 'fails to find closure through meat' (2015: 79). While this refers to a very particular constellation of gustatory practices of a particular time, place and culture, we might nevertheless draw from it a question of the narrative 'closure' of a meal: that felt experience that the meal is done, that it contained what it ought to have contained. This is not just about feeling full (it is easy to imagine a condition of being unable to eat more and yet feel somehow unsatisfied by a meal), but the requirement for certain cultural and personal narratives to be fulfilled for the meal to be fulfilling.

The tasting menus at each of the restaurants seem to navigate a fine line, subscribing to certain cultural traditions and narratives of a meal (a broad progression from savoury to sweet, the inclusion of meat for meat-eaters, serving individual courses *à la russe*, in sequence, rather than *service à la française*, where all the food is served together in an elaborate display) while experimenting with other elements. In other words, the experience is never wholly experimental or radical but navigates between cultural narratives of the meal and explorations and experimentations. For instance, elBulli's 'avant-desserts', which were small dishes that acted as a transition between the savoury and sweet, continue to subscribe to that savoury to sweet progression, but mark the moment *as* a transition. Alinea employed something similar, coupling the degrees of sweetness throughout the menu (discussed above) with transitory dishes between savoury and sweet; for instance, a dish called 'Graffiti', served on a block of concrete, consisting of a meringue and sorbet, which brought together hazelnut and Périgold black truffles. This was sprayed at the table with balsamic vinegar, by the waiter as if graffitiing a wall. In being neither wholly sweet nor wholly savoury, the dish not only marked a transition in the meal but also had substance as a dish in its own right; indeed, being served on a large slab of concrete, with a short performance by the waiter, it was a substantial moment.

For these narratives, tropes and motifs to emerge through the meal, for conceptual continuity to linger throughout the experience, the experience requires the diner to be attentive in various cognitive and embodied ways to the multiple elements at work through the meal. Some of the narratives emerge by a process of 'readership'; a self-aware process of questioning, teasing out the various elements of a dish, identifying them in order to recognise when they reemerge as the meal progresses. But there is also something less self-aware and more felt in the continuities. In a complex of memories, the meal operates as a felt or sensed experience, in its sensory continuities and ruptures or interruptions; not merely cognitive recognition of returning elements, but a felt return to an experience. In Heidegger's writing on 'mood', he argues that the mood or '"one's state-of-mind is grounded primarily in having been" [which] means that the existentially basic character of moods lies in *bringing* one *back to* something' (1962: 390, original emphasis). Narrative continuity is not just an acknowledgement of particular elements, recognised and brought to mind, but a felt continuity, a return to earlier sensations, re-felt and re-experienced in a sensate and embodied manner, but slightly altered. As such, the meal begins to hold together as a series of sensations, emerging in relatively close temporal proximity, suggesting not only continuities through the meal, but a continuous sensate body that experiences and can recognise in and for itself that which it experiences sensorially.

We might think about this in relation to memory. In *Matter and Memory*, Henri Bergson writes of pure memory as an 'image-remembrance', an unrepeatable representation of the past (2004: 194). Bergson furnishes us with a visual rendering of memory, which allows it to be easily connected to images, texts and representations. But might we not conceive of a sensorial memory beyond the visual – a continuity that allows sensory experience to unfold as continuous? In Paul Riceour's reflections on Bergson's 'memory-image', he reflects that it is '[...] an intermediary form of imagination, half-way between fiction and hallucination [...]' (2012: 70). To fold this understanding of memory into the present allows us to think of the continuity of sensory experiences (or presentifications) as a kind of hallucination, an imagined continuity that nevertheless has 'reality' as it is the only way in which we experience.

The qualities of performance of the meal are perhaps most apparent in its engagement with time and temporality. The meal unfolds in time, is time-based and like performance marks out its ephemerality and transience as a key factor of its ontology. Indeed, it heightens the logic of the ephemerality of performance, as it not only disappears, but the work presented to the diner has to be carefully planned so that the food object appears at the table at the right moment for its qualities to appear to the diner in the way precisely designed and delivered by the chef. Its ephemerality extends beyond its disappearance into the past as the food object itself never exists as a static and stable object: it disintegrates, warms up, cools down, melts, congeals, rots. While some of these processes will take longer than the duration of the meal and so are not an apparent concern, others happen much more quickly.

In de Certeau et al.'s *Practice of Everyday Life* on *Living and Cooking*, they write that 'In the kitchen, *one battles against time*, the time of this life that is always heading towards death. The nourishing art has something to do with the art of loving, thus also with the art of dying' (1998: 169, original emphasis). There is a complex of ideas at work here in relation to the arts of gastronomy. They acknowledge the time-based art of preparing food – actions unfolding and experienced in time, with time itself lingering as a concern in the experience. But the gastronomic and culinary arts also implicitly (and sometimes explicitly) invoke the time of life and death: the requirement of various kinds of death and destruction for the creation of the meal (the death of animals, the plucking of plants from the earth and the ceasing of their growth) and the continuation of the body and life of the diner through eating (with lingering questions of nutritional value and sustenance). Eating itself contributes to the 'battle against time' that inevitably leads to death. They also describe it as an 'art of loving' (loving, not living; it is not a typo). To think of it in this way suggests an intimate and sensual contact in and through the food, with implications of reproduction and continuation (especially understood through the lens of Georges Bataille's argument that food, sex and death are the fundamental areas for the economy [1991: 33]).

Time itself lingers throughout the experience as a concern. This arises partly from the structure of the tasting menu; more courses of differing sizes draws greater attention to the time of the event than the 'traditional' three-course structure, with a roughly equal weighting of time and size of the starter and dessert, and the 'main' having greater material and temporal substance. The experimental nature of many dishes from the tasting menu involve processes of production that are both precise and intimately bound with time. Processes of spherification, making foams or blast freezing mean the food has a very brief window of time in which to be served in order to retain the qualities those techniques produce.

The time of production is also implicit and lingering in the dish presented to the diner. For Heidegger, in 'The Origin of the Work of Art', a work's 'createdness is part of the created work. [...] createdness is expressly created into the created being, so that it stands out from it [...]' (2011a: 122). The work's 'having been created' lingers in the art object, beyond its more general 'having been brought forth' (2011a: 122). For Heidegger, this is not the lingering of the work of the particular artist, the 'the impression of having been made by a great artist' (2011a: 122).[2] While at each of these restaurants the identity of the celebrity proprietor lingers through the experience and goes some way in framing it, the work presented is never that of an individual, but is rather the productive of a collaborative effort (as is made apparent through the kitchens often being on show, demonstrating the team of chefs, as well as the role of the waiting staff in presenting and framing the dishes as they emerge). Each dish carries its own createdness and thereby implies the time and effort of its acts of creation. In foregrounding the provenance of the ingredients, the createdness of the dish moves beyond even the work of the chefs. The weight of time of production bears down on the dish, in its complexity and care. The relatively brief moment of consumption is loaded with the weight of time in production, producing a sense of sensory, emotional and economic richness. The createdness (the intervention of bodies and actions to transform from the 'raw' to the 'cooked') is a defining characteristic of the gustatory work as art precisely when the createdness itself comes to the fore of the experience; the encouragement to acknowledge the creative work and to experience the dish as not *merely* 'natural' but a delicate and precise construction and curated experience.

This lingering createdness of the work, and its implication of the time and labour of production, encourages a particular mode of care and engagement on the part of the diner and attentiveness to the constructed nature of the meal and the ideas and narratives it may be exploring. In other words, the implication of the work of the chefs encourages the diner to seek out meanings, narratives and ideas in the meal and connections between dishes. For instance, the dish 'Dry Shot' at Alinea (in Achatz 2008: 156–57) is sent to the table in a folded, vellum envelopes, containing dried red bell pepper, dried Niçoise olives, fried oregano leaves, dried garlic, toasted breadcrumbs and fried capers. In being presented as an envelope, the dish highlights its 'having been sent' from the kitchen and encourages the diner to 'read' and make sense of it, both in terms of the mixture of ingredients and in its relation to the rest of the meal.

The curation of the tasting menu oscillates between two separate approaches, each with its own processes and practices of sense-making of the experience. These can be characterised in terms of the distinction between the 'map' and the 'tour', as articulated by Michel de Certeau in the first volume of *The Practice of Everyday Life*. In the chapter 'Spatial Stories', de Certeau discusses the intrinsic spatialising of narratives, writing of the distinction between the map and the tour as an oscillation '[...] between the terms of an alternative: either *seeing* (the knowledge of an order of places) or *going* (spatializing actions). Either it presents a *tableau* ("there are..."), or it organizes *movements* ("you enter, you go across, you turn...")' (1998: 119, original emphasis). These are two fundamentally incompatible modes of space: the map presents a bird's eye view, showing the relation of elements in space to one another, and the tour is an experiential navigation of space. Together they offer two modes of thinking about the tasting menu. To see it as a map is the perspective of the written menu, which is a cartography that places dishes and elements in relation to one another, allowing for the diner to see the overall progression of the meal, to see various times of experience simultaneously in front of them and to acknowledge, moving across the menu in any direction, the motifs, themes and narratives. The tour is the experiential perspective; bound in the progression of experienced time, it moves in only one direction and unfolds, including the body of the diner in the processual nature of the meal. In the tour, memory is the means by which narratives emerge. These two perspectives cannot be experienced simultaneously, though they can speak to one another. In each case, they offer a particular perspective on the meal and its construction. The map is an abstracted knowledge, taken out of bodies' sensory experiences, teasing out particular elements and traits in order to furnish the meal with intellectual consistency. The tour is the fully sensory, embodied experience, where traits might be foregrounded and backgrounded in terms of the attention of the diner, but nevertheless dwells in the messy, noisy world that spreads out from the diner.

This sensory touring that is at work in the tasting menu has been explored in contemporary artistic practice. Bompas & Parr's *The Waft That Woos* (2012–13), installed at the Royal Shakespeare Company, was a mirror maze 'navigable by nose'. Each participant entered a complex maze of mirrors, in which they had to follow the increasing intensity of a smell released by a vaporiser at the end of the maze. The smell was supposedly an aphrodisiac, composed of blackberry, figs, juniper, polished leather, oak, smoked and cured venison, bilberries, wild cherries with the 'naturally occurring aphrodisiacs' phenylethylamine and yohimbine. It was a rich and heady smell, which increased in intensity as one moved through the maze. The maze was difficult to navigate by sight and so the smell became more important. As one approached the end of the maze, the smell became stronger and more of its elements, layers and complexities were noticeable. The work highlighted the lack of a 'map' for navigated and foregrounded the experience of the 'tour' and the increasing visual disorientation alongside the increasing intensity of the smell created an experience of increasing sensory overload. Much like the tasting menu, the intensification of embodied awareness and sensory sensitivity encouraged a future orientation; to move towards the end, to come to understand how the experience will unfold rather than a sense of the whole journey, mapped and understood in its entirety.

Perhaps even closer to the structure of a meal, given the discrete courses or sections offered, Jennifer Rubell's *Icons* (2010) took participants on a journey between rooms in a gallery. *Icons*, at the Brooklyn Museum in New York, began in a room reminiscent of Vito Acconci's *Seedbed*, with baby carrots seemingly growing out of the floor, which participants picked and took to the next room to wash and eat. The next room contained a series of aperitifs and canapés: a huge pile of crisps alongside a pile of dips in paint tubes, both on wooden pedestals; canvases on the walls, each with a protruding tap, from which the guests could pour themselves a gin and tonic, bourbon, a screwdriver, a Dirty Martini, rum and coke, white wine, lemonade or water; champagne fountains; and seven casts of the artist's head made of cheese suspended from the ceiling, slowly being melted by heat guns and dripping onto a pedestal of crackers below. In the penultimate space, nine pedestals were heaped with different foods, included roast beef, lamb, pork, turkey, rabbits and vegetables. Finally, after eating, the participants were invited into the museum lobby, where they broke open a twenty-foot tall piñata of Andy Warhol's head, filled with commercial, prepackaged desserts. The work clearly followed the traditional structure of a meal (though extended to include an act of preparation: picking and washing carrots). The meal was turned into a tour, moving between different rooms, with different moods and ending in a riotous and playful act. The separate rooms drew out the distinction between different sections of a meal – not just the shifts in mood at one table in a restaurant, but the journey one takes through a meal.

As mentioned above, the written menu can offer a counterpoint to the touring of the tasting menu, by setting out in a fixed form a map of the meal. Each of the restaurants offers a copy of the menu experienced by diners as a memento of the experience to take away with them. As such, the menu functions not only as a cartography in anticipation of a future journey but also as an *aide memoir*, a way of looking back over the terrain that has been traversed. But the menu is not the only form of 'map' apparent in the restaurant. In David Leatherbarrow's 'Table Talk', he writes

> Inscribed onto the table's surfaces are traces of what just occurred, in all its particularity. [...T]his cloth, china, and cutlery fully attest to the ways they were used. *Service* is a term we sometimes use to name tableware. It denotes two things: the physical premises of a meal and their readiness to assist whoever wants to eat.
>
> (2004: 211)

The tablecloth, cutlery and crockery leave behind traces of the experience. It forms a rudimentary map: the layering of a temporal unfolding onto a singular surface, where the various experiences of the meal linger in co-existence. The tabletop bears the traces of the actions undertaken and food eaten, not indexical documentation but a document of a performance.[3]

In a similar way, Daniel Spoerri's 'trap-paintings' offered a mapping of an event. He set up a meal for an artist and, once the meal had been eaten, Spoerri glued down everything that was left on the cloth and hung the 'paintings' vertically. The 'trap-paintings' are maps that point to a contingent and temporal experience, its ephemerality foregrounded in the detritus of the event that marks an absence of bodies and action. It is an attempt to fix in place the final moment of the experience, which bears the weight of the actions that precede the 'ending'. The tabletop surface of the restaurant operates in the same way, as a cartography of documenting. The seemingly blank tablecloth attempts to act as a *tabula rasa*, though inevitably contains the anthropological history of its usage as an object in the cultural history of the meal. By the end of a meal, it contains spillages, marks, indentations and crumbs from the event; those accidental leftovers that accumulate and are apparently worthless, but nevertheless offer a retrospective mapping of the meal for the diner – the final image before leaving.

The construction of narratives in and through the tasting menu emerges from the relations between elements: between different sensations in a mouthful; between different mouthfuls and elements that make up a dish; and between the dishes themselves over the course of the meal. But as these narratives emerge in the experience of dining, they are then folded into the experience, guiding how the diner might experience and understand later dishes and courses. As the meal progresses, the narratives may emerge more forcefully and clearly, refining the experience of eating by furnishing it with narratives for making sense of the dishes. Equally, later dishes in the meal can interrupt or disrupt the emerging narratives, forcing the diner to rethink, re-evaluate and re-engage in the process of making sense of the meal. The incompatibility of the map and the tour is mirrored in this process of understanding narratives in and of the meal: the meal can only be considered in its entirety from a retrospective position, once it is over; and once the meal is over, the individual parts (sensations and dishes) that make up the meal have disappeared, been consumed and cannot be revisited or re-experienced in such a way that, in the experience of eating, their significance can be fully appreciated.

Aesthetic Processing

The tasting menu follows a dramaturgical structure. Beyond individual courses, the meals are constructed as sections, with each progressing the 'narrative' of the meal and moving towards its conclusion and the emotional and gustatory satiation of the diner. The Adrià brothers and Soler explicitly framed the elBulli experience as broken into 'acts':

> Act One: 'To welcome guests, cocktails, aperitifs and snacks are served, usually on the terrace.'
> Act Two: 'This is the most substantial part of the menu and consists of the savoury tapas-dishes; in other words, the dishes that are eaten with cutlery.'
> Act Three: 'Guests now immerse themselves in the sweet world, beginning with the avant-desserts and going on to the desserts.'
> Act Four: 'The final act, during which morphings are served, often takes place back on the terrace, and has no time limit. It lasts as long as the after-dinner conversation, the coffee, liquors and cigars.'
>
> (Adrià et al. 2008: 272.3–72.4)

While this structuring seems to place elBulli within a theatrical framework, it is not in the borrowing of artistic and theatrical terminology that the work of the restaurant moves beyond the everyday and becomes artistic. This final section of this chapter turns explicitly to the artistic and aesthetic work of the restaurant, considering how the food event can be legitimately thought as an aesthetic experience, beyond its appeal to pleasure as part of an economy of experiences.

In 'The Origin of the Work of Art', Heidegger marks art as separate from 'useful equipment' (2011a: 97). Art is not equipment but rather has a revelatory function of disclosure or unconcealment, as 'the truth of beings setting itself to work' (102). Art's revealing is bound within its worldliness, its belonging to a particular time and context (106), and the 'work-being' of art is itself to set up a world, one that makes space for liberation (108–09). Art's work-being is not of the realm of usefulness or equipment but rather like a temple: a consecrated space where materials do not disappear into utility but are rather caused to come forth (109). Art goes beyond craft and is of the nature of *technē*, where craft meets knowing (118–19), and the createdness of the work comes forth as a dominant trait (122). Art transports us 'out of the realm of the ordinary' (123) into a world that takes itself and its own operations as an issue in experience through revelation and disclosure. It encourages an 'authentic' experience of and for Dasein.

What emerges here is a definition of art that is close to philosophy: a practice that does not merely subsist in craft or making but rather sets up its own world outside of the quotidian. For the restaurant to be considered artistic in this sense means moving beyond everyday food cultures and enacting something more creative, which brings to the fore its own createdness, self-reflexively engages with its own materials and most significantly encourages a reflective attitude towards itself, to consider what is revealed in and through the experience. This revelation might be about the material qualities of the food, a disruption to the continuity of our own sensory experience or an unearthing of the ideological and/or cultural enframing of our quotidian and often unconsidered experience (those things that are taken for granted). For the meal to be considered as both artistic and allowing for an aesthetic experience, it needs to move beyond or outside of the quotidian experience of dining and, by so doing, open space for an intellectual and embodied reflection on the processes of eating itself: the ways in which we sense, the ways in which we make sense and encouraging a defamiliarised awareness of the various discourses that operate through the meal that allows continuous experience to happen. In other words, like Heidegger's concept of 'authentic' and enowned Dasein, it takes itself as an issue.

In his book *Event*, Slavoj Žižek reflects on Heidegger's use of '*ereignis*' (sometimes translated as 'event'): '[…] for Heidegger, Event has nothing to do with processes that go on out there in reality. Event designates a new epochal disclosure of Being, the emergence of a new "world" (a horizon of meaning within which all entities appear)' (2014a: 31). The Heideggerian event is a process of disclosure or unconcealment, though it might be more useful to think of this in the Žižekian mode of a new frame (horizon of meaning). While Žižek writes of this in grand terms ('a new epochal disclosure of Being'), we can think of the event at the level of an artwork: a work that, in its work, reveals or discloses; the work that troubles, cracks, reconfigures or breaks the frame. And this 'frame' is our conditioned enculturation, which continually allows sense to emerge; it is the 'horizon of meaning', the taken for granted background assumptions that allow intelligibility. The work of art is to not merely reproduce the sensible status quo, to merely subsist within existing frames of meaning and intelligibility (what we might call a cultural product), but needs this disruptive and revelatory character. The work of art is to 'de-second-nature'. This is Simon Jones' term, which he defines as 'True discontinuity, the actually felt interruption of *out-standing standing-within* [...] felt as both a *mood* of de-naturing and an *instant* when-where one's self is forced out of its self, interested in (in the sense of *esse*/being *inter*/between) the world' (2012: 36–37, original emphasis). The encounter with the work of art unfolds and troubles. It is not a creation of absolute originality, but instead a process of revealing, uncovering and disclosing that 'second nature'.

In *Mindfulness*, Heidegger explores the tension between art in the sense of the *work* of art (from 'The Origin of the Work of Art') and 'Art in the Epoch of Completion of Modernity'. In the latter, art is transformed into an 'installation', an arrangement of elements in such a way that 'organises beings'; appealing to its audience 'in the sense of *calling out* what already exists in the domain of the all-deciding and all-securing public' (2016: 23, original emphasis). When 'art' appeals to these public and general forms of knowing and experiencing, it ceases to operate as an aesthetic experience of revelation and disclosure. Instead, it continues the machinational work of modern technicity and technological thinking, treating its audience as something to be controlled and manipulated, operating within the coordinates of meaning taken from the public world of the *they*. There is a sense in which this could be said to be at work in the restaurants, especially in their deployment of technological and scientific knowledges to manipulate the diner into experiences that have been pre-planned. However, the restaurants also engage in the acts of revelation and disclosure. This is the truly aesthetic experience of art. The restaurants' experimental, creative and spectacular cuisine can provoke the diner to question their own sensory apparatus, defamiliarising the experience of eating and calling the body (and its experiences) into question. In this way, the experience of the work of the restaurants is aesthetic, because it ruptures those everyday, public modes of understanding and experiencing – not merely in a distanced and reflective way, but in a way that is folded into the experience itself.

Given the processual and temporal nature of the artwork's unfolding and disclosure, there is a performative dimension to Heidegger's writing on art (though he does not use the term 'performative'). This is not merely a reflection of the temporal quality of the encounter with art, but more significantly that the work becomes itself in and through the encounter; its 'workly' qualities appear in its work. Art's identity *qua* art is performative in that it becomes itself in its process of unfolding and revelation. It is temporally bound and only works in relation to the one who encounters. To ground this more clearly in food as performance/performative: a dish presented at the table is only partially revealed to the diner; its important sensory qualities discovered through the process of eating are not given over until it is eaten. The work of the dish as art unfolds in the act of eating, never showing itself fully. Though it is not just the process of its becoming that makes it art in the Heideggerian sense. It goes further, where one is brought into the world of the world set up by the dish, to dwell within it and, in the dwelling, the encounter becomes an issue for itself.

Following Žižek and Heidegger, the artistic and philosophical notions of 'event' have the possibility to coincide, where the artistic work sets up its own world, framing the experiences it contains as alongside, outside or beyond the 'everyday' experience of experience. Within an artistic-philosophical event, experience itself is made strange or becomes something different, altered; what Jones describes as 'Out-standing, standing-within'. It is not wholly divorced from the body and the everyday world, but neither is it fully coherent with it. From this position, the event sets up a world by creating a conceptual space that distances one from, or reconfigures, the quotidian. The nature of performance as event (as both artistic and philosophical) is the bringing into being of this world, allowing it time and space, opening itself out to the bodies and experiences of its audiences or experiencers. It is perhaps easier to conceive of this at work in immersive and participatory performance practices, which explicitly and overtly open up a material space to include the bodies of its audience within the world of the work, a physical setting up of a world. But for Heidegger, it is a conceptual setting up of a world that is open to other art practices (indeed, for Heidegger, it is often explored in relation to painting). The event allows for the physical and conceptual dwelling in the world of the work that is marked as different from the everyday world. Through this framing as 'different', as 'unusual', as 'strange' or 'spectacular', we are encouraged to engage in an act of revelation or disclosure of the nature and construction of materials, ideas or the functioning of bodies within the everyday world.

We might think of the restaurant as a particular kind of immersive or participatory performance practice. In overtly bringing the diner within the world of the work, and in using the diner's body as a key site of the operations and the artistic and conceptual work of the work, it solicits an attentiveness to one's body, one's mood, one's acts of making sense and one's sensory experience. Each of these things is unsettled, unable to operate continuously and unconsciously as they might otherwise do. Experiments with the food, the performances of the restaurant and its spaces move us out of the everyday world of eating (whether domestic or high street dining).

161

There are moments in the meal when the experience is so overwhelming that everyday forms of experiencing and understanding seem to fail. At these moments, the diners are called to 'own' themselves – to acknowledge the insufficiency of the modes of knowing of the *they* and confront their own experience. This can be conceived in relation to Heidegger's 'call of conscience' (from *Being and Time*). For Heidegger, conscience is not used in its everyday manner, as a sense of morality, but rather as a summons to take ownership of oneself, to take responsibility.[4] This is experienced as part of Being-towards-death, Heidegger's conceptualisation of authentic Dasein, where Dasein truly recognises death as its own limits of Being and therefore as the absolute horizon of Dasein's possibilities. The readiness or capacity to face up to death as the ultimate limitation of Dasein, to recognise that death is always already a possibility, ruptures the all-knowing and organising idle talk of the *they*, which distances Dasein from its authentic self by framing (Dasein's experience of) the world in such a way that it is knowable. The call of conscience operates 'in the mode of keeping silent' (1962: 318) and 'summons the Self' from the all-knowing world of the *they* 'to its potentiality-for-Being-itself' (319): 'Conscience summons Dasein's Self from its lostness in the "they"' (319). The overwhelming moments of the meal, when words fail to provide an adequate account of the experience, when the experience exceeds everyday frames and modes of understanding, institute a silent call of conscience. Words and discourse fail, everyday modes of understanding fail, and the diner is confronted by a more fundamental experience of their own experience: becoming aware of their own sensory apparatus and modes of making sense; becoming aware of the various narratives that make sense of the meal; and becoming aware of the ways in which those narratives furnish the experience with a sense of substance and meaning that is constructed. In these moments, death appears as an absence, as a failure, as the lack of inherent meaning, significance and substance. The experience is revealed as performative, as a fantastical construction of meaning, and the self itself as containing no substance beyond its attempts to make sense of sensory experiences of the world.

Throughout this book, there has been an attempt to articulate the multiple and intricate ways that the restaurant can and does open up an artistic and conceptual space – the ways it unsettles or makes strange. It reveals, unsettles and discloses our everyday encounters with food (and the means we have at our disposal, without thinking, to make sense of those encounters and how they are framed). The practice implicitly and explicitly draws attention to those things that can often be taken for granted or unconsciously assumed, subsumed within the everyday performances of the body and forgotten. But they are not given absolutely. The restaurant, in its unsettling, through setting up a strange, unusual or experimental world, encourages reflection and lays the ground for revealing the ways in which the body and experience are both produced and constructed. Perhaps at the most fundamental level, the experiments with dining and eating at these experimental restaurants demonstrate that eating could be different. They pose an open and unsettling question: if it could be different, if our sensory, emotional and intellectual appreciation of food could be constructed another way, then how did it become as it is in everyday experience? This is both a personal and political question. It is one that is not answered in the work of the restaurant. Through their respective practices, chefs such as Ferran Adrià, Heston Blumenthal, Grant Achatz and René Redzepi offer experiences that are not merely a continuation of the quotidian experience of eating but instead set up their own worlds, which implicate, trouble and question the everyday practice of eating, intervening in that practice. Through those interventions, the diner is encouraged to engage with the contexts of eating, the social rituals of dining and the seemingly unmediated experience of the senses. In Heideggerian language, the practice engages with its own 'worldliness'. It goes beyond 'craft' and utility to reveal or disclose our ways of knowing.

NOTES

1. The idea of a set tasting menu is not of elBulli's design. A sequence of small courses was a core part of *nouvelle cuisine*, which itself was inspired by Japanese *Kaiseki*. Set menus are a common staple of restaurants and were once the standard offering in inns for travelers (see Clintberg 2018: 207). However, elBulli engaged in a significant development of the *experimental* tasting menu.

2. Indeed, for Heidegger, 'where the artist and the process and the circumstances of the genesis of the work remain unknown, this thrust, this "*that* it is" of createdness, emerges into view most purely from the work' (2011a: 122–23, original emphasis).

3. Following Angela Piccini and Caroline Rye's distinction between 'document' and 'documentation': the former, 'the unintentional traces, detritus, residues left over from practice-as-research in the form of coffee cups, cigarette butts and the hair, skin and sweat of our bodies that may later be identified as important by the archaeo-archivist' and the latter 'the intentional desire to create the indexical sign *out of which* meaning may be *revealed*' (2009: 35, original emphasis).

4. This is connected to Heidegger's notion of 'being-guilty', which is not about shame for doing wrong, but a more fundamental capacity to acknowledge one's own limitations, to take responsibility and become accountable for one's own life, experiences and actions (1962: 327).

Interlude 4

Posterity: Documenting Experiences

In 2013, Somerset House (London) hosted a retrospective exhibition of the work of elBulli entitled *elBulli: Ferran Adrià and the Art of Food* (in partnership with Estrella Damm, directed by Carme Cañadell). The exhibition included details of the development of elBulli, reflections on the work, documentation of the development of some of the dishes, parts of the elBulli catalogue and creative works responding to elBulli. Lingering throughout the exhibition was a question over the ability (or, rather, limitations of the attempt) to document an experience that was so reliant on taste, smell and touch – the inability to capture that embodied experience through images, text and models. This final interlude turns to questions around the attempt to document, capture or record an experience of the gustatory, to transform it into a lasting or durable form. It picks up on ideas of the retrospective reflection on the meal from the last chapter, considering strategies for how the meal is transformed into a durable object, which itself then becomes an object that supports the cultural capital acquired through dining at an elite restaurant (which forms part of the subsequent and last chapter).

Perhaps one of the most obvious ways in which an experience of the restaurant is both retained and shared is through language, attempting to give an account of the experience (descriptive, evocative and evaluative) to oneself or to others. The different modes of language might become entwined with one another, and it might be held just in memory or shared through writing or spoken language. But that language must inevitably fall short of the experience itself. As discussed in the 'Perception' chapter, language enters into experience itself, but the kind of conscious reflections at work in and around sensory experience, both producing and reflecting upon it, might figure in later accounts, but is in important ways different. It shifts tense, from present to past, and is distanced in time from the sensory encounter. As such, it becomes something different. We might remember thinking a particular thing during the experience, but that is not the same as the thinking itself becoming entangled with and in the experience.

In *The Practice of Everyday Life*, de Certeau et al. discuss the problems of attempting to find an appropriate language to give an account of the 'gestures' of 'culinary practices'. They write

How can one choose words that are true, natural, and vibrant enough to make felt the weight of the body, the joyfulness or weariness, the tenderness or irritation that takes hold of you in the face of this continually repeated task where the better the result (a stuffed chicken, a pear tart), the faster it is devoured, so that before the meal is completely over, one already has to think about the next.

(1998: 199)

They draw out how language falls short of giving a full account of the experience of preparing and eating a meal. The experience itself might carry so much, which might be unacknowledged or unknown, but it nevertheless weighs down on the palate and the body in the moment of eating, so that words must fail to encapsulate it fully. More generally, we might say that the sensory, sensual, emotional and embodied experience always resists a full incorporation into any system of representation.

There are various ways in which the experience of each of these restaurants can be documented by the diner. Photographs taken at the table, of the food and those with whom one is dining, are not uncommon, and often copies of the menu are provided by the restaurant for the diner to take away. The menus offer a map of the meal and act as an *aide memoire*. Alinea's menu, with its graphic notation of the meal, gives more details as an *aide memoire*, as well as offering more in terms of documentation of the experience. However, this is documentation produced in advance of the event and not by the one who experiences the meal. As such, it seems to work more as a kind of script than documentation, producing the experience of the event in advance by suggesting, framing and beginning to determine what the diner will notice.

There is a difference between documents of an event and an attempt to index that event through documentation. The menu has the potential to function as both, given that it is an object leftover that was part of the event and that it provides an indexical map of what took place and how the various elements relate to one another. Daniel Spoerri's 'trap paintings' equally seem to traverse this line between document and documentation, as they are formed of the detritus of a meal, but nevertheless begin to map out what took place, though there is an absence of temporal ordering, as the residue of the event is mapped onto a single surface. In 'Table Talk', David Leatherbarrow discusses Nicole La Rossa's *Three @ Kisso* (2001) and Ariane Sphikas' *Meal Time* (2001). Both attempt to document in visual form, on a canvas, the experience of a meal. Leatherbarrow describes them as 'A pair of drawings that explore [the] delicate choreography of a meal in time [...]' (2004: 217). In both cases, images of the meal are layered onto one another and, from left to right, they map out a certain progression through the meal. Images are foregrounded and backgrounded, some opaque and some dense. In both works, there is an attempt to articulate not only the materiality of the meal (the actual, physical components and materials that were encountered) but also to render on canvas a sense of what it was to move through it; what elements were more significant or bolder than others. The stability of the canvas is used to reflect the shifting nature of the meal. As Leatherbarrow argues in his analysis of the works, '[...] the notion one has of [the table's] permanence or fixity is replaced by a more accurate idea of change or shifting positions' (2004: 217).

The documentation of elBulli's practice in the exhibition makes use of various modes of documentation, including images, film, text, models and sounds. While the exhibition did include images of dishes from elBulli's catalogue, it went further and included contextual information and documentation of the development of ideas and presentations for dishes. The exhibition offered a wider notion of documentation – not just the dining event itself, but drawing attention to how the practices were developed and what the restaurant was attempting to do. In other words, it sought to place the practice in a number of contexts (the location of the restaurant, the chefs, the ideas and the practices), to furnish the documentation of the dishes themselves with a horizon of meaning and to historicise the work. As with any exhibition, the labels on individual objects and items provide some information and explication. However, a broader positioning of the visitor in relation to an individual object takes place through the ways the different parts of the exhibition speak to one another and contextualise each other within a broader period of, and approach to, practice. The exhibition made apparent how each dish itself indexed a period of experimentation, creativity and labour; those things subsumed within the object of the dish, but without which the dish could not have come into being. For instance, in one case was displayed a series of clay representations of component parts of elBulli's cuisine, annotated use of these to show the plating of a particular dish and then a photograph of the final dish itself. This kind of documentation of process and development draws attention to the intellectual and creative labour that is subsumed within a dish; those things that can go unnoticed as the diner engages with and enjoys the various pleasures of eating but nevertheless are important in documenting the processes of production of the dining event.

In these objects, what is inevitably omitted or excluded are the gustatory, olfactory and haptic elements of the encounter with the food object – those things that are perhaps most integral to the work of the restaurant. An image might solicit a particular kind of imaginary, an affect by virtue of imagination and association, but this is not the same as the material, sensory encounter. However, given that documentation is an attempt to evidence and index a live event, there must be a transformation that takes place, which marks it as separate from, and not the same as, the live(d) experience. The food itself cannot become an archival material, because like the body, it too is live and subject to decay. The ephemerality of the food object is like the ephemerality of performance and so, following Peggy Phelan (in *Unmarked*) becomes something other than itself in documentation. For the documentation to be congruous, but not synonymous, with the live(d) experience, it should perhaps draw on implied sensory experience but not seek to emulate or directly mediate the live(d).

In Adair Rounthwaite's article, 'From This Body to Yours: Porn, Affect, and Performance Art Documentation', she draws a comparison between documentation and pornography. She writes that pornography 'is a form of performance documentation that is designed to create a new performance – of a sexual sensation, and often masturbation, accompanied by orgasm – in the viewer' (2011: 63). She continues that, as documentation of a live performance, pornography 'not only records past performance but also projects forward a future performance in the form of the new bodily pleasure it will generate' (2011: 64). Rounthwaite proposes a model for performance documentation that mirrors pornography – something that records or preserves the live event but transforms it into something anticipatory, which leaves space for, or indeed solicits, a new affective experience in the act of encountering the documentation. She calls this 'masturbatory spectatorship' (2011: 78). This kind of documentation, where the solicitation of an experience is embedded in the documentation itself, relies on the imaginative engagement of the spectator. However, as has been discussed earlier in the book, a large part of our sensory experience operates at the level of the imaginary – anticipation producing experience, conscious reflection directing and framing one's attention, past experience directing both an understanding and appreciation of the sensory input. As such, documentation that solicits this kind of imagined sensation is closer to the live(d) encounter than it might first appear. There is an embodied and experiential dimension to documentation, which is implied and produced through imagination and a referential relationship, not just between images and the live event, but between images and imagined or remembered live experience.

In some ways, this was potentially at work in the elBulli exhibition. One of the first objects on display when entering the exhibition was a model of a box of chocolates served at the end of the meal at elBulli (Figure 5). The exhibit contained realistic models of the selection of chocolates and, as it was contained within a glass display case that denied the viewer the opportunity to touch or smell the model, became all the more 'realistic'. It did not include the sensory information of touch, smell and taste that would have confirmed it as a model rather than the 'real thing'. As such, the model can become as enticing as the 'real' version it was emulating, whetting the appetite and soliciting the same kinds of desire as if it were real chocolate served at elBulli. The object encouraged the same kind of imaginative and anticipatory gaze that would have been at work when the box was served in the restaurant (though with the obvious caveat that one's curiosity and appetite could not be satiated in the gallery).

In another exhibit, a table was set up onto which was projected video footage of a meal being served and eaten, from a bird's eye view perspective, where visitors were invited to sit at the table in the position of the diner. The image played out on the table showed dishes being placed down, arms extending from the edge of the screen in front of the exhibition visitor, picking up cutlery and consuming the meal. Here, the visitor is positioned in a virtual reality experience of dining at elBulli, with the meal presented and eaten as a series of moving images and, perhaps even more so than the model chocolate box, encouraging the visitors to imagine themselves as diners. Both of these enacted the same logic as what is often called 'Food Porn': hidden behind glass or a screen, the manipulated object solicits a desiring and hungry gaze, which can never be satisfied, which in turn allows for its work to continue. The image is not transformed into a live encounter; it relies on imaginative work on the part of the viewer and, as such, can become an image of pure desire, untroubled by the object's inability ever to fully encapsulate that which the individual wants.

FIGURE 5: 'Chocolate Box' (2009), elBulli archive. Photo by Francesc Guillamet.

In Matthew Reason's *Documentation, Disappearance and the Representation of Live Performance*, he proposes a synaesthetic approach to writing around performance as a mode of documentation. He argues that

> synaesthetic comparisons provide a broader and more multidimensional sense 'picture' of the event being described, establishing a rich and full impression of the live performance. Synaesthesia offers the opportunity for the extension of sensual perception and the 'thickening' of the reader's descriptive experience. These values – multidimensional, richer, fuller – are ones associated with, defined by and defining liveness. Synaesthetic writing seeks to affirm perception of the presence of human performers and audiences at the performance, marking it out as an event experienced live – and therefore involving all the senses.
>
> (2006: 228)

While Reason's proposal is for a mode of writing, it might also suggest a kind of experientially grounded performance documentation, through which an experience is transformed by an artist-documenter into another sensory form. In this, an experience is both documented and reflected upon, as well as mirroring the multisensory modes of perception that are always already at work in experience.

Documentation of this kind was included in the elBulli exhibition in the form of Bruno Mantovani's symphony, *Le Livre des Illusions (Homage à Ferran Adrià)* (2009). Mantovani's symphony was based on his experience of dining at elBulli in 2007 and contains 35 movements, which map on to the 35-course tasting menu. The symphony '[...] represents a musical transcription of the textures, flavours, impressions and sensations that the composer experienced when tasting the menu at elBulli' (Serrano and Pinto 2013). The exhibition included a recording of Mantovani's symphony alongside an outline of the menu it sought to emulate, so the visitor could listen and allow the music to evoke elements of the meal.[1] As a creative form of documentation, the symphony attempted to transpose the gustatory, olfactory, haptic and emotional sensations of Mantovani's dining experience into a musical form. By so doing, it documented the experience in a way that continues that openness to an imaginative engagement of the part of those who encounter the documentation. It indexes the event, but in an oblique way that foregrounds the appeal to imagination, emotional and sensation rather than the logic of the photographed image, which appeals to a distanced kind of knowing.

The problems of documentation of a sensory experience are not just esoteric; they have a part to play in the transformation of an event into cultural capital, into a commodity that can be incorporated into an economy of experiences. The documentation, evidencing and sharing of an event are integral to the functioning of an economy of selling and paying to participate in experiences as they offer material support for the cultural capital potentially derived from those experiences. As documentation inevitably omits or cannot fully incorporate the sensory experiences of the body, it raises two key ideas in relation to the 'experience economy'. First, the documentation, which might circulate more easily than a live experience, is always deficient, and so there is encouragement to pay to participate in the live event. Second, the documentation provides material evidence and reminders of participation, thus furnishing the diner with objects that allow the experience to be shared and for the ephemeral cultural capital to be rendered as a material artefact. The following chapter turns to the political discourses surrounding the food event and, in considering the restaurants' position within an economy of experiences, place this kind of material documentation within an economic frame.

NOTE

1. In *Distinction*, Bourdieu writes that 'As mystics speak divine love in the language of human love, so the least inadequate evocations of musical pleasure are those which can replicate the peculiar forms of an experience as deeply rooted in the body and in primitive bodily experiences as the tastes of food' (2010: 73). In this way, Mantovani's symphony can be thought not just as an expression of the meal but also vice versa: for those who ate at elBulli, the meal could be understood as an appropriate means of explicating and deciphering the music, a way of rendering the abstract forms, motifs and ideas of the music in a concrete and experiential way.

5

Payoff: Political and Economic Frames of Experience

The restaurants under consideration in this book all sit within 'high-end' cuisine. This sphere of activity is not of the order of quotidian domestic eating nor the realm of high-street restaurants. They do, though, continue some of the political food discourses that are more generally encountered in terms of food production and consumption, as well as contributing to the hegemonic production and dissemination of those discourses. This final chapter turns to questions of the politics and economics of the restaurant, considering the ways in which they work, and broader political and ideological contexts within which the work operates and how it manifests certain political, social and economic relations. It is not an investigation of the labour of the restaurant but rather how that work enters into a context of political exchanges, particularly considering the so-called economy of experiences, with its invocations of desire, pleasure and enjoyment.

Political and economic discourses frame, guide and contribute to producing the experience of the restaurant. This chapter examines three different areas of contemporary (Western) food politics, which can be, and indeed are, found in restaurants and food production generally but are heightened in the work of the Michelin-starred experimental restaurant. The chapter begins with an examination of the structural relationship between enjoyment and excess. The restaurants' focus on pleasure and enjoyment is a core part of the experience and a major element of what is sold to the diner. This section considers how that pleasure is constituted as an excess or luxury, beyond what, in eating, might be deemed 'necessary'. The second section turns to the politics of seasonality and locality in dining – those dominant political frames for apparently 'ethical' eating. This section examines how discourses of the seasonal and local are co-opted as part of the fine dining experience – performed in and through the meal as a means of intensifying pleasure, assuaging guilt and sustaining an ideological position. The final section of the chapter addresses directly how the restaurants operate as part of an economy of experiences, commodifying live experience and selling it as a form of cultural capital. In each case, these political and economic discourses and frames are understood not only as circulating around the experience but also as a force that permeates the experience itself, inflecting the attitude of the diner and what they experience in the tasting menu and the restaurant.

Enjoyment and Excess

In *The Sublime Object of Ideology*, Žižek writes of enjoyment,

> It is this paradox which defines surplus-enjoyment: it is not a surplus which simply attaches itself to some 'normal', fundamental enjoyment, because *enjoyment as such emerges only in this surplus*, because it is constitutively an 'excess'. If we subtract the surplus we lose enjoyment itself [...].
>
> (Žižek 2008: 54, original emphasis)

Žižek theorises that enjoyment itself always already operates at a level of excess, as a surplus beyond necessity. Enjoyment proper is not in 'use-value' but rather in an excess or surplus. While we might say, superficially, that eating is necessary for the continuation of the body, it is difficult to articulate what precisely constitutes necessity in terms of eating. In Carol J. Adams' *The Sexual Politics of Meat*, she charts one line of the historical contingency of notions of necessity, observing that meat was reserved for those with power, while carbohydrates (bread, potatoes) were the staple of labourers' cuisine (2015: 4). She also acknowledges a gendering in the ideas of food and what is considered beneficial, noting that 'meat is a masculine food and meat eating a male activity', while women, in patriarchal culture, are more likely to eat fruits, vegetables and grains (2015: 4). What is considered *necessary* for the continued life and existence of the body, and beneficial for particular bodies, is clearly not fixed and static. It is dependent on the activities of the body and the cultural constructions of the body's position and needs. It is a moveable feast. Any notion of 'necessity' around eating harbours within itself an attitude towards the body – what the body should be capable of doing, how long it should last and what is considered desirable or healthy for the body.

In this contingency of food needs, Ferran Adrià's hierarchy of levels of pleasure in dining (of the satiation of hunger, sensory pleasure, emotional pleasure and intellectual pleasure [Adrià et al. 2008: 318]) is complicated. This pyramidical structure postulates that the satiation of hunger, what we might intuitively call the necessary condition of food and eating, is nevertheless a form of pleasure or enjoyment. Indeed, the alleviation of hunger is often experienced as pleasurable. But for Žižek, for this to operate as an enjoyment, it must structurally be a surplus. The 'surplus' at work in the enjoyment of the satiation of hunger is a temporal and embodied one – it allows the body to continue. But for many people hunger itself is not immediately a threat to existence. Hunger is also psychosomatic: it is grounded in expectations (of when we should eat, whereby a mealtime creates hunger rather than vice versa); it is affected by our emotional state and our activities (we can be distracted from hunger); and its satiation is equally grounded in past experiences and expectations (the same amount of food on a smaller plate can make us feel fuller). As such, the alleviation of hunger is not a simple pleasure and cannot be understood merely in terms of eating enough.

Levels of necessity and excess are always produced, the result of a particular cultural-ideological position, which produces ideas of who needs what. Of course, this is not to say that any particular culture is static in terms of its construction of necessity and excess but rather that there are a constellation of positions that broadly define them and, in so doing, define individual bodies, their social-political roles and functions and their economic position. A clear example can be drawn from Carol J. Adams' *The Sexual Politics of Meat*. She writes of 'the white Western world's enactment of racism' in relation to meat-eating: that meat is a necessity for White people and only available to all if it is in plentiful supply (2015: 8). Adams continues that 'The hierarchy of meat protein reinforces a hierarchy of race, class, and sex' (2015: 8). The connection between meat consumption and White masculinity is troubled by Adams, as she argues that it is not a necessity but a political choice. The myth of the White male body requiring protein and therefore to be given privileged access to meat reinforces the White male body as the pinnacle of the food chain. Cultural food practices enact, as well as reiterate and reinforce, cultural hierarchies and positions. Perhaps even more dangerously, they have the potential to 'naturalise' those hierarchies by directly suggesting that they are grounded in the 'truth' of biological differences.

Adrià's hierarchy of pleasures mirrors Marvin Harris' pyramidical model of food in human and social life, where the base of the pyramid concerns the environment and the acquisition of food and sustenance, the middle concerns the socialisation of food in terms of socio-political structures such as family and nationality and the apex concerns food's role in 'superstructural' discourses, such as art and religion (in Jones 2007: 4). This hierarchy naturalises the distinctions between food as sustenance and food as participating in the social, religious or artistic sphere, which invokes a class distinction between those who eat for apparent necessity and those who are able to eat for emotional or intellectual pleasure. Indeed, in *Distinction*, Bourdieu argues that the apparent distance from 'economic necessity' is a precondition for the cultivation of cultural ideals of an 'aesthetic disposition' (2010: 46). The naturalisation of the hierarchy of needs and pleasures (in Harris and Adrià, respectively) presupposes a distinction that is, in fact, constructed, where the 'aesthetic disposition' is not a natural distance from necessity but rather institutes a distance from necessity. To take an aesthetic or pleasurable approach to food is to demonstrate that one does not need to eat but rather chooses (what) to eat. It is an assertion and performance of a class position.

Notions of luxury, excess and enjoyment are culturally produced and, therefore, subject to change over time and between cultures. We can discover both continuity and disparity in constructions of luxury in 'Beef Royal (1723)', a dish served at The Fat Duck in 2007. The dish was based on a historical recipe from *Court Cookery: or, the Compleat English Cook*, a document of the dish served at the coronation feast of James II in 1685. The original dish, as the name suggests, was an opulent and luxurious one, containing 'the best of beef', expensive spices (cloves, mace), truffles and oysters. Blumenthal's re-creation of this dish attempted to 'capture something of the spirit in which the dish was conceived – its magnificent extravagance – and bring that to a new audience' (Blumenthal 2009: 385). Blumenthal's version was split into three courses: the first, fried sweetbreads and oysters with a truffled emulsion; the second, braised beef short ribs with ox tongue, a beef sauce, onions and turnips; and the third, beef crackers with mushroom ketchup, bone marrow and onion gel (Blumenthal 2009: 390–97). While a number of the component parts are the same as the original dish, there are discrepancies in where the luxurious nature of the dish is to be found. For the seventeenth-century diner, the spices would have been expensive and the oysters a common food of the working classes. For the twenty-first-century diner, the oyster has become a luxury and the spices are readily available and not expensive. Truffles remain a luxury across the time, as do prime cuts of meat (though the latter has, of course, become more accessible in Britain). Some of these changes stem from changes in the processes of production and relative ease of global food transportation, which manifest themselves at the level of individual tastes for luxury. Access to ingredients and repeated exposure contribute to our experience of quotidian taste; greater access and eating lead to familiarity and the formation of tastes. What is perhaps more interesting in this case is the use of offal, which is currently a cheap meat source and yet is increasingly gracing the menus of high-end cuisine. Relatively recently, offal has decreased in popularity, in favour of more expensive cuts of meat, and, as such, its rarity in everyday cuisine has led to a resurgence of its use in fine dining. The luxury of offal, and this dish specifically, is not only grounded in the economics of food production but also in cultural trends. The surplus enjoyment of this dish, its luxury, is found in the rarity of its ingredients, some of which are costly, but others are rare in terms of everyday dining. There is a kind of perverse reversal at work in the dish: two ingredients once closer to notions of necessity for survival (offal and oysters), connected to the lower classes, have been transformed into the luxurious, the excessive and, therefore, potentially pleasurable.

In a similar way, Noma has explored this cultural production of luxury. In 'Trash Cooking of Fish Scales and Livers' (in Redzepi 2013: 56–57), cod livers are brined, spiced, smoked and frozen, served with fish scales fried in clarified butter and served on a frozen plate with a broth and rapeseed oil. The name of the dish acknowledges that it is made with leftovers, offcuts, those things usually discarded. There are two political narratives operating simultaneously in this dish. First, the dish engages with an ecological agenda of avoiding waste, making use of ingredients that would ordinarily be thrown away and considered unworthy of use. The second narrative is one that transforms 'trash' into something luxurious, by virtue of its inclusion in the repertoire of an expensive and elite restaurant. While the overall agenda and ethos of the restaurant would seem to foreground the first of these narratives, given the focus on the environment and extolling the virtues of the local, Nordic ingredients, the second is nevertheless at work. And as with Blumenthal's 'Beef Royal (1723)', there is an inversion whereby the food that is usually discarded or reserved only for the poorest is transformed into luxury and excess. The pleasures of both of these dishes seem to reside in not only the craft of their preparation or the luxurious, fine dining context within which they are served but also the superficial undermining of that excess. By using 'traditionally' discarded or working-class ingredients, the restaurants appropriate a 'lower class' gastronomy and, of course, charge a not inconsiderable price for it. Because of the context of these restaurants as fine dining, there is no escape from their luxurious and elitist framing, and the ecological credentials of the work (avoiding wastefulness) are not sufficient to destabilise the excess. While the use of ingredients or presentations of a 'working class' cuisine might superficially suggest a universal collectivism (where everyone eats the same), those who eat have to pay for the privilege.

Within the arts, we find a mirror of Noma's 'Trash Cooking', but framed in a different way. Piero Manzoni's *Artist's Shit* (1961) comprised 90 tins of his own excrement, numbered and signed by the artist and sold at the same rate as the day's price of gold (Berghaus 2005: 95). While the work does raise questions about edibility, what is perhaps more prominent is the question of value. The excremental and the discarded are transformed into a commodity by virtue of the signature of the artist and its framing as a work worthy of attention and purchasing. In the same way, Noma's 'Trash Cooking' takes the discarded and transforms it not only through the processes of production but also in the context of the restaurant as a legitimising force. The operations of the value of the work are not to be found in its nutrition or deliciousness or in its sensory pleasure but rather in its signalling of a particular attitude or position, purchasing in order to show an appreciation of art that takes up a particular political position. For Manzoni, it is a critique of the commodification of art and the fetishisation of the artist; for Redzepi, it is a critique of wastefulness. In both cases, the irony of the works is apparent; that they both operate within, and continue, the very context they seek to critique.

The seeming contradiction of hedonist culture begins to come to the fore with these examples: that the enjoyment of the meal is solicited in relation to the cultural politics of prohibition and sensitivity. The enjoyment is always in some way an excess because it is derived from the surplus (surplus itself produces enjoyment and pleasure). As such, for hedonism as a cultural ethos to take hold, it requires an officially sanctioned austerity; an austere and ascetic status quo that nevertheless allows for, even unofficially solicits, pleasure, enjoyment and excess. In *The Five Senses*, Michel Serres writes of this apparent contradiction, stating that 'No culture every achieved the degree of asceticism that our so-called consumer society, our banquet, imposes on us today' (2016: 234). Of course, in the political context of contemporary Western Europe, 'austerity' is not merely a definition of strict discipline but encapsulates a social-economic agenda. Contained within this is an attitude towards the body and necessity – a cultural construction of the ascetic subject, for whom (sensory) pleasure is an indulgence and therefore should only be available to those who can pay for it themselves. This austerity is devoid of sensory pleasures and richness. Indeed, it constitutes the senses themselves as a structural excess, with the body as something that merely subsists. Food is reduced to data around the continuation of the body. Yet this occurs alongside the emergence of the economy of experiences that is an economy grounded in pleasures, 'excesses' and sensory experiences, with the invocation to experience and enjoy as a cultural duty.

To understand this supposed contradiction, in *Event*, Žižek discusses the nature of prohibition in relation to pleasure, using the analogy of a father and son. He writes,

> While prohibiting his son's escapades, the father not only discreetly ignores and tolerates them, but even solicits them. It is in this sense that Father as the agent of prohibition/law sustains desires/pleasures: there is no direct access to enjoyment since its very space is opened up by the blanks of the Father's controlling gaze.
>
> (2014a: 127–28)

For Žižek, pleasure is not just an excess or surplus but arises as a tension between the official sanctioning of behaviour (for him, the image of the Father as representative of patriarchal law), the 'blind spots' of the controlling gaze and those things that, in the unwritten but nevertheless practiced law, are solicited even though they might run counter to the officially sanctioned.[1] Indeed, even in 'sanctioning' there is a doubling, in its double meaning of both allowing and punishing. Prohibition has a positive and productive function – not merely denying but making space for the solicitation of pleasure and enjoyment as a surplus or even a violation of the law or cultural status quo. This manifests itself in the restaurant as a tension between, on the one hand, capitalist hedonism, which posits the seeking of pleasure and enjoyment as the primary goal of the neoliberal subject (the injunction to choose what you want, though within the market place), and, on the other hand, ideals of beauty and the desirable body, which is thin, lean or toned and is the result of an ascetic lifestyle. Pleasure is both solicited and denounced. The pleasure of the experience of dining is at least intensified, if not created, in the oscillation between these two positions: guilt intensifying enjoyment.

The desire for, and pleasure in, tasting experiences brings together both the sensory-experiential and the social. We take pleasure not only in the sensory and experiential qualities of eating but also in the demonstration of our tastes as social citizens. In part, those things we eat and demonstrate that we eat (the cultural capital of announcing how we partake in particular experiences) form a means of presenting ourselves and demonstrating our involvement in the socio-political system as good citizens, who desire and pay for novel experiences. In Gallegos and McHoul's 'It's not about good taste. It's about tastes good', they suggest three distinctions of taste: '1. Taste as a physiological fact', '2. Taste as subjective judgement' and '3. Taste as public judgement' (2006: 173). But these are not separate spheres of activity or judgement; they are inherently interconnected. Those things that 'taste good' are influenced, framed and even produced by the cultural realm(s) of 'good taste', and, vice versa, good taste can be produced, iterated and reiterated through what is experienced as tasting good. Pleasure and desire in eating straddle these different forms or modes of taste and begin to collapse the distinctions between them. They work in conjunction with one another to produce the pleasures of eating.

In 2006, The Fat Duck introduced a new dish titled 'Chocolate Wine, Millionaire Shortbread'. Blumenthal describes the genesis of the idea as coming from hearing of 'chocolate wine' at Hampton Court: 'Combining two of the guiltiest pleasures, the biggest indulgences, in one dish, Chocolate Wine seemed beyond luxury, the kind of thing you read about in old books, served to some absurdly wealth potentate perhaps, reclining on silken pillows' (2009: 275). Served as chocolate-infused Maury or Banyuls wine with a gold-topped salted caramel millionaire's shortbread, the dish brings together different notions of luxurious tastes to mutually reinforce one another. The luxury associated with wine and chocolate, as indulgent forms of consumption or 'guilty pleasures' as Blumenthal has it, is combined, using the rich qualities of the foods themselves to reinforce their luxurious cultural status and vice versa. The three forms of taste outlined by Gallegos and McHoul are inseparable, precisely because what we think of as the physiological qualities of eating chocolate or drinking wine cannot be split apart from their cultural construction as luxurious items (in part a result of various cultural histories and narratives, in part a result of the labour of their production).

A similar idea is at work in Noma's 'Egg Cured in Fermented Beef'. While this dish does not evoke the same kind of cultures of luxury as chocolate and wine, it plays with the blurred distinctions between categories of taste. Served as a warm egg yolk with meaty qualities from being cooked in a fermented beef stock, encircled with rounds of slightly crunchy potatoes and surrounded with a nasturtium sauce with rose oil, the dish was described as 'rich' when presented by the waiters. That framing, as a 'rich dish', begins to lead the diner to acknowledge the deep complexity of the flavour and to encounter the dish as a form of luxury – by implication, something for the wealthy or for a refined palate to appreciate. The slippage in 'richness' as a description moves between the two modes of taste: good taste and tastes good.

Blumenthal's 'Chocolate Wine' forces together two luxurious items into a single dish, bringing together the various social and sensory luxuries of both its constituent parts (chocolate, wine) and, by so doing, attempting to double the sense of luxury and its associated pleasure through their combination. However, while this was the aim, the name itself does not necessarily designate luxury; it has the potential to disrupt (or at least interrupt) usual luxurious tastes through the unusual combination. In Novero's *Antidiets of the Avant-Garde*, she writes of the Dadaists that their 'antidiets' 'through a *performative* textual repetition of apparently nonsensical forms of consumption, based in disgust and indigestibility, a repetition that is always excessive, *construct* bourgeois taste and its reproducibility as indigestible and insufferable' (2010: x, original emphasis). In much the same way, Blumenthal's 'Chocolate Wine' begins to engage with notions of high-end taste. Through the combination of two luxurious items, the dish has the potential to move explicitly into a realm of excess and to undo itself and the tastes to which it is attempting to appeal – to destabilise those tastes through its sheer excessiveness. Enacting a kind of reversal of the Dadaists' dwelling in disgust, Blumenthal dwells instead in notions of luxury, which can become 'too much'.[2]

A part of this disruption to luxurious tastes is found in the disjunction between the imagined combination of the two constituent luxurious and pleasurable items and their actual articulation or presenting as a live object. The experience of the dish itself can only fall short of the imagined combination as it remains a mixture of chocolate and wine rather than a 'true' synthesis of the two parts. The imaginary or image of the dish, suggested by its title, remains an elusive fiction – partly because the dish *merely* allows the two parts to sit side by side and partly because of the personal histories, memories and associations of their luxury, which are individual and cannot be incorporated into the object. The dish is included in Blumenthal's *The Fat Duck Cookbook* and the fixed image, the photograph in the book, devoid of the haptic, gustatory and olfactory experience, makes greater space for an imagined experience – for the sensory gaps in the encounter to be filled in by the imagination. It becomes a fixed fantasy image of pleasure and luxury, a form of 'food porn' (to use the colloquial expression), endlessly reproducible, not disappointing, dwelling always in anticipation that cannot be satiated.

This idea of the fixed image of food as a reproducible, pleasurable commodity is both explored and problematised by Klaus Pichler's photographic series *One Third (Cherries; Octopus; Cheese)* (2011–12). Included in these four photographs, rotting and mouldy cherries and strawberries are presented in elegant and intricately decorated bronze and silver bowls against a deep black background. Within the images, the luxurious is reconfigured and transformed into the disgusting. While Pichler's aim was to engage with issues of global food waste (see Howells and Hayman 2014: 164), the works engage with a context of 'food porn' and unsettle the fixed image – no longer one that strives for perfection and to tease and titillate the imagination, the photographs fix in place rot, decay and disgust. The series troubles the circulation of beautiful (and ultimately unattainable) images and fantasies of dining experiences and instead offers a comment on the wastefulness and disgust that must surround or underpin privileged tastes of luxury. Unlike Noma's 'Trash Cooking', which transforms leftovers into something that can be enjoyed and sold, Pichler allows the leftovers to become fixed *as* leftovers (though, like both Noma and Manzoni, ironically transformed into something 'productive' in their status as art object).

Enjoyment is not deployed in the restaurants as a 'pure' experience. It always emerges in tension, or in a differential relationship, with asceticism, guilt and disgust. The food at elBulli, The Fat Duck, Noma and Alinea is not designed merely for the continuation of the body as a necessary condition of continued bodily existence; it is eating for pleasure. Pleasure always has the potential to fragment, to break apart, to be interrupted and to provoke questions around the nature of pleasure itself. Pleasure is experienced in a way that is somewhat anxious – navigating the distinctions between pleasure and asceticism or guilt. The cost of the meals plays a considerable role in this: the expense means that for the meal to be 'worth the cost', the diner needs to continually be in a state of ecstatic pleasure (which itself is an exhausting experience). There is a latent anxiety in the pressure to enjoy, which threatens to disrupt the very enjoyment of the meal – though it can also have a productive force. The Fat Duck's famous 'Snail Porridge' (braised snails on a bright green porridge) requires that the diner moves through the potential disgust of being confronted with snails on a surface reminiscent of grass, a reminder of the live snail, in order to enjoy the rich and delicious combination of snails, parsley, duck, garlic, walnut and fennel. Luxurious pleasure can give way to disgust, but disgust can also lead to luxurious pleasure.

Politics of the Seasonal and the Local

In Julian Baggini's *Virtues of the Table*, he articulates a contemporary food politics in theological language as '[...] the holy trinity of seasonal, organic and local'

(2014: 29). This has become the mantra of contemporary cuisine, not merely within fine dining but across food cultures in the Western world. It proposes an ethical standard of food production and consumption, which implicates ecological, class-based, political and economic concerns. While distinctly 'middle class' in its apparent concerns, it is a ubiquitous mantra and one that is found in high-end and high street restaurants, supermarkets, local stores and farmers' markets. It operates as a kind of virtue signalling in food production – so taken for granted that the use of any one of the terms seems to position the food product as both higher quality and ethically sound. Yet, it is a highly problematic triad, in part because of its operation as a shorthand for ethical consumption, which leaves it open to manipulative usage for promoting and selling food products. Attach any of the three monikers (seasonal, local, organic) and a product can be increased in price, with the reason displaced from increasing profits to an apparent implication of greater labour in production.

In *The Practice of Everyday Life*, de Certeau et al. discuss the drastic ways in which food production has changed in a relatively short period. They write that the developments in the speed and efficiency of transportation have radically altered the production and distribution of food, including through the increase of global trade in food and the ways in which food can be processed and preserved (1998: 172). This has led to greater availability, variety and longevity of food (particularly in the West). This globalised and industrialised production process forms the background to contemporary food politics. The concern with seasonal, local and organic is one that is *of* the contemporary world, rather than the moments in history when hunger, starvation and scarcity of resources were a pressing and often lethal concern, because it emerges at a moment of choice. Where there is no choice over consumption, this ethics is not just obsolete but unthinkable. In elBulli's 'philosophy' document, points five, six and seven deal with their 'philosophy on sourcing and purchasing ingredients'. The document articulates 'respect for the environment', that 'local produce is always the first choice' and that 'every ingredient should be judged on its gastronomic merits, rather than on its price [...]' (Adrià et al. 2008: 72.3). The very ability to make choices over ingredients grounded in anything other than strict availability articulates a kind of privilege. Whereas once it was a marker of luxury and privilege to be able to eat beyond the seasonal and local, there has been an ironic and troubling inversion. The ability to eat seasonally and locally is no longer a sign of being tied to the necessary conditions of life in an environment but instead is a sign of a level of privilege. This is compounded by the costs of seasonal, local and organic produce, which remove them from the material means of those who cannot afford them. The *desire* for seasonal, local and organic foods only emerges after it has ceased to operate as an everyday and necessary mode of living.

The framing of a particular food product as seasonal, local or organic is not an essential property of the product itself. Instead, it is enacted through a series of performances: the performances of the labour of production (where it is produced, how and by whom), the performances of food presentation (how explicitly the presentation speaks of the connection between the food and the 'land') and the performances of consumption (the articulation of noticing particular qualities, to draw attention to the *terroir* or taste of the land, to praise oneself for eating 'ethically'). As Leda Cooks writes in her article 'You Are What You (Don't) Eat', 'The connection of food to the land has always been part of human discourse and performance, but, as the bourgeois emphasis on taste gained cultural value, "refined" food became the mark of one's status in society' (2009: 103). She continues that '[...] to disconnect one's (high) culture from association with land and labor remained consistent throughout the rise of industrial class society until more recent times' (2009: 103). While the seasonal, local and organic might offer a (re)connection between bodies and land, countering the alienation instituted through the process of industrialisation, it does so at a cost. The cost is to the consumer who purchases that connection, separate from the costs of time, energy and labour of production, which remains elsewhere, undertaken by others.

In the foregrounding of seasonality and locality in the high-end restaurants, what is on sale is a marketised experience of a connection to 'nature'. It is not a 'genuine' connection, the process of producing one's own food, but rather a quick solution to capitalist alienation remedied through an act of expensive purchasing. This is more overt at elBulli and Noma than Alinea and The Fat Duck, though the latter restaurants engage in it. elBulli and Noma both foreground and reinforce a particular kind of cultural narrative that connects the food to the land. The discourses of seasonality and locality that operate through the work of these restaurants are sound enough in principle (to connect the final dish with the land or sea from which it comes), though remain problematic because it is never a *full* account of the production of the food. There is a romantic idealising that takes place, where the food performs an element of the rustic and rural while hiding the labour and processes of its production.

elBulli's 2007 dish, 'Burnt Earth' (Dish Number 1427 in Adrià et al. 2014c: 330–32), is a mixture of different kinds and forms of chocolate arranged to look like soil (Figure 6). Its title suggests an ecological agenda: bringing together the pleasures of elBulli's cuisine with a stark reminder of the consequences of ecological exploitation. The lingering irony of the dish is that it pretends to be 'of the land', performing a connection between food and its production, while hiding the excessive processes of its production (melting, blending, cooking, siphoning, freeze-drying, piping, bathing in ice, draining, refrigeration) in service of chocolate appearing as land. The presentation of the dish reinforces the idea of the 'natural': connecting food to the land (although, quite clearly, not the land in which the cocoa bean would have been grown) and the chef attempting to hide – to present the food in a 'natural' form, as though the chef merely *represents* an environmental ecology rather than being part of that ecology. The dish requires a lot of preparatory processes and transformations of the raw ingredients. It is not a simple presentation of the natural produce that allows its 'natural gene' (the elBulli term) to emerge. It makes use of potentially environmentally damaging processes (the use of gas in the siphon, heavy use of refrigeration, a number of electric technologies) to make a statement about ecological disaster (the name: Burnt Earth) and then wraps the whole experience up as part of a pleasurable dining experience, with guilt mitigated by the apparent environmental message. 'Nature' or 'the land' is constructed in a particular way, performing an idealised construction of the 'natural world' while masking the potentially less appetising aspects of the ecological effects of its production.

FIGURE 6: 'Burnt Earth' (2007), elBulli archive. Photo by Francesc Guillamet.

In a similar presentational mode, there was a dish served in KILN's performance *Eat Your Heart Out* (2009–11) that explored ecological catastrophe. *Eat Your Heart Out* was an immersive 'Edible Performance', made in collaboration with the food artists Blanch & Shock. In the performance, the audience were invited into a post-apocalyptic world to take part in a celebratory feast made in the remnants of a kitchen. One of the dishes served in the performance was 'Burnt Soil', which included an edible flower served in a jar on soil made from chocolate and chilli, scented with alderwood smoke. This dish did not perform that same kind of idyllic connection between food and land as 'Burnt Earth'. Instead, the dish itself and the post-apocalyptic frame of the performance world positioned this dish as something wrenched from the land – a desperate attempt to find food. It performed a desperate attempt to find food in a world that was scorched by an unknown disaster. Where 'Burnt Earth' performed an idealised connection between food and the land, covering over the processes of its production, the performance frame of *Eat Your Heart Out* (a world where food had to be sought and discovered) positioned 'Burnt Soil' as open to two readings: either as the last remnants of the edible (soil and a flower) or as a hopeful image of a direct reconnection between land, food and consumption. In either case, the dish unearthed and drew attention to a process of production (and the implied fictional labour involved) rather than covering over that labour for the sake of a pleasant experience.

The externalising narrative of a connection to the land functions to allay the fears and the guilt of consumer capitalist systems of production and alienation. The 'superiority' of the seasonal and the local is found, in a circular fashion, in the construction of seasonal and local as ethically sound, mitigating the potentially dubious aspects of systems of consumption. It intensifies the experience of enjoyment as it simultaneously contains and then rectifies the guilt that might accompany consumption.[3] It could equally be said to be at work in the use of leftovers and waste, where the use of leftovers and things usually wasted enacts another narrative of 'respect for the environment', irrelevant of the broader systems within which that production and consumption operate. The narrative of respect for the environment and not wasting potential food sources from a local supplier institutes another ethical quandary: a lack of respect for the artisanal skill of the farmer and their produce. The labour of the farmer can be ignored – as though the farmer's work is irrelevant because 'bountiful nature' will provide.

Again, ideas of the ethical impact on the experience in the restaurant. Charles Spence has observed that 'labeling food as organic can give rise to increased activity in the ventral striatum, a part of the brain that is involved in controlling our motivation to acquire and eat food' (2018a: 65). This labelling can work either as a textual label or through the performance of a dish, when it suggests a connection to the land or to nature. The idea of ethical consumption in the seasonal, local and organic enters into a feedback loop, in experience, of pleasure: enjoyment in the seasonal, local and organic reiterates that these are qualities and traits to be desired, which in turn heightens the desire for and enjoyment in their consumption. There is an ethos always already at work in taste (as both an experiential and a figurative notion of taste), where the ethical and political frames play a role in 'good taste' and 'tastes good'.

The idea of the superiority of the 'local' is dubious. It certainly can counter the environmental impact of global food transportation. But to assert its superiority in terms of quality only works if one assumes that our tastes are ultimately determined by our place of consumption (which itself is highly problematic given the global food trade). In *Cross-Cultural Consumption*, David Howes uses Coca-Cola as emblematic of 'global homogenization' of tastes and the eradication of regional differences in food cultures (1996: 3–4). While he goes on to problematise the easy dissemination of an ideological system through the exporting of its goods, with the goods disseminating the political system from which and through which they have been produced, nevertheless he acknowledges that this is the 'contemporary thinking about the cultural effects of the migration of food within the world market system' (1996: 3). The attachment to local produce, cuisines and tastes, then, seems to be a form of resistance to globalisation – food politics that revel in regional differences. But taking this logic too far and assuming that one is absolutely a product of a particular locality (in both tastes and attitudes) begins to naturalise distinctions between communities – to suggest 'you are what you eat' and that you are, in identity and essence, irrevocably localised. As a key coordinate between body and land, food and its localisation can create a kind of essentialism: my body, my tastes and my habits a product of, and forever connected with, this land, this space and this region. When local produce is considered superior, this reiterates not just distinctions between groups but also value judgements – one community over another. Food has the potential, therefore, to essentialise, naturalise and internalise a particular political ideal or ideology, asserting that 'as particular foods from my locale appeal to me, I am therefore absolutely of that place'.

At work in this is a kind of perceived or experienced essentialism, both in terms of the food and collective identities. This is not to say that a food or location has an essence but rather that a kind of essentialism is performatively constructed, played out through our interactions with food and our tastes. These interactions (retroactively) create a sense of self and identity that comes *after* but is experienced as the substrate *of* an eating experience. In the culinary notion of *terroir* (which is more often associated with wine, but can be thought to be conceptually at work in food discourses), the product is perceived to have been imbued with particular qualities and traits of the land from which it emerges.[4] It is a performative interplay that produces this. Knowledge of the land can begin to frame the eating experience and draw the diner's attention to those particular qualities, tastes or flavours. This compounds the connection between individual taste and space/land, suggesting that the flavour of the land itself (or region or nation) is contained within the food, which is why it appeals. This kind of localism not only produces a connection to the land but also enforces that connection as 'innate' rather than performative. It is the interplay of language, presentation and experience that causes particular elements of a dish, those that solidify the superiority of the locally produced, to be foregrounded.

Despite each of the restaurants professing, to varying degrees, a desire to make use of local ingredients, their work nevertheless draws on ingredients and food cultures from beyond the immediate locale, crossing regional and national borders. Julian Baggini argues that the desire for the local is an attempt to 'recapture the human dimension in economic life', to combat the alienation from the land and the seasons instituted by modern technology and industry. He continues that the 'cult of localism [...] misunderstands the problem' because the ethical dimension of food production is not about whether it is local but whether it is located: 'whether it comes from a particular place and a producer we can, however indirectly, treat with respect and fairness' (2014: 23–24). Baggini supplements the distinction between the local and the located with an ethical call for respect and fairness. The major political/ethical call inherent to the 'located' is that it counters the alienation of globalised food production and transportation, attempting to forge that connection between land and food. However, this ethical call is not strictly connected to locating the provenance of ingredients. Rather, it is a structural political ethics about respect for producers, including pay, working conditions and acknowledgement of the quality of what is produced. Locating the ingredient and its processes of production is merely a means of facilitating this 'respect and fairness', by encouraging attentiveness to that process. The located remains just as susceptible to the issues of the local, as it continues to naturalise and essentialise regional differences of identity and taste and reiterate a particular kind of localised conservativism.

Within the context of fine dining (and more broadly in food cultures that foreground the local/located), the 'local(ised)' produce is transformed into commodity-form, where the various ways it performs its localisation allow for increases in monetary and cultural capital. The Fat Duck's 'BFG' (Black Forest Gateau) is accompanied with a spray of kirsch around and over the table; the diner is explicitly told that kirsch comes from the Black Forest. The implication is that the dish is somehow more 'authentically' local – that the kirsch carries within it a trace of its provenance. In triangulating the Black Forest kirsch with the name of the dish (*Black Forest* gateau) and the taste and smell of cherries in both the kirsch spray and the dish, different aspects of the experience begin to reinforce one another. Much like the Symbolist notion of correspondences, taken from Baudelaire's poem of the same name, which sought to establish connections between sensory experiences as a way of bringing to the fore the interconnected nature of things, the dish uses the correspondence of flavours and the name to consolidate a sense of the 'completeness' of the experience. A significant aspect of this is its connection to the Black Forest, where the naming principle at work in the dish inflects the sensory experience (the smell and taste of cherries), forging a connection between them that allows mutual reinforcement and the sense that somehow the dish is revelling in and revealing an essential property of that location in and through the food. It is a subtle yet complex operation, where the placing together of the name of a place and a particular sensory experience forges a link that might unthinkingly be regarded as essential – that something of the Black Forest is captured in the flavour of cherries. Ultimately, this apparent exploration of the Black Forest and its gateau namesake is not merely a sensory, intellectual and/or artistic exercise but is an experience sold to the diner. Foregrounding the 'located' qualities of the dish starts to mask over its form as commodified experience.

The locating of a dish takes place through various kinds of performances around and in the food. In the case of the 'BFG', it is the way the dish is framed by the waiter (explicitly stating the connections to the Black Forest) that foregrounds its locatedness. But it can also be performed in the dish itself. At Alinea, a series of three dishes perform a different kind of narrative that nevertheless locates the food. In 'Hamachi (shishito, bean, pine branch)', a small campfire built from blocks of charred wood is set alight on the table and the diner is invited to char their own kebab over it. This is served with 'Matsutake (pine, abalone, tapioca)', a charred mushroom and a small cup of cider. Once the plates are cleared, the diner is left to watch the fire burn out, before a waiter moves the wood aside to reveal that the fire has been cooking the next course, 'Pork Belly (parsnip, black trumpet, kombu)'. From the centre of the fire, a piece of pork belly is taken and placed on a plate, alongside one of the charred pieces of wood, which is revealed to be parsnip. In writing on seasonality in Alinea's cuisine, Achatz states that in developing new ideas, they not only look for seasonal ingredients but also think about activities associated with a particular season – what he calls 'the expression of the season' (2008: 34). Beyond the playfulness of the series of dishes, its suggestion of a camp-fire makes a connection to the land, to being outdoors and to a seasonal activity. The diner is brought into the actions of the dish, through finishing the cooking of their kebab on the fire, and so is positioned in the narrative. The dish performs bringing outside activities inside and, by implication, suggests a modern form of 'primitive' cooking (over an open campfire). But the dish is left open enough for the diner to 'fill in the gaps'; it makes space for any personal memories or associations of outdoor food production and so gives a general 'air' of locatedness without specificity. It articulates Baggini's 'desire to recapture the human dimension' in food production, but in aesthetic rather than content.

Constructions of the seasonal and local in the restaurant are ubiquitous and operate as though the work of the chef is to allow 'nature' to come forth in the food and the chef merely facilitates the actualising of the ingredient(s) in the dish. This is evident in writings from each of the chefs running the restaurants under consideration: 'In the past, critics have commented that elBulli does not value the quality and purity of natural ingredients […] in a way that ignores or overlooks their intrinsic qualities. This is not, in fact, the restaurant's philosophy' (Adrià et al. 2008: 72.2); 'Farmers and artisans devote their lives to cultivating and creating wonderful produce, and part of the skill of the chef is to understand and respect this so that he or she can then get the best from that product' (Blumenthal 2009: 131); 'You have to become aware of the history of the raw material or the farmer's passion [...]. This encounter means that you wouldn't dream of manipulating the materials excessively' (Redzepi in Skyum-Neilsen 2010: 17) and 'The primary focus here is to let the ingredients talk' (Achatz 2008: 30). They all profess a respect for the natural, for ingredients and their producers, as though the work of the restaurant is to merely draw out or accentuate those 'natural' or 'essential' qualities, rather than constructing them through their practice. In Heideggerian terms, nature operates as a standing-reserve, waiting to be subjected to technological thinking and practice to yield an economically productive work (an experience as product). Where the restaurants are purportedly revealing the natural, they are in fact engaging in another mode of concealment: *producing* the idea of the natural under the guise of merely representing it. In this way, the restaurants are asserting a lack of intervention while constructing the very desires and discourses on which the selling of their product rests. The restaurants continue constructions of the seasonal and the local, as well as respect for the intrinsic qualities of the produce and the ingredients, as a core part of their practice, while their practice itself is a part *of* the construction of what constitutes the seasonal and the local.

Experiences

In Pine and Gilmore's *The Experience Economy: Work Is Theater and Every Business a Stage*, they offer a model for businesses to think about the transformation of their work into 'experiences', performances or events – a guidebook for capitalising on 'experiences' rather than the selling of mere commodities, goods or services (1999: 6). As a continuation of the drive towards 'mass customization' (72), the customers themselves become the product (163), are given experiences and guided towards personal 'transformations' (189). Pine and Gilmore outline the now fairly ubiquitous idea of an economy grounded in experiences: not just the selling of a product that performs certain functions or provides the consumer with particular kinds of social prestige but one that furnishes them with cultural capital and plays a significant role in the forging of one's social, cultural and, indeed, personal sense of self and identity. The final section of this chapter turns to a reading of the work of the restaurants as participating in the ideas and the practices of the experience economy, considering the ways in which the restaurant produces commodified experiences, relying on various kinds of labour on the part of the diner – the political discourse that plays a significant role in framing the entirety of the event.

To view the restaurants as an experience, rather than selling goods or services, acknowledges that the food is not just served for its nutritional value or the alleviation of hunger. Instead, it is an experience that brings together the experimental cuisine with the various performances of the restaurants (its site and staff) as a whole, creative event and a form of cultural capital accessible only to those who can afford to pay for it. The experience operates as cultural capital precisely because of its exclusivity. The experience economy can be thought as a reaction to the mass production of culture by providing something seemingly momentary, unique and addressed to the individual. Warde argues that there is a bourgeois cultural fear of uniformity, which arose in reaction to mass production of the industrial revolution (1997: 36). He argues that this is an elitist fear 'that all people might share similarity of condition, experience or taste' and that it 'offends against the dominant favourable image of individuality' (1997: 36). The experience economy, including how it is manifested in the restaurant, speaks to and of this fear. By uniformly addressing the diners as individuals, with a product that can only come into being in the individual experience of the diner, the restaurant continues the economics of mass production (the honed and efficient delivery of a product through workers trained to perform particular functions) but combines it with an ostensible individualism (seeming to cater, and provide an experience, for the individual). Importantly, the restaurants offer an elite experience, appealing to the desires and proclivities of the privileged classes, distinct from the uniform mass production of fast food and high street restaurants.

In their writing on the workings of elBulli, the Adrià brothers and Soler reflect that

> The frenetic speed the chefs work at during service is confined to the kitchen, and they try not to allow it into the dining room. Here, the distance between the tables and the air of tranquility mean that guests can relax with their friends. A peaceful atmosphere is also essential for experiencing the full sensory impact of each dish.
>
> (2008: 394)

This is emblematic of the experience economy and the workings of the restaurant within that frame. There is hidden labour. The work of the chefs is hidden from the dining room and the diners; the intensity and exhaustion of the chef is sublimated into, but not explicitly referenced in, the food. In much the same way, the experience relies on sensory and emotional labour on the part of the diner. They are not mere 'receivers' of the work. Instead, they are required to engage in overt performances of its consuming and the labour of interpretation, processing and emotional connections. To leave any of this behind enacts a kind of failure of appreciation. The diners' bodies are both the focus of the address, the thing to which the work of the restaurant is aimed, and the site of the work, which does not take place in the dish on the table but in the sensory and emotional apparatus of the diner. The diner does not purchase the food but the opportunity to experience the food – a subtle, yet important, difference that marks the experience rather than the food itself as the commodity.

The food event becomes a commodity not only through paying for the experience, but, in the various ways, the experience is transformed into cultural capital and its material markers and support. While one does pay in order to eat (which seems to position the event as the provision of a mixture of 'goods' and 'services'), it is not a quotidian experience of eating – the continuation of the body through eating. Rather, it is marked as a 'special' event, in part through the price, in part through the difficulty in securing a reservation (often months in advance) for the 'exclusive' restaurant and in part through the encounter with the celebrity chef. The restaurant becomes a brand, and the diner both experiences and embodies that brand in and through the event. Maurya Wickstrom, in *Performing Consumers*, argues that '[…] corporations produce subjectivity as aspects of their brands through mimetic and identificatory processes akin to those of performance, somatic and embodied' (2006: 2). She continues that companies do not focus on the particular traits and qualities of their commodities but rather emphasise 'experiential environments' in which the customer or the consumer embodies and experiences ideas connected to the brand as 'feelings, sensations, and event memories' (Wickstrom 2006: 2). The sensory and sensual appeal of the restaurants, in the food, the performances of the staff and the construction of the space, all make up the multisensory horizon of the experience-as-brand. The diners take it upon themselves to embody the brand, to furnish it with a body and its 'completion' through its lived quality. It is a performative fantasy: that the brand somehow exists 'in its own world' and that to participate, to reserve a table, to pay for the experience, to be there and to eat produce the very branded experience that purports to exist in advance, waiting for the diner.

At the heart of the experience economy is a quest for novelty. It is grounded in the pursuit of new, exciting experiences, which increase the account balance of one's cultural capital. It solicits a form of curiosity that seeks out the novel in order to have experienced it. In the restaurants, the novelty is partly derived from their experimentations with food – presenting unusual ingredients and preparations, spectacular presentations and moving sensual experiences. At elBulli, The Fat Duck, Noma and Alinea, the experience is almost invariably geared towards a pleasurable experience – one that plays on desire and pleasure, encouraging it as a positive reinforcement to take enjoyment and, by extension, to value the experience (to share it and perhaps pay to experience it again).

In Heidegger's *Being and Time*, 'curiosity' is a mode of care (with care being the fundamental mode of our engagement with the world). Curiosity, though, is a deficient mode of care for Heidegger. Heidegger writes that curiosity restlessly seeks 'the excitement of continual novelty and changing encounters' and 'the constant possibility of *distraction*' (1962: 216, original emphasis). It constitutes part of Dasein's fallenness into the world of the *they* (Dasein's inauthentic *they*-self) because it is not an authentic entanglement with one's own self and its possibilities but a distraction of giving oneself over to the *they* (220). The experience economy works as part of the *they*: a reassuring and comforting appeal to the pleasures of superficial novelty, a kind of (economic) activity that requires no thought and the transformation of the fundamental anxiety surrounding one's own existence into a concrete and directed fear (the fear of missing out, of not having experienced enough). Curiosity provides us 'with the guarantee of a "life" which, supposedly, is genuinely "lively"' (217). Heidegger continues that curiosity 'concerns itself with a kind of knowing, but just in order to have known' (217). Heidegger's framing works for understanding the experience economy, which is grounded in this restless pursuit of novelty – knowing in order to have known, doing in order to have done.

Curiosity, as the drive for novelty and new experiences, allows the experience economy to keep working. It is never satiated because it continually seeks out the next new experience, the next new sensation. It is because it dwells in the sensory and the sensual experiences of the live(d) body that it resists being accumulated as owned objects. It is able to bring bodies back time and again, for slightly new experiences or even for the same experience again. The spectacular restaurant provides a space for this kind of novelty – an ephemeral experience that cannot be entirely owned because of its relational qualities. It requires the chefs, the space, the food and the bodies of the diners. It cannot be recreated at home. It provides a sensory experience that is unusual, new, outside of the everyday. It is a space of fantasy. The spectacular and sometimes seemingly magical work with food brings to life a fantasy that speaks of the work of Willy Wonka or the food in *Alice in Wonderland*. The diner becomes absorbed in the fantasy, given over to the world of the restaurant, which provides food for curiosity – a multisensory experience that seems to enliven and awaken the body (though always at a price).

For Heidegger, 'This "absorption in..." has mostly the character of Being-lost in the publicness of the "they"' (1962: 220). In terms of the experience economy, the absorption is into the public (i.e. ideological) world of the drive to 'experience' ('experience' as both noun and verb) and is characterised by what Heidegger calls 'ambiguity': 'the sort of thing which is accessible to everyone, and about which anyone can say anything', meaning it is 'impossible to decide what is disclosed in a genuine understanding, and what is not' (1962: 217). As the personal or individual quality of the experience is foregrounded, any diner can make any claim about the experience. It allows anyone to say anything about it. However, this also allows for a more complex engagement with the experience, to read against the grain of mere pleasure or novelty and draw out its more unsettling or defamiliarising qualities. In other words, the experience is ambiguous because it can be discussed both in terms of novelty and in terms of revelation.

The experiences offered by the restaurants are, in part, an attempt to offer a counter to the visual logic of the virtual. In a world dominated by images and screens, the restaurants attempt to reinvigorate the 'lower' senses of taste, touch and smell, providing an experience that enlivens these senses and (re)awakens the sensual and sensate body. In reflecting on Noma, Olafur Eliasson writes that 'We are constantly confronted with a trivialized sensory world, largely the product of banal commercialization. [...] The senses are blunted. By contrast, what is continually being developed at Noma helps to keep our senses keen' (2010: 8). Equally, Blumenthal reflects on the work of the psychologist Charles Spence that 'He has done fascinating work on how the modern-day, sedentary, indoor lifestyle gives a thinned-down sensory experience (particularly since there is now an emphasis on the value of sight at the expense of the more emotional senses of touch and smell) [...]' (2009: 208). The experience sold is one that is both spectacular and (re)invigorating for the senses. It attempts to counter the potential alienation of dwelling in images, sights and screens.

However, in its framing as a purchasable experience, and operations as part of an experience economy, their work has the potential to produce rather than mitigate alienation. Heidegger argues that fallenness into the world of the *they* is a form of alienation, where inauthentic Dasein is calmed, tranquilised and, thus, removed from the unsettling entanglement with one's 'ownmost potentiality-for-Being' (1962: 222). It is precisely the fallenness of Being into the world of the 'they', the world of the general political status quo, that leads to alienation. While it might appear to be a political act to reinvigorate the senses in order to combat the alienation of the virtual, in operating within an economic frame of experiences, the restaurants continue that idle curiosity and ambiguity that is easily knowable, thereby continuing the very political system they might attempt to counter. Far from being released from alienation, the engagement with the senses in these restaurants, for as long as they operate within an experience economy, continues that very alienation by tranquillising (offering the comfort of a knowable experience), by attempting to facilitate pleasurable experiences (enjoyment as the primary goal, which sets the diner at ease rather than unsettles them) and by reiterating and deepening the grasp of commodification (through appealing to the so-called baser and more emotional senses of touch, taste and smell). The alienation of which Heidegger writes is an alienation from 'authentic Being', from the entanglement with our own Being as an issue for itself, via a process of setting at ease that brings us wholly within the grasp of the *they* – the status quo of commodification, consumerism and the purchasing of experiences.

191

In discussing the marketisation of sensory experience, David Howes argues that as a counter to the 'visual fatigue' that can set in through advertising, 'Touch revivifies. [...] Adding feel provides an additional dimension for product differentiation' (2005: 287). While sensory experience beyond the visual is always already at work in any encounter (even with visual materials, given that we cannot absent our own embodiment), Howes discusses the foregrounding of other kinds of sensory encounters and their explicit inclusion within a given commodity. Within the dominance of the visual, the other senses might in some way be understood as resisting the totalising logic of the commodity. In an experience economy, different kinds of sensory experience are folded into the form of the commodity, furnished with a body to 'flesh out' the experience, with multiple aspects of the experience becoming integral to the commodity-form itself. In other words, where the visual logic of advertising and selling might be troubled by their disjunction with other kinds of sensory experience, in the experience economy, the totalising logic of capitalism extends into the entire body, bringing more sensory and embodied elements under its reign. The body is not merely a receiver of commodities but is the site where commodities are enacted and articulated. The experience economy is not an economy of ownership but rather one where the act of consuming itself is purchased.

For Žižek, the 'latest ideological triumph of capitalism' is that 'each worker becomes his or her own capitalist, the "entrepreneur-of-the-self"' (2014a: 181). While Žižek is explicitly referring to work and labour, we might extend this, and by so doing acknowledge the extension of capitalism itself, into a more personal and intimate reading of the 'entrepreneur-of-the-self', whereby one's subjectivity itself is conceived and managed as an actor in the accumulation of capital. The experience economy engages with this kind of self, through the accumulation of cultural capital, purchasing experiences and encouraging a building of oneself as a brand – a brand that is built through the series of experiences in which one has engaged and for which one has paid. Rather than a lived life, authentic in the Heideggerian model because of its own existence or state being a continual issue for itself, a 'lively' existence becomes a series of experiences, one after another. The restaurant has the possibility to operate within this framework – perhaps most especially because of the ephemeral nature of its work. It can only continue, after the event, through memories, photographs and stories. For it to continue to circulate as commodity, its work must be as cultural rather than strictly material capital.

To dine at any of these restaurants costs a considerable amount. In 2008, the average cost at elBulli was €230 per person, including drinks (Adrià et al. 2008: 496.2). The Fat Duck cost £225 per person in 2013, Alinea was $298 in 2014 and Noma was DKK2700 in 2015. The cost is not indicative of the 'use-value' of the food or experience, but it does not pretend to be, given that the luxurious framing of the restaurants, as high-end or Michelin-starred cuisine, positions the work as experience and event rather than quotidian eating. The cost goes some way to solidify the position of the restaurants and reiterate their place as providers of an experience. Rather than the food or experience justifying the cost, the cost works to justify the experience. It is 'worth' the money insofar as the cost marks it as a special and worthwhile experience. But more than this, the framing of the cost enters into the experience itself. While money is perceived to have value, its exchange for the experience encourages an attitude that seeks to 'make the most' of the experience – to engage with and appreciate it. This is not absolute but is part of the encouragement to participate in such a way that the cost becomes justified. So, in a complex manoeuvre, the cost encourages a 'discerning' disposition, to appreciate the care and complexity of the food and the experience, which in turn justifies the cost. Given the considerable difference between costs of food day-to-day and the price of the Michelin-starred restaurant, the experience introduces an anxiety to enjoy it and appreciate it as much as possible. It begins to draw attention to the temporality of the experience, a greater attention to the passage of time and the slipping away of the experience, as well as a desire to save and savour it. It not only encourages a greater appreciation of the food, to notice its subtleties and complexities but also further solicits a rich and multilayered appreciation of the food – its sensory, sensual, emotional and conceptual workings. These are perhaps made more apparent as the diner seeks out the reason for its expense.

The restaurants sell an experience. They sell the opportunity to experience the food, the curation of a multisensory event and an (in)direct encounter with the celebrity chef. But the experience economy, understood not just as purchasing an experience but as the commodification of an experience that is novel, embodied and producing cultural capital, is perhaps grounded more in the approaches taken by the restaurant and diners than something inherent to the experience itself. The experience is neither absolutely a commodity nor absolutely aesthetic. The aesthetic potential of the experience, to reveal, disclosure or defamiliarise the experience of eating and making sense, is neither precluded by the restaurants' position in an economy of experiences nor does it counter the commodification of experience itself. While the cost and the act of paying can and do enter into the experience and play a role in inflecting, framing and shaping it, the experience has the potential to be more than, or at least different from, a novel commodity. It can still be unsettling, conceptually driven and take itself as an issue. In other words, it can be art.

NOTES

1. While Žižek is writing within a Lacanian-psychoanalytic approach, this can be thought in terms of a Heideggerian understanding of inauthentic or everyday Dasein: rather than the

image of the Father, we can posit the world of the *they* as the ideological realm that teaches us how to live and how to experience. To take this perspective means that the understanding of pleasure as a solicited transgression of an official rule is not innate to pleasure, but something learned. Pleasure, as something both prohibited and solicited by the world of the *they*, is part of the inauthentic experience of Dasein. The authentic experience would be to become aware of how pleasure itself is a mechanism of interpellation, particularly in late capitalism, to encourage participation in an economy grounded in and on the seeking of pleasure. This is an efficient procedure in the neoliberal capitalist world of the *they*, where the desire for pleasure is a motivating factor, rewarded with pleasure itself; that pleasure is always fleeting, carries the guilt of the prohibition, and so is limited, allowing more pleasure to be sought. The system becomes self-perpetuating.

2. Janine Antoni's *Gnaw* (1992) explored a similar tension between luxury and its slippage into disgust. The work included a 600 lb cube of chocolate covered in teeth marks. The excessive luxury of so much chocolate was literally and figuratively marked with a failed attempt at consumption, suggesting that the chocolate was too much. Also, in covering the chocolate with teeth marks, the work slips from an excessive and desirable luxury into something repellent.

3. There is still an awareness of guilt, which itself is part of the intensification of enjoyment. That guilt is assuaged so that the enjoyment might be enjoyed more fully.

4. The idea of *terroir* has undergone a transformation: Strattor and Young note that, historically, in France, *terroir* was 'associated with the filth of the provinces and the savagery of more distant lands' and that it has not been 'reappropriated as a powerful vehicle for regional pride and identity' (2018: 193). This shift, whereby the once-working class is appropriated by 'high culture', is a mirror of the appropriation of the seasonal, local and organic more generally (once a necessity for the least wealthy, now a choice for the privileged) and the appropriation of once-lower class tastes as part of an elite taste (such as in The Fat Duck's 'Beef Royal [1723]').

Conclusion

To think of each of the restaurants as a site of performance opens a perspective on the work that shifts it away from static conceptions of the food object and towards an acknowledgement of the temporal nature of the experience. The restaurants operate as a performance world, akin to that of immersive or site-specific practices, where the site itself performs and includes performances of the front of house staff, performances around and through the food and performances of the diners, including the performed nature of their own acts of perception and making sense. elBulli, The Fat Duck, Noma and Alinea each operate within two broader conceptions of the work of performance. On the one hand, they offer the performance of a commodified experience, which works within the hedonistic logic of capitalist structures, where the experience itself is a purchasable commodity, appealing to pleasure and pre-existing tastes. On the other hand, the restaurants have the potential to enact an artistic-aesthetic practice, where the experience becomes an issue for itself: defamiliarised or estranged, unsettled and revealing, combining artistic processes of creation with an aesthetic experience for the diner.

The restaurants engage in a performance practice that is marked by a series of tensions encapsulated by the tension between commodified experience and the artistic-aesthetic. There is a tension between the evocative and the provocative, between evolution and revolution, between the quotidian and the unusual, between *technē* and technology, between the Heideggerian authentic and inauthentic (between enowning and giving oneself over to the world of the *they*) and between product and art. These are not mutually exclusive. They co-exist as potential readings and experiences of the meal and can be teased out as the quality of the relationship between the material practice of the restaurant and the approach and perspective of the diner.

The artistic and performance work of the restaurants, as with any artistic practice, operates within the creative methods and approaches of exploring materials, engaging with technologies of creating, developing ways of preparing and processing the material and articulating styles of presentation. The *work* of the artwork becomes itself through a process of appearing: it is never grasped as a stable and absolutely present whole; it carries within it its own createdness, its having-been-made; and it becomes itself through the experience of the audience or diner. It is in the experience that the artistic process of making becomes aesthetic and the audience or the diner is brought into the world of the work, which works to unsettle, defamiliarise, make strange and question the experience; in other words, to take itself as an issue. In the restaurant, this is characteristically an engagement with the sensory apparatus of the body, the processes of making sense and the everyday discourses surrounding the production, consumption and understanding of food. The *process* of discovery, unconcealment, revelation and disclosure constitute the aesthetic nature of the experience, not directly as a preserving of truth in the work (as Heidegger suggests), but as a result of the encounter with the work. In this, the work becomes itself and does not rely on the identity or intentions of the artist or chef to be understood as an artistic-aesthetic practice. The work establishes its own world (the world of the restaurant, the world of individual dishes, the world of the meal entire), and while this world is sometimes a continuation of the everyday world (hedonic, spectacular, 'lively' and reassuring), it can also grapple with the everyday world, which transforms the experience from product to art.

Experience has an imaginative quality. It is not merely the gathering of information through the senses (the material encounter), which is then processed by the body and consciousness. Rather, experience is always already framed and guided in advance. This happens through the inherited and learned ideas of the sensible, of what could make sense, which guides attention and frames understanding. This framing can come from the world in general (from the world of the *they*, from political, historical and cultural discourse), from previous personal experience and from the material practice of the restaurant (the performances of the front of house staff, the language used around a dish, the way that a dish is presented). In this way, the division between perception and reception is problematised, because the judgements and reflections of reception bear down on and permeate acts of perception. There is no neutral encounter, through the senses, with the world.

Often positioned as the power of performance in a world of recording technologies, immediacy is an illusion that can be ruptured by the intensified sensory experience of the restaurants. The idea of the immediate (present and unmediated) is subjected to three challenges: the unfolding of time, the rupturing of the holistic body and the mediations of culture, history and ideology. The restaurants' practice challenges immediacy by drawing attention to: the ways in which the body is always catching up to an experience that has disappeared, the ways that the senses work in relation to one another in experience, and how sense requires background knowledge that can be insufficient. The food object cannot be grasped, at one moment, entirely and completely; the experience is not stable and the same for all diners; and processes of sensing and making sense constitute the experience, but not in an unthinking and everyday manner. The force of language becomes palpable in the experience itself, both in how it is used to describe dishes and as a component of perception in consciousness. Language can produce, conjoin and discriminate between sensations, both creating and mediating the experience.

In a similar way, political and economic discourses manifest themselves as a force in experience: framing it, guiding it and forming a core part of the processes of making sense. The restaurants are not free of the politics of the everyday world, including class, gender, race, food production and the experience economy. At times, the restaurants continue these political discourses; at times, they encourage the diner to forget or ignore them; and at times, they problematise and challenge them. The drive to pleasure in the restaurants is itself a political drive – a key aspect of the commodification of experience, appealing to the hedonic impulse that is integral to an economy of commodified experiences. This produces sense-in-enjoyment, where enjoyment and pleasure make sense of the experience and the potentially more radical qualities of the meal are mitigated by their framing as an enjoyable and novel experience.

While the restaurants do conform to the logic of commodified experience and perpetuate elements of both the everyday experience of food and the superficial pleasures of spectacle, they also offer something more provocative, defamiliarising and unsettling. The experimental nature of the cuisine can frame the chefs as both producers of a commodity and as artists and can frame the diners as both customers and as aesthetes. The restaurants can be experienced as a site of distraction and pleasure, but they can also be conceived in the realm of art.

Bibliography

Abend, L. (2011), *The Sorcerer's Apprentices: A Season at elBulli – Behind the Scenes at the World's Most Famous Restaurant*, London and New York: Simon and Schuster.

Achatz, G. (2008), *Alinea*, Berkley: Ten Speed Press.

Achatz, G. and Kokonas, N. (2011), *Life, on the Line: A Chef's Story of Chasing Greatness, Facing Death, and Redefining the Way We Eat*, New York: Gotham Books.

Adams, C. J. (2015), *The Sexual Politics of Meat: A Feminist-Vegetarian Critical Theory*, London and New York: Bloomsbury.

Adrià, F., Soler, J. and Adrià, A. (2008), *A Day at elBulli: An Insight into the Ideas, Methods and Creativity of Ferran Adrià*, London and New York: Phaidon.

Adrià, F., Soler, J. and Adrià, A. (2014a), *elBulli 2005 Catalogue*, London and New York: Phaidon.

Adrià, F., Soler, J. and Adrià, A. (2014b), *elBulli 2006 Catalogue*, London and New York: Phaidon.

Adrià, F., Soler, J. and Adrià, A. (2014c), *elBulli 2007 Catalogue*, London and New York: Phaidon.

Adrià, F., Soler, J. and Adrià, A. (2014d), *elBulli 2008 Catalogue*, London and New York: Phaidon.

Adrià, F., Soler, J. and Adrià, A. (2014e), *elBulli 2009 Catalogue*, London and New York: Phaidon.

Adrià, F., Soler, J. and Adrià, A. (2014f), *elBulli 2010–11 Catalogue*, London and New York: Phaidon.

Adrià, F., Soler, J. and Adrià, A. (2014g), *elBulli 2005–2011: Evolutionary Analysis*, London and New York: Phaidon.

Arenós, P. (2009), 'Periods, Movements, Avant-garde and 20th and 21st Century Styles in Western Haute-Cuisine', in Richard Hamilton and Vincente Todolí (eds), *Food for Thought, Thought for Food*, Barcelona and New York: Actar.

Baggini, J. (2014), *Virtues of the Table: How to Eat and Think*, London: Granta.

Bataille, G. (1989), *The Accursed Share: An Essay on General Economy, Volume 1: Consumption* (trans. Robert Hurley), New York: Zone Books.

Ben Chaim, D. (1984), *Distance in the Theatre: The Aesthetics of Audience Reception*, Ann Arbor: UMI Research Press.

Berghaus, G. (2005), *Avant-garde Performance: Live Events and Electronic Technologies*, Basingstoke and New York: Palgrave Macmillan.

Bergson, H. (2004), *Matter and Memory* (trans. Nancy Margaret Paul and W. Scott Palmer), New York: Dover Publications.

Blanch & Shock (2018), 'Exploding Cake', https://www.blanchandshock.com/explodingcake. Accessed 2 March 2018.

Blumenthal, H. (2009), *The Fat Duck Cookbook*, London and New York: Bloomsbury.

Blumenthal, H. (2010), *Heston's Fantastical Feasts*, London and New York: Bloomsbury.

Blumenthal, H. (2011), *Heston Blumenthal at Home*, London and New York: Bloomsbury.

Boisvert, R. D. and Heldke, L. (2016), *Philosophers at Table: On Food and Being Human*, London: Reaktion Books.

Bourdieu, P. (2010), *Distinction: A Social Critique of the Judgement of Taste* (trans. Richard Nice), London and New York: Routledge.

Butler, J. (2015), *Senses of the Subject*, New York: Fordham University Press.

de Certeau, M. (1998), *The Practice of Everyday Life*, vol. 1 (trans. Steven F. Rendall), Berkley and London: University of California Press.

de Certeau, M., Giard, L. and Mayol, P. (1998), *The Practice of Everyday Life, Volume 2: Living and Cooking*, New Revised and Augmented Edition (ed. Luce Giard, trans. Timothy J. Tomasik), Minneapolis and London: University of Minnesota Press.

Clark, L. B. and Peterson, M. (2017), 'Ways of Eating: Tradition, Innovation, and the Production of Community in Food-Based Art', in Silvia Bottinelli and Margherita d'Ayala Valva (eds), *The Taste of Art: Cooking, Food, and Counterculture in Contemporary Practices*, Fayetteville: University of Arkansas Press.

Clintberg, M. (2018), 'Local, National, and Cosmopolitan: The Rhetoric of the Museum Restaurant', in Nina Levent and Irina D. Mihalache (eds), *Food and Museums*, London and New York: Bloomsbury.

Cooks, L. (2009), 'You Are What you (Don't) Eat? Food, Identity, and Resistance', *Text and Performance Quarterly*, 29:1.

Deleuze, G. (2004), *The Logic of Sense* (trans. Mark Lester), London and New York: Continuum.

Derrida, J. (2001), *Writing and Difference* (trans. Alan Bass), London and New York: Routledge.

Deschamps, P. (2015), *Noma: My Perfect Storm*, UK: Studio Canal.

Dewey, J. (2008), 'Art as Experience', in Steven M. Cahn and Aaron Meskin (eds), *Aesthetics: A Comprehensive Anthology*, Maldon and Oxford: Blackwell Publishing.

Di Benedetto, S. (2010), *The Provocation of the Senses in Contemporary Theatre*, New York and London: Routledge.

Domene-Danés, M. (2013), 'El Bulli: Contemporary Intersections Between Food, Science, Art and Late Capitalism', *BRAC: Barcelona Research Art Creation*, 1:1.

Douglas, M. (1982), *In the Active Voice*, London and Boston: Routledge and Kegan Paul.

Dudek, N. (2008), 'Reading a Plate', *Gastronomica: The Journal of Food and Culture*, 8:2 California: University of California Press, pp. 51–54.

Eliasson, O. (2010), 'Milk Skin with Grass', in René Rezepi (ed.), *Noma: Time and Place in Nordic Cuisine*, London and New York: Phaidon.

Foucault, M. (2002), *The Order of Things: An Archaeology of the Human Sciences*, London and New York: Routledge.

Fried, M. (1998), *Art and Objecthood: Essays and Reviews*, Chicago and London: University of Chicago Press.

Gallegos, D. and McHoul, A. (2006), '"It's not about good taste. It's about tastes good": Bourdieu and Campbell's Soup... and Beyond', *The Senses and Society*, 1:2 Oxford: Berg Publishers, pp. 165–181.

Govan, E. and Rebellato, D. (1999), 'Foodscares! The Pleasures and Dangers of Culinary Theatre', *Performance Research: On Cooking*, 4:1.

Hamilton, R. and Todolí, V. (2009), *Food for Thought, Thought for Food*, Barcelona and New York: Actar.

Heathfield, A. (2004), 'Alive', in Adrian Heathfield (ed.), *Live: Art and Performance*, London: Tate Publishing.

Heidegger, M. (1962), *Being and Time* (trans. John Macquarrie and Edward Robinson), Oxford: Blackwell Publishing.

Heidegger, M. (2011a), 'The Origin of the Work of Art', in David Farrell Krell (ed.), *Basic Writings: from Being and Time (1927) to The Task of Thinking (1964)*, London and New York: Routledge.

Heidegger, M. (2011b), 'Letter on Humanism', in David Farrell Krell (ed.), *Basic Writings: from Being and Time (1927) to The Task of Thinking (1964)*, London and New York: Routledge.

Heidegger, M. (2011c), 'The Question Concerning Technology', in David Farrell Krell (ed.), *Basic Writings: from Being and Time (1927) to The Task of Thinking (1964)*, London and New York: Routledge.

Heidegger, M. (2016), *Mindfulness* (trans. Parvis Emad and Thomas Kalary), London and New York: Bloomsbury.

Helstosky, C. (2017), 'Time Changes Everything: Futurist/Modernist Cooking', in Silvia Bottinelli and Margherita d'Ayala Valva (eds), *The Taste of Art: Cooking, Food, and Counterculture in Contemporary Practices*, Fayetteville: University of Arkansas Press.

Heston's Feasts (2009–2010, UK: Channel 4).

Howells, T. and Hayman, L. (2014), *Experimental Eating*, London: Black Dog Publishing.

Howes, D. (1996), 'Introduction: Commodities and Cultural Borders', in David Howes (ed.), *Cross-Cultural Consumption: Global Markets, Local Realities*, London and New York: Routledge.

Howes, D. (2005), 'Introduction: Empires of the Senses', in David Howes (ed.), *Empire of the Senses: The Sensual Culture Reader*, Oxford and New York: Berg.

Howes, D. and Classen, C. (2014), *Ways of Sensing: Understanding the Senses in Society*, London and New York: Routledge.

Husserl, E. (1964), *The Phenomenology of Internal Time-Consciousness* (ed. Martin Heidegger, trans. James S. Churchill), The Hague: Martinus Nijhoff Publishers.

Jameson, F. (1999), *Brecht and Method*, London and New York: Verso.

Jones, A. (1998), *Body Art/Performing the Subject*, Minneapolis and London: University of Minnesota Press.

Jones, M. (2007), *Feast: Why Humans Share Food*, Oxford: Oxford University Press.

Jones, S. (2012), 'Not Citizens, But Persons: The Ethics in Action of Performance's Intimate Work', in Maria Chatzichristodoulou and Rachel Zerihan (eds), *Intimacy Across Visceral and Digital Performance*, Basingstoke and London: Palgrave Macmillan.

Jouary, J.-P. and Adrià, F. (2013), *Ferran Adrià and elBulli: The Art, the Philosophy, the Gastronomy*, London: André Deutsch.

Kear, A. (1999), 'Cooking Time with Gertrude Stein', *Performance Research: On Cooking*, 4:1.

Kirshenblatt-Gimblett, B. (1999), 'Playing to the Senses: Food as a Performance Medium' *Performance Research: On Cooking*, 4:1.

Kirshenblatt-Gimblett, B. (2007), 'Making Sense of Food in Performance: The Table and the Stage', in Sally Banes and André Lepecki (eds), *The Senses in Performance*, New York and London: Routledge.

Kokonas, N. (2008), 'How to Use this Book', in *Alinea*, Be rkley: Ten Speed Press.

Langer, J. (2006), 'Television's "Personality System"', in David Marshall (ed.), *The Celebrity Culture Reader*, New York and London: Routledge.

Leatherbarrow, D. (2004), 'Table Talk', in Jamie Horwitz and Paulette Singley (eds), *Eating Architecture*, Cambridge, MA and London: The MIT Press.

Lévi-Strauss, C. (1969), *The Raw and the Cooked: Introduction to a Science of Mythology*, vol. 1 (trans. John Weightman and Doreen Weightman), New York and Evanston: Harper and Row.

Machon, J. (2011), *(Syn)aesthetics: Redefining Visceral Performance*, Basingstoke and London: Palgrave Macmillan.

Machon, J. (2013), *Immersive Theatres: Intimacy and Immediacy in Contemporary Performance*, Basingstoke and London: Palgrave Macmillan.

Marinetti, F. T. (2014), *The Futurist Cookbook* (trans. Suzanne Brill), London: Penguin.

McClusky, M. (2008), 'Postmodern Pantry', in *Alinea*, Berkley: Ten Speed Press.

McDonnell, E. M. (2016), 'Food Porn: The Conspicuous Consumption of Food in the Age of Digital Reproduction', in Peri Bradley (ed.), *Food, Media and Contemporary Culture: The Edible Image*, Basingstoke and New York: Palgrave Macmillan.

McKenzie, J. (2001), *Perform or Else: From Discipline to Performance*, London and New York: Routledge.

McLean, A., Cayley, K. and Legere, S. (2018), 'Approaching Ambient Drama: Reflections on Two Immersive Experiments', *Canadian Theatre Review*, 173, pp. 21–25.

Merleau-Ponty, M. (2002), *Phenomenology of Perception* (trans. Colin Smith), London and New York: Routledge.

Miller, T. (2007), *Cultural Citizenship: Cosmopolitanism, Consumerism, and Television in a Neoliberal Age*, Philadelphia: Temple University Press.

Novero, C. (2010), *Antidiets of the Avant-Garde: From Futurist Cooking to Eat Art*, Minneapolis and London: University of Minnesota Press.

Peterson, A. R. (2005), 'Between Image and Stage: The Theatricality and Performativity of Installation Art', in Rune Gade and Anne Jerslev (eds), *Performative Realism: Interdisciplinary Studies in Art and Media*, Copenhagen: Museum Tusculanum Press.

Phelan, P. (1993), *Unmarked: The Politics of Performance*, London and New York: Routledge.

Piccini, A. and Rye, C. (2009), 'Of Fevered Archives and the Quest for Total Documentation', in Ludivine Allegue, Simon Jones, Baz Kershaw and Angela Piccini (eds), *Practice-as-Research in Performance and Screen*, Basingstoke: Palgrave Macmillan.

Pine, B. J. and Gilmore, J. H. (1999), *The Experience Economy: Work is Theater and Every Business a Stage*, Boston: Harvard Business School Press.

Plato (1994), *Symposium* (trans. Robin Waterfield), Oxford: Oxford University Press.

Raviv, Y. (2018), 'Food and Art: Changing Perspectives on Food as a Creative Medium', in Kathleen LeBesco and Peter Naccarato (eds), *The Bloomsbury Handbook of Food and Popular Culture*, London and New York: Bloomsbury.

Reason, M. (2006), *Documentation, Disappearance and the Representation of Live Performance*, Basingstoke and New York: Palgrave Macmillan.

Redzepi, R. (2010), *Noma: Time and Place in Nordic Cuisine*, London and New York: Phaidon.

Redzepi, R. (2013), *Journal*, London and New York: Phaidon.

Ricoeur, P. (2012), 'Memories and Images', in Ian Farr (ed.), *Memory: Documents of Contemporary Art*, London and Cambridge: Whitechapel Gallery and MIT Press.

Rounthwaite, A. (2011), 'From This Body to Yours: Porn, Affect, and Performance Art Documentation', *Camera Obscura*, 26:3.

Schwarz, D. (1998), 'Chronology', in Peter Kasperak and Dieter Schwarz (eds), *From Action Painting to Actionism Vience 1960–1965: Günter Brus, Adolf Frohner, Otto Mühl, Hermann Kitsch, Alfons Schilling, Rudolf Schwarzmaler*, Klagenfurt: Ritter Verlag.

Serrano, S. and Pinto, J. M. (2013), 'Exhibition Guide', *elBulli: Ferran Adrià and the Art of Food*, Somerset House, July–September 2013.

Serres, M. (2016), *The Five Senses: A Philosophy of Mingled Bodies* (trans. Margaret Sankey and Peter Cowley), London and New York: Bloomsbury.

Skyum-Nielsen, R. (2010), 'The Perfect Storm', in René Redzepi (ed.), *Noma: Time and Place in Nordic Cuisine*, London and New York: Phaidon.

Spence, C. (2018a), 'The Neuroscience of Flavor', in Nina Levent and Irina D. Mihalache (eds), *Food and Museums*, London and New York: Bloomsbury.

Spence, C. (2018b), 'The Art and Science of Plating', in Nina Levent and Irina D. Mihalache (eds), *Food and Museums*, London and New York: Bloomsbury.

Steingarten (2008), 'Experiencing Alinea', in *Alinea*, Berkley: Ten Speed Press.

Strattor, J. J. and Young, A. R. (2018), '*Terroir Tapestries*: An Interactive Consumption Project', in Nina Levent and Irina D. Mihalache (eds), *Food and Museums*, London and New York: Bloomsbury.

Styler, C. (2006), *Working the Plate: The Art of Food Presentation*, Hoboken: John Wiley & Sons.

Szanto, D. (2018), 'Performing With(in) Food', in Kathleen LeBesco and Peter Naccarato (eds), *The Bloomsbury Handbook of Food and Popular Culture*, London and New York: Bloomsbury.

This, H. (2006), *Molecular Gastronomy: Exploring the Science of Flavor* (trans. M. B. Debevoise), New York: Columbia University Press.

This, H. (2009), *Building A Meal: From Molecular Gastronomy to Culinary Constructivism* (trans. Malcolm DeBevoise), New York: Columbia University Press.

Volgelzang, M. (2018), 'Teardrop', https://marijevogelzang.nl/portfoliopage/teardrop/. Accessed 31 January 2018.

Warde, A. (1997), *Consumption, Food and Taste: Culinary Antinomies and Commodity Culture*, London: Sage Publications.

Weiss, A. S. (2004), 'Culinary Manifestations of the *Genius Loci*', in Jamie Horwitz and Paulette Singley (eds), *Eating Architecture*, Cambridge, MA and London: The MIT Press.

Weiss, A. S. (2007), 'Artaud's Anatomy', in Sally Banes and André Lepecki (eds), *The Senses in Performance*, New York and London: Routledge.

Wetzell, G. (2010), *El Bulli: Cooking in Progress*, Germany: Artificial Eye.

Wickstrom, M. (2006), *Performing Consumers: Global Capital and its Theatrical Seductions*, London and New York: Routledge.

Žižek, S. (2008), *The Sublime Object of Ideology*, London and New York: Verso.

Žižek, S. (2009), *First as Tragedy, then as Farce*, London and New York: Verso.

Žižek, S. (2014a), *Event*, London and New York: Penguin.

Žižek, S. (2014b), *Žižek's Jokes* (ed. Audun Mortense), Cambridge and London: The MIT Press.

Index

Lightning Source UK Ltd.
Milton Keynes UK
UKHW032123090122
396795UK00001BB/18